Posting for Power

LEGISLATIVE POLITICS & POLICY MAKING

Series Editors

Jamie L. Carson, University of Georgia

James M. Curry, University of Utah

RECENT TITLES IN THE SERIES:

Posting for Power: Congressional Partisanship on Social Media
JEREMY GELMAN AND STEVEN LLOYD WILSON

*Broken Record: The Origins and Evolution of Recorded Voting
in the U.S. Congress*
MICHAEL S. LYNCH AND ANTHONY J. MADONNA

*Waves of Discontent: Electoral Volatility, Public Policymaking,
and the Health of American Democracy*
JACOB F.H. SMITH

Strategic Responsiveness: How Congress Confronts Presidential Power
SCOTT H. AINSWORTH, BRIAN M. HARWARD, AND KENNETH W. MOFFETT

*Home Field Advantage: Roots, Reelection, and Representation in the
Modern Congress*
CHARLES HUNT

*The Committee: A Study of Policy, Power, Politics, and Obama's Historic
Legislative Agenda on Capitol Hill, Second Edition*
BRYAN W. MARSHALL AND BRUCE C. WOLPE

Minority Party Misery: Political Powerlessness and Electoral Disengagement
JACOB F. H. SMITH

The Politics of Herding Cats: When Congressional Leaders Fail
JOHN LOVETT

Committees and the Decline of Lawmaking in Congress
JONATHAN LEWALLEN

Losing to Win: Why Congressional Majorities Play Politics Instead of Make Laws
JEREMY GELMAN

It's Not Personal: Politics and Policy in Lower Court Confirmation Hearings
LOGAN DANCEY, KJERSTEN R. NELSON, AND EVE M. RINGSMUTH

For a complete list of titles in this series, please see www.press.umich.edu.

POSTING FOR POWER

Congressional Partisanship on Social Media

Jeremy Gelman and Steven Lloyd Wilson

University of Michigan Press
Ann Arbor

For questions or permissions, please contact um.press.perms@umich.edu

Published in the United States of America by the
University of Michigan Press
First published February 2026

A CIP catalog record for this book is available from the British Library.

Library of Congress Control Number: 2025030403
LC record available at https://lccn.loc.gov/2025030403

ISBN 978-0-472-07792-2 (hardcover : alk. paper)
ISBN 978-0-472-05792-4 (paper : alk. paper)
ISBN 978-0-472-90570-6 (open access ebook)

DOI: https://doi.org/10.3998/mpub.13031478

The University of Michigan Press's open access publishing program is made possible thanks
to additional funding from the University of Michigan Office of the Provost and the generous
support of contributing libraries.

The authorized representative in the EU for product safety and compliance is Easy Access
System Europe, Mustamäe tee 50, 10621 Tallinn, Estonia, gpsr.requests@easproject.com

Contents

List of Figures   vii

List of Tables   ix

Acknowledgments   xi

1. Introduction   1
2. Why Partisanship?   17
3. Moving Beyond Votes: Defining and Measuring Partisan Intensity   45
4. Bickering or Cheerleading: The Tone of Congressional Team Play   73
5. The Determinants of Congressional Partisanship   93
6. The Negligible Connection Between Legislating and
   Partisan Intensity   115
7. A Very Affordable Consequence: Estimating Partisanship's
   Electoral Penalty   155
8. Conclusion   173

Notes   185

References   197

Index   213

Digital materials related to this title can be found on
the Fulcrum platform via the following citable URL:
https://doi.org/10.3998/mpub.13031478

Figures

2.1	Major Factors That Predict a Legislator's Partisan Intensity	19
3.1	Distribution of Legislators' Partisan Intensity	69
3.2	Dot Plot of Legislators' Partisan Intensity	69
3.3	Scatter Plot of Partisan Intensity and Ideology Measures	71
4.1	Legislators' Partisan Intensity and Tone	79
4.2	Legislators' Ideological Extremity and Tone	80
4.3	Factors That Affect a Member's Partisan Tone	86
4.4	Legislators' Partisan Intensity and Tone, by Total Number of Tweets	90
6.1	Partisan Balance of Cosponsorship Coalitions	121
6.2	Predicted Bipartisanship Score as Partisan Intensity Changes	123
6.3	Party Unity and Presidential Support Scores, 2015–20	125
6.4	Predicted Party Unity Voting as Partisan Intensity and Ideology Change	127
6.5	Predicted Presidential Support as Partisan Intensity and Ideology Change	128
6.6	Partisan Intensity's Predicted Effect on Legislative Effectiveness	132
6.7	Partisan Intensity's Predicted Effect on a Legislative Section Becoming Law	137
7.1	The Effect of Excessive Partisanship on Predicted Vote Share	161
7.2	The Effect of Partisan Tone on Predicted Vote Share	164
8.1	Scatterplot of Partisan Intensity and Ideology Scores, 2015–22	174
8.2	Partisan Intensity by Congress for All Members and Freshmen	179

Tables

2.1 Reelection and Collective Party Goals Expectations   27
2.2 Power Seeking's Expected Effect on Partisanship   32
2.3 Personal Factors' Expected Effect on Partisanship   33
2.4 Partisanship's Hypothesized Effect on Legislative Effectiveness   37
2.5 Partisanship's Expected Electoral Consequences   42
3.1 Votes and Cosponsorship Opportunities for 12 Partisan Events   58
3.2 Partisan Tweet Coding Rules   63
3.3 Example Tweets About Donald Trump   64
3.4 Out-of-Sample Performance of Neural Network   66
3.5 Total Tweets, by Congress   68
3.6 Party Accounts' Partisan Intensity Scores   70
3.7 Partisan Intensity and Ideology Correlations   71
4.1 Tone and Partisanship Example Tweets   78
4.2 Number and Percentage of Strong Partisan Types, by Congress   82
4.3 Measurement of Factors Used to Predict Partisan Tone   85
4.4 Factors that Differentiate Strong Partisans Based on Tone   88
4.5 Determinants of a Legislator's Partisan Tone   91
4.6 Determinants of Strong Partisans' Tone   92
5.1 Potential Explanations for Legislators' Partisanship   99
5.2 Determinants of Congressional Partisanship   102
5.3 Common Explanations for Legislators' Partisanship   103
5.4 Determinants of Partisanship, by Chamber   105

5.5   Predicted Change in Partisan Intensity When the Least
       Competitive House Seats Become More Competitive   111
5.6   Determinants of Partisan Intensity, by Chamber   113
6.1   Association Between Partisan Intensity and Cosponsor
       Partisan Balance   120
6.2   Association Between Partisan Intensity and Legislative
       Effectiveness Scores   131
6.3   Effect of Partisan Intensity on Legislative Effectiveness in
       Different Specifications   134
6.4   Independent Variables Included in Enacted Policy Idea Models   136
6.5   Tracking If Partisan Intensity Is Negative and
       Statistically Significant   138
6.6   Likelihood Partisans Engage in Bipartisan Cosponsorships 141
6.7   Partisanship's Effect on Party Unity Voting   142
6.8   Partisanship's Effect on Presidential Support   143
6.9   Effect of Partisan Intensity on Legislative Effectiveness
       in Different Specifications, Full Models   144
6.10   Partisanship's Effect on Probability Bill Section Is Enacted
       (Volden & Wiseman Approach)   146
6.11   Partisanship's Effect on Probability Bill Section Is Enacted
       (Gelman & Wilson Approach)   147
6.12   Robustness Checks for If Partisan Intensity Is Associated
       with Section Passage Rates   148
6.13   Robustness Checks for If Partisan Intensity Is Associated
       with Section Passage Rates (Gelman & Wilson Approach)   150
6.14   Decision Tree Performance Metrics   153
7.1   The Electoral Costs of Partisanship   159
7.2   The Electoral Consequences of Partisan Tone   163
7.3   Determinants of Being Primaried, 2015–20   167
7.4   Determinants of Being Primaried, with Lagged Partisan Intensity   170
7.5   Determinants of Being Primaried, Robustness Checks   171
7.6   Determinants of Being Primaried, Two-Stage Model   172

Acknowledgments

Looking back seven years to when we started this book, we are struck by the immense role serendipity played in reaching this point. We began faculty positions at the University of Nevada, Reno (UNR) at the same time, and through sheer randomness, we found ourselves in offices very near one another. Our close proximity led to many conversations about what we were working on, and eventually we connected the dots that Jeremy's substantive interests and Steven's data collection efforts could be combined to answer some interesting questions about modern congressional politics. If one of us had been placed in the vacant office on the other side of our building, where our third colleague who was hired with us ended up, we doubt this book would have ever been written. So, it seems appropriate to begin an acknowledgments section by acknowledging the incredible role serendipity had in catalyzing this research.

But serendipity, mutual interest, and hard work only get you so far. We greatly benefited from our colleagues' insights as we developed this book together at UNR and after our coauthor relationship became a long-distance collaboration when Steven moved on to Brandeis University. Without their support, we doubt this book would have ever been finished, and even if it had been, the final version would not be what it is today. We thank Sean Theriault for his help and encouragement when this project was in its earliest stages. Sean generously came to Reno and read an early draft of what became our initial *Legislative Studies Quarterly* article on this topic and also became parts of chapters 2, 3, and 5. Most of the conference papers related to this book were presented online during the COVID-19 pandemic. We sincerely thank

Larry Evans, who luckily for us was assigned our discussant a few times, for his comments on multiple chapters. Christian Fong similarly provided excellent virtual comments on an initial draft of chapter 7. Finally, we thank our anonymous reviewers for providing insightful reviews and catching the many ways we misspelled various members' names throughout our draft manuscript.

We thank our colleagues at UNR, including Allison Evans, Ian Hartshorn, Callum Ingram, Brad Johnson, Elizabeth Koebele, and Carolyn Warner, for reading early chapter drafts, providing comments during the department's faculty research workshop, and offering their support as we navigated the book publishing process. We also thank the generous support of the Brandeis academic computing staff, who provided servers, troubleshooting, and bandwidth at every step of the way. We could not have asked for a better, more responsive, and more encouraging editor than Madison Allums at the University of Michigan Press. In our view, she is the gold standard.

Jeremy thanks his family for the joy they brought him during the years he spent on this book, especially at its most frustrating moments. As always, Scott and Cindi were supportive and encouraging parents. Michelle provided the time and space (unfortunately sometimes on weekends) to meet deadlines or to just think hard about some particular point we were trying to make. This project wouldn't have been possible without her support. Ruby and Talia did a fantastic job of slowing down the book's progress by growing up while we wrote it. I'm so glad they did.

Steven thanks Anne-Marie for her endless support and patience both in life and in the endurance of secondhand discussions of the technical details of scraping and neural networks. Lloyd and Kathy deserve the same thanks and also acknowledgment of the parental support in the form of mailed boxes of baked goods. Merry, Oliver, and Alison provided the support that only cats can, simultaneously completely unhelpful and absolutely essential.

ONE

Introduction

In the early morning hours of October 23, 2019, the plans for a partisan confrontation began to emerge. Hard-line House Republicans, furious that Democrats were impeaching Donald Trump (for the first time), began a coordinated messaging campaign on Twitter.[1] They accused Adam Schiff (D-CA), the chair of the House Intelligence Committee, of deposing witnesses in secret. In fact, members of both parties were participating in the depositions, but the leak on October 22 of acting Ambassador to Ukraine Bill Taylor's damning testimony of a Ukrainian quid pro quo sparked some 30 House Republicans into engineering a distraction. According to them, Schiff, a Democrat they had spent weeks vilifying, was holed up in a room in the Capitol basement, building his case against the president in secret.

Even before sunrise, their plan was clear. Steve Scalise (R-LA), the minority whip, blessed and participated in their stunt by reposting Bob Aderholt's (R-AL) complaint that "this impeachment process is literally being conducted in the basement of the Capitol, behind closed doors, to keep you from seeing what is taking place. It is a mockery! #StopTheSchiffShow" (Scalise 2019). Other Republicans adopted the #StopTheSchiffShow hashtag, and at 12:50 p.m., Paul Gosar (R-AZ) announced that he was "joining [Matt Gaetz (R-FL)] and other colleagues this morning demanding transparency in this sham impeachment inquiry" (Gosar 2019). Other Republicans quickly echoed Gosar and, following the same talking points, used nearly the exact same language in publicly laying out their plans.[2]

To someone watching from the House gallery, though, the day began just like any other in Congress, with representatives from both parties conduct-

ing business as usual. At 10:00 a.m., Bobby Rush (D-IL) called the House of
Representatives to order. During the morning hour speeches, Betty McCollum (D-MN) demanded that Washington's NFL team change its name and
Rodney Davis (R-IL) eulogized his friend and constituent Thomas Tracy Jr.
Beneath the mundane daily speeches and procedures on the House floor, the
hyper-partisanship that defines the contemporary Congress was roiling just
under the surface.

This description is not purely metaphorical. Somewhere in the basement
below the House chamber is a sensitive compartmented information facility
(SCIF), in which the House Intelligence, Foreign Affairs, and Oversight Committees were deposing Deputy Assistant Secretary of Defense Laura Cooper as
part of Donald Trump's first impeachment. Around 11:00 a.m., approximately
30 House Republicans, as they promised on social media, entered the secure
room and disrupted Cooper's testimony.

The partisan bickering over this saga quickly metastasized. Democrats
accused Republicans not only of disrupting the deposition and intimidating
a witness but also of compromising national security by bringing their cell
phones into a SCIF. The Republicans pivoted, claiming that Mark Meadows
(R-NC), Trump's future chief of staff, had collected their phones and taken
them out of the room and that the tweets they apparently sent from within the
SCIF were actually sent by staff.[3] By the end of the day, Democrats were con-
demning Republicans for endangering the country's national security and participating in a charade. The nearly three dozen Republican disrupters cheered
their own exploit, claiming they had pulled back the curtain on Democrats'
secret hearings.

Media reports from the day took a somewhat breathless tone.[4] The AFP
International Text Wire headline and article lead, reproduced for audiences
in Spanish, French, and Portuguese around the world, described Republicans
as storming the room (Mathes 2019). The Associated Press depicted a "chaotic scene" (Balsamo and Jalonick 2019). Cable TV shows, and their panel-
ists, all had something to say about the SCIF incident. On Fox News's *Lou
Dobbs Tonight*, the event was evidence that Republicans were ready to fight
for Trump (Dobbs and Roberts 2019). Other shows, like *The Lead with Jake
Tapper* on CNN, focused on the cell phone–related national security concerns
(Tapper 2019). Rachel Maddow began her primetime MSNBC show by telling the audience that "this was—this is one of those days, this was another
one of those days, right, not just a lot of news or just, you know, fast-moving
news, but shocking and jarring developments one after the other. By the end of
the day, like, just feel like too much, right? This is overstimulation" (Maddow
2019). International news outlets, in the United Kingdom, Canada, and even

Bahrain, all ran their own news stories about the event. Multiple *Washington Post* opinion columnists devoted their next day's columns to it. In total, hundreds of news outlets in the US and around the world, via the wire services or their own original reporting, covered what happened in the Capitol basement.

For someone hearing about these events for the first time, a natural reaction would be that the SCIF incident ignited a partisan dispute that roared through Congress. In reality, it was one of many partisan quarrels that day. Before Republicans marched into the Capitol basement, Democrats fumed that Trump had called his impeachment a lynching the day before. While those 30 or so Republicans occupied the SCIF, other congressional Democrats excoriated the president for his Syria, family separation, and healthcare policies. They lambasted their Republican colleagues for not advancing election security legislation and for misrepresenting how their recently passed tax cuts affected the economy. Other Republicans not in the SCIF alleged that Democrats were socialists and hypocrites, that they were pursuing partisan solutions on issues like prescription drug pricing, and that they were harming America by not voting on the United States–Mexico–Canada Agreement trade deal. These were only some of the partisan clashes from that day.

The partisan events from October 23 are notable for two reasons. First, although it seems like that day was some exhausting low point of partisan bickering, in fact, it was a fairly normal day. The SCIF disruption was unusual, which is why Republicans thought it would be effective, but headline-catching partisan stunts from both parties are relatively common. Such a level and tone of partisanship, on a wide range of topics, is typical fare on Capitol Hill. What is notable, and what the events of October 23 reveal, is the sheer volume of partisanship that permeates Congress *every day*. Members are constantly trying to politicize issues by framing them in partisan terms. This includes hot-button issues like impeachment, healthcare, and immigration and the more mundane ones such as the debt limit, the interpretation of the monthly jobs report, and claims that a political party upholds an important American ideal.

Indeed, the relatively brief media frenzy around the SCIF incident highlights how fleeting these partisan disputes are. Later that week, House Democrats released the articles of impeachment against Trump. Talk of the October 23 "chaos" nearly disappeared from public discussion. It mostly became a line used by Democrats to discredit Republicans' impeachment-related antics in TV interviews.[5] Republicans mostly stopped talking about it, with a few reminding voters about the incident in their press releases denouncing the articles of impeachment. By early November, the incident almost entirely disappeared from public discourse.

Second, the vast majority of this politicization happens "off the record." It is not cosponsored, introduced, and voted on as a bill or debated in speeches on the House or Senate floors. Take the SCIF incident. No bills were introduced and no votes were taken to sanction the Republicans who participated. The congressional record includes few mentions of it. Only Ron Wright (R-TX) took to the House floor on October 23 bragging about what he and his fellow Republicans had accomplished. The next day, Chuck Schumer (D-NY), the Senate minority leader, briefly mentioned it in a speech. After that, the incident almost entirely disappeared from the congressional record. Yet another very clear, comprehensive record of the incident exists. The buildup, stunt, and reaction are carefully cataloged through members' statements, mostly on social media. From the early morning posts in which Republicans outlined their plans, to their alleged posts from within the SCIF, to the Democrats' furious reactions that afternoon, we can closely track this partisan dispute.

More broadly, the events of October 23 epitomize what congressional observers mean when they describe a hyper-partisan legislature. Lawmakers, split into their respective partisan teams, take nearly every opportunity to improve their side's brand while tarnishing the other party. Sometimes this means adding a partisan dimension to ideological disagreements. To Democrats, the 2017 GOP-written tax cuts became the GOP tax scam. Republicans rebranded the Affordable Care Act as Obamacare, and Democrats returned the favor, calling the attempted repeal Trumpcare. Other times, the bickering is nonideological. High-profile events, like Trump's impeachments and the Benghazi hearings used to tarnish Hillary Clinton's reputation, and low-profile ones, such as concerns about the Secret Service staying at Trump-owned properties, become wrapped up in partisan bickering. The result is a constant drumbeat of Democrats and Republicans arguing about issues big and small.

This book's purpose is to understand the causes and consequences of this daily partisan behavior in which legislators are engaging. To do so, we develop a theory of legislators' partisanship. Our argument is that a lawmaker's partisan actions help them achieve two of their goals—winning reelection and becoming more politically influential. In appealing to voters, lawmakers adopt partisan personas that reflect their district's preferences and help burnish their party's collective reputation. Once in office, their partisan behavior supports their party's collective goal of gaining or maintaining majority status. But it has an individual component as well. For politically ambitious members, winning party and committee leadership races requires that they win support from their fellow copartisans in the House or Senate. Being a good team player is a prerequisite for winning the rank and file's favor, so candidates for these roles increase their partisan behavior to show that they can be relied on to support the party. Aspirants for higher office follow a similar practice by raising their partisan profiles in order to appeal to the extended party network that they hope will support their candidacy. Put simply, a member's partisan persona reflects both voter demands and their ambitions to become more politically powerful.

We argue that any excessive partisan behavior from lawmakers in pursuing these goals comes with minimal consequences. Although members from the other party may not like strong partisans, these members are constantly looking for partners to legislate with and are generally willing to ignore someone's behavior as long as that person possesses a shared interest. At the ballot box, some voters may penalize excessive partisan behavior. But we argue that even if incumbents lose some vote share, for most legislators the price is more nuisance than real electoral concern. As we show later in the book, only those representing the most competitive districts risk losing their seats for such conduct. Consequently, we argue that lawmakers are mostly free to act as partisan as they like.

To test our argument, we create a new measure of members' partisanship. We calculate lawmakers' partisan intensity, which is the "time and . . . effort they devote" to partisan activities (Hall 1996, 3). Our approach differs from previous research that uses votes, speeches, or bill cosponsorships to study legislators' "revealed preferences" of partisanship (3). Our intensity measure is based on lawmakers' Twitter posts and allows us to examine congressional partisanship in a detailed and comprehensive manner not afforded by other preference-based data sources.

By quantifying partisanship this way, we show that it differs a great deal among members and that this variation is predictable. Partisan intensity changes as legislators work to build their personal and their party's political brands. As such, increases are associated with seat safety, majority party status, small majorities, and membership in the party opposite the president. However, legislators' personal ambitions also affect their partisanship. To get ahead in contemporary Washington, DC, legislators need to show that they are good team players. Ambitious members who hold or seek leadership positions appeal to their copartisan officeholders, their constituents on Capitol Hill, by raising their partisan intensity. Those running for higher office also act more partisan to display their partisan bona fides to the extended party network, upon whose electoral support they rely. Once lawmakers no longer need to present themselves as reliable team players, because they lost their leadership race or they are no longer running for higher office, they decrease their partisanship.

Unlike their ideology, legislators' partisan intensity fluctuates. Yet, for most members, raising or lowering their intensity is not a problem. We find that strong partisans receive less cooperation from opposition copartisans early in the legislative process; however, partisan intensity is not associated with their legislative effectiveness. On Election Day, stronger partisans pay an electoral price, but it is small and one that almost all members can afford. We also do not find consequences to being a reluctant team player. Lower partisan intensities are not associated with attracting primary challengers. Instead, we show that voters strongly prefer negatively toned partisan rhetoric and that by shifting to more bickering, legislators can recover any electoral penalty they incur for their excessive partisanship.

Our results present a clear and novel explanation for why some lawmakers are constantly politicizing issues while others are less willing to do so. Members use partisanship to help them stay in Washington, DC, and to become more influential once there. They need to show that they are good team players to many of their voters—and ambitious lawmakers need to do the same to their copartisans and to the extended party network. Adopting a more partisan persona is not a consequence-free action, but for most legislators, it presents a reasonable trade-off. The effect of fewer cosponsors on their bills from the other party and a slightly smaller vote share on Election Day is a price most members are willing to pay to enter the party leadership ranks, lead a committee, or run for higher office.

For reformers who worry about excessive partisanship poisoning the legislative process, our findings are concerning. Getting ahead in Congress demands that members be good team players who are willing to politicize issues to score political points. Moreover, the consequences for this behavior are the opposite of what many congressional observers might hope for. Voters reward negatively toned bickering but not positively toned partisan cheerleading. At the ballot box, the electoral penalty is minimal, and legislators can recoup it by attacking the other party more frequently. Members from the other party do not ostracize strong partisans during the legislative process. Despite that politicizers are less likely to work collaboratively, the ideas they push are regularly passed. Put simply, the incentives are heavily stacked toward higher, negatively toned partisan intensities.

Yet, to the extent that partisanship is a problem, our study also offers clear remedies to reining in its excesses. Members from safe seats respond to their partisan voters by bickering with the other party. Ambitious members appeal to their copartisans in the same way. As such, two institutional remedies can lower the partisan temperature in Congress. More competitive districts are associated with lower partisan intensity. Changing House committee leaders' within-Congress constituents from the party caucuses/conferences to another group, like committee members, would reduce the partisan demands on those ambitious members. Some congressional partisanship is inevitable and is not necessarily bad. Its excesses and the politicization it creates, however, can be problematic. Right now, the incentives are clearly tilted toward extreme levels. That said, our analysis shows that both electoral and institutional changes can make a difference.

The Importance of Partisanship

The case for studying partisanship is often an institutional one. Congress watchers worry that this sort of behavior affects the legislature's ability to function. Certainly this is an important concern, and we make the case for it as motivation for our research below, but it is not the most important reason to write about this topic. Instead, studying partisanship is essential for behavioral reasons, namely, how it affects the citizenry.

Political scientists who study Americans' political behavior consistently show that today Democratic and Republican citizens are split along any number of dimensions. Their views on issues have diverged ("The Partisan Divide on Political Values Grows Even Wider" 2017). Their attitudes toward one another have soured (Iyengar et al. 2019), and their social circles have become more politically homogenous ("The Partisan Divide on Political Values Grows Even Wider" 2017; Huber and Malhotra 2017). Even issues or situations that begin with no political content become politicized, with Republicans holding one view and Democrats the other (Gadarian, Goodman, and Pepinsky 2021; Nyhan 2014; Baum 2011). This can even extend beyond policy or cultural preferences, as a partisan divide often emerges concerning facts themselves (Gerber and Huber 2010).[6] For many, their partisan affiliation has become a social identity that colors their views of politics and policy, culture, the state of the world, and their fellow citizens (Mason 2018).

Just as these partisan schisms have been carefully documented, researchers have shown that people do not just decide on their own that Democrats will take one side of an issue and Republicans the other. Rather, these divides are created by a top-down information exchange from political elites to the public (Wang and Klar 2022). People use their party as a heuristic when evaluating information, which affects their opinions and attitudes in a wide range of settings. When voting, party labels are important cues for voters, especially in low information environments (Garlick 2015; Schaffner and Streb 2002). Citizens use partisan endorsements to formulate their opinions on issues (Barber and Pope 2019; Hill and Huber 2019; Druckman, Peterson, and Slothuus 2013; Slothuus 2010; Pink et al. 2021). This effect is even more pronounced in contemporary politics, since the parties are polarized and voters perceive a variety of issues as central to partisan conflict (Slothuus and de Vreese 2010; Druckman, Peterson, and Slothuus 2013). Even different perceptions between partisans that often flip when control of the presidency shifts between the parties, such as views on the economy or whether the country is on the right track, are driven by frames disseminated by partisan elites (Bisgaard and Slothuus 2018).

Put simply, nature does not make voters from different parties disagree. Politicians do so by politicizing issues. One of the most common ways this occurs is by framing a topic in partisan terms. Political elites will say their party is for X while the other party, who is obviously wrong, is for Y. To the extent that politicians, through partisan framing, affect peoples' opinions, an important question is, Which politicians are doing this? And why? Who wants citizens to view the world through blue- or red-tinted glasses and who does not?

To date, few studies systematically examine which officials politicize our politics. Some recent research begins taking steps in this direction (Gelman and Wilson 2021; Russell 2021a), but it is mostly descriptive. A common retort is that this question does not need to be studied because all politicians engage in this behavior. Yet, as we show in chapter 3 and as others consistently find (Mann and Ornstein 2012; Russell 2018; Gelman 2020b; Sinclair 2006), this simply is not the case. In Congress, some legislators are much more partisan than others. Describing who these legislators are and what motivates their behavior is essential to understanding who tries to politicize nearly everything in our politics. Political scientists have clearly shown the consequences of this behavior on the public. We seek to explain who traffics in this kind of rhetoric and to what end.

In addition to the compelling behavioral argument, the more traditional institutional reasons for studying partisanship are valuable as well. Today's Congress is a polarized, hyper-partisan place. In explaining how Congress has moved away from the mid-20th century's decentralized, textbook version to its modern version, the dominant explanation has been ideological polarization. Although we do not dispute this cause's contribution to creating today's more centralized, divisive Congress, we argue that much of the day-to-day conflict on Capitol Hill over the last generation is pure partisanship, increasingly divorced from ideology.

This is not a new phenomenon. For instance, take Newt Gingrich's rise through the Republican leadership ranks. Gingrich was certainly conservative, but he "was much more flexible than ideologically rigid" (Mann and Ornstein 2012, 33). His strategy for gaining power in his party and winning the House majority centered on partisan confrontation, not selling conservative ideas. Gingrich, and his Republican acolytes, avoided cooperating with Democrats, smeared them as corrupt, and sought conflict whenever possible. Some of these tactics had the veneer of policy content. Gingrich famously railed in floor speeches that Democrats were soft on communism. A good deal of these tactics did not. In 1994, Gingrich "instructed [Republican congressional candidates] to use certain words when talking about the Democratic enemy: *betray, bizarre, decay, anti-flag, anti-family, pathetic, lie, cheat, radical, sick, traitors,* and more" (Mann and Ornstein 2012, 39). Understanding Gingrich's politics, his rise to power, and his effect on the House means viewing him principally as a partisan, not an ideologue.

Similarly, the contemporary Congress is often better understood through a partisan lens rather than an ideological one. Major political disputes, like Hillary Clinton's use of a private email server or Donald Trump's impeachments, devolved into pure partisan politics. There is no liberal or conservative stance on those disputes as ideological issues. Rather than addressing the issues on their merits, legislators almost always determined their positions by whether they happened to be a Democrat or a Republican. Common negotiating strategies, like Mitch McConnell's (R-KY) now widely used approach of starving the opposition of bipartisan legislative victories, have no ideological underpinnings. Lee (2009) moves beyond anecdotes and finds evidence that a great deal of legislative conflict comes from the parties acting as teams, not from disagreement over policy.

This hyper-partisan environment has changed how Congress operates. It incentivizes constant confrontation, which affects Congress's agenda, the bill development process, and the way the chambers work (Gelman 2020a; Curry 2015; Sinclair 2016).[7] Partisan warriors have torn at the Senate's conciliatory fabric (Theriault 2013, 2015), and for many members, scoring political points has become a daily imperative.

For congressional reformers, both the institutional and the behavioral cases for understanding this behavior should be compelling. Political observers and lawmakers cite rampant partisanship as a problem afflicting Capitol Hill (Dingell 2014; Zapler 2012). The complaints, including their causes and consequences, may vary, but a common underlying theme is that partisanship, not ideological polarization, often stands in the way of cooperation. In this telling, negotiating a compromise is possible, but hyper-partisan legislators politicize issues and frame conflict as between the two parties. Consequently, a potential deal stops being politically viable, even if more compromising members could have set aside their differences. To the extent that politicizers are affecting what Congress can accomplish, then just as it is important to identify the ideologues and their influence, which has produced a mountain of research, it is important to identify the partisans and the motivation for their behavior.

In addition to their concerns about legislative gridlock, reformers worry about the politicization of issues among the public. As we discuss above, researchers have convincingly shown that political elites, including lawmakers, drive this behavior. Studies on messaging politics show that among members this emphasis on politicization is increasing and coming at the expense of expertise building (Crosson et al. 2021). For most members, partisan messaging has become a dominant daily activity that far outstrips the time they spend attempting to legislate (Gelman 2018). Put simply, members are spending more time and effort trying to politicize issues, and that trend shows no sign of abating. To the extent that this politicization is a concern, then a first step to addressing it is better understanding what benefit members get from it.

Our Approach to Studying Partisanship

Congressional partisanship is a well-trodden subject. However, there is a great deal that we do not know or that we have contradictory results for that need more exploration. Our research approach includes three features that, in combination, present a fresh and clarifying perspective on this topic.

First, we carefully define what "partisan behavior" is and what it is not. In doing so, we disentangle a term too often used as a catchall from other distinct concepts such as "partisan polarization" and "incivility." Partisanship is when legislators support their party or oppose the other party. It arises due to "competing political interests" (Lee 2009, 3) and manifests when members seek to advantage their side, usually at the expense of the opposition. Members are being partisan when their actions benefit their party at the expense of the other party. We operationalize this concept through rhetorical analysis of members' Twitter posts, classifying a tweet as partisan if it creates a party-based frame that supports their party or attacks the other party. We use terms like "partisanship," "partisan intensity," "partisan demeanor," and "partisan persona" synonymously and are referring to the frequency that lawmakers use these party-based frames.

Second, we examine individual members of Congress, not parties (Lee 2009, 2016; Koger and Lebo 2017; Gelman 2020a), leaders (Jenkins and Monroe 2012), specific legislative cohorts (Theriault 2013; Ragusa 2016; Sinclair 2006), or case studies tracking how important events have increased partisanship over time (Smith 2014; Mann and Ornstein 2012; Sinclair 2006). This is a departure from the excellent studies that explain how parties work together as teams or how some particular group of lawmakers contributes to partisan quarreling. That said, we take insights from this research and apply it to understand legislators' behavior. For example, Lee's (2009, 2016) theory of partisan teamsmanship contends that members' linked electoral fates, due to their party affiliation, encourage them to stick together on issues to build a stronger partisan brand. The idea that members work in teams is foundational to the argument later in the book.

Other political scientists have studied lawmakers' partisanship, but the third difference in our approach is how we measure this concept. A common strategy to understanding partisan behavior is to examine who is willing to break with their party and work with legislators from the other side of the aisle ("Bipartisan Index" 2021; Harbridge 2015; Harbridge-Yong, Volden, and Wiseman 2023; Lawless, Theriault, and Guthrie 2018). These studies of bipartisanship, which often imply that partisanship is some natural state that members overcome when working together, are problematic for studying partisan behavior for a few reasons. They assume that partisanship and bipartisanship are opposites. As we discuss in chapter 3, that is not necessarily the case. Usually these studies use votes or bill cosponsorships to construct their measure of bipartisanship, which weakly proxies for a member's partisan behavior. More importantly, these data are preference based, whereas a better measure is an intensity-based one. Other studies use different vote-based measures, like party unity scores (Carson et al. 2010). These suffer from the same problems, being weak proxies and only measuring revealed preferences, not behavioral intensity.

Additionally, we do not analyze an area that others have shown is an important aspect of modern partisan behavior: incumbents' donation and contribution strategies. On Capitol Hill and in the political science literature, it is common knowledge that money is related to being a good partisan team player. Leaders fundraise on behalf of the rank and file and donate generously to their campaigns (Currinder 2008). Those aspiring for higher positions on committees or in the party leadership structure strategically donate to win their copartisans' support (Currinder 2003; Heberling and Larson 2012; Kanthak 2007; Deering and Wahlbeck 2006; Green and Harris 2019). The parties themselves ask members to pay dues to their campaign arms, and members are open about party pressure to constantly fundraise and distribute those funds to vulnerable colleagues (Nocera 2014; Buck and Blankschaen 2017; Franken 2017). Put simply, we know that money functions as a partisan tool for promotion-seeking behavior, including building loyalty among one's copartisans. Given these findings, we choose not to focus on the link between partisanship, fundraising, and power-seeking behavior. Instead, we explore other important but less studied consequences of members' partisanship.

Partisan Intensity

Our approach follows recent research that uses social media posts, specifically from Twitter, to measure lawmakers' partisanship. Russell (2018, 2020) has examined senators' partisan tweets, and our previous research has explored partisan behavior on Twitter more broadly (Gelman 2020b; Gelman and Wilson 2021). Unlike other data sources, social media allows us to measure an individual member's partisan *intensity*, by directly measuring the time and effort they devote to supporting their party. Other methods only capture partisan preferences, which is just a member's position on the issue. These different conceptual approaches produce different patterns in partisan behavior.

For instance, consider how measures of partisan intensity and preferences capture one of the most contentious issues in Congress today: judicial nominations. A preference-based measure weights all votes the same and can produce misleading conclusions. Just by counting votes, we might infer that Howard C. Nielson Jr.'s straight party line confirmation to the US district court in Utah created more partisan conflict than Brett Kavanaugh's Supreme Court nomination, during which two senators voted against their party's dominant position. Of course, Nielson's confirmation was much less contentious. Senators spent months sparring over Kavanaugh's nomination. It dominated politics for weeks once sexual assault allegations against him became public. Nielson was confirmed with barely a partisan peep from either side.

Measuring a member's partisan intensity with social media posts allows us to explore partisanship in a way that was not possible with previous research. We can assess differences in this behavior that is independent of leadership arm-twisting, agenda-setting effects, and rules about when members can speak on the floor. Unlike votes or cosponsorships, we can measure partisanship's tone and lawmakers' reactions to the continual stream of clashes that never reach the House or Senate floor. Put simply, partisan intensity allows us to study congressional partisanship much more comprehensively.

Scope, External Validity, and Overview

Our study covers three congressional terms, from 2015 through 2020 (the 114th through the 116th Congress), which include the final two years of Barack Obama's presidency and nearly all of Trump's first term. As a consequence, this book describes contemporary partisanship in the US Congress. We use Twitter posts by members of Congress to create our measures of partisan intensity that form the basis of our analyses throughout the book.

Using six years of data on a social media platform that has since dramatically changed raises important questions about our study's scope and external validity. Is this book about a very specific moment in American politics? And can this tell us anything else about politics beyond this time and place? When we began writing this book, we did so with the view that our argument has some exportability beyond what American politicians posted on Twitter in 2017, so we will spend a few pages here explaining our thinking.

We limit the project's scope to this specific time period and social media platform for practical reasons. Although it seems commonplace as we write now, social media use among legislators, including on Twitter/X, is a recent phenomenon. Not until 2015, when our data begins, was Twitter's use ubiquitous among members (Golbeck, Grimes, and Rogers 2010; Straus et al. 2014). We use Twitter data because, for this brief moment, it was the central location where legislators sent easily accessed public messages and often interacted with one another.[8] Donald Trump's reliance on Twitter during this first presidential term amplified its importance, as it was the place that he often announced new policies (usually without warning).

This social media hub for congressional communications was short-lived. In 2022, Elon Musk purchased Twitter and rebranded it as X. After the change in ownership and by 2024, congressional Democrats had largely moved on from the platform, no longer making it a useful place to study all legislators' partisan behavior (Elkind 2024).[9] The upshot is that for six years, we have excellent social media data—ubiquitous, public, accessible, and comparable—that allows us to examine the partisan personas that lawmakers cultivate.

One of the most common adages of our times is that social media is not real life. Even though it was an important place as American politics unfolded in the 2010s, it is true that for most people Twitter wasn't real life or even part of their life. It is well documented that most of the public never used it and that its user base tilted to the more politically engaged (Wojcik and Hughes 2019). Yet, as we note in chapter 2, widespread use among voters is not essential to our argument. Rather, the social media website's public-facing nature, where anyone could easily see what legislators were posting, is the more significant underlying component to our theory. Put simply, the nature and role of Twitter as a centralized, easily accessible hub for consistent congressional communications during this six-year period make it an ideal time span to study public-facing legislative partisanship.

Even so, the admittedly narrow time period we study raises important questions about what this research can say about congressional partisanship more generally. After all, partisanship on Capitol Hill is not new.[10] Are we describing an odd moment in American politics? Is our theory and these social media posts only useful for understanding this particular time, or do our ideas speak to broader, long-term dynamics in politics?

Although we will tread very lightly here, it is worth connecting ideas from our research to some larger ones. First, we are limited to analyzing what lawmakers posted on Twitter. However, they engage in other public activities where they display their partisan personas for similar reasons. Their propensity to go on television, for instance, and use partisan frames may stem from the same political incentives we explore throughout the book. Put differently, we are observing a certain type of behavior on Twitter, but it likely manifests in other public-facing communications for similar reasons.

Additionally, a natural question relates to time and how partisanship has changed relative to the past. We cannot say whether members' partisan intensities are higher than in previous decades or even centuries, although others have argued this is the case (e.g., Mann and Ornstein 2012). If so, our theory provides a few reasons for this increase and gives context for why we live in such partisan times. First, promotion-seeking behavior has evolved for reasons related to changes internal and external to Congress. Inside the House and Senate, there are very few ways to accrue power that do not require being a team player. Broadly speaking, House committee chairs maintain their positions by winning party caucus elections instead of rising through a seniority system.[11] For House Republicans, term limits for chairmanships likely exacerbate this behavior, because any prospects for leading another committee require having been a good partisan in their previous role.

Becoming a party leader and keeping that job is likely more about cultivating an intensely partisan persona when compared to the past. Certainly, leaders have always needed to be good team players, but what that means has likely changed in recent decades. More recent political science scholarship emphasizes that party leaders are delegated power by their backbenchers to build and maintain the party brand (e.g., Cox and McCubbins 2005). This responsibility has become especially important in an era of nationalized elections. Because backbenchers are increasingly unable to build local support divorced from the national party (Jacobson 2017), they need a positive partisan image on which to run. As such, they require leaders who are intensely partisan and invest in brand building. In previous eras, where national party brands were less relevant, leaders emphasized other parts of their jobs. Democratic leaders during the early and mid-20th century famously had to balance the policy interests of an ideologically diverse coalition (Polsby 2004). Scoring political points at the expense of Republicans was not the same daily imperative as it is today. Put simply, seeking promotion and maintaining party leadership roles likely did not require building the same type of partisan persona.

Nationalized politics has also likely changed promotion seeking to higher office. If we believe the old saying and suppose that every senator believes they will be president and that most House members believe they will be a senator, then how these ambitious politicians rise to these offices affects their partisan intensities. Decades ago, presidential and senatorial candidates relied on local bases of political support to win their party's nomination (albeit in very different ways). Now, these races are highly nationalized. Often, winning means highlighting your partisan bona fides to party leaders, donors, and primary voters as a prerequisite to be taken seriously. Jacobson (2017, 58) provides a small caveat that "a handful [of legislators] may still be able to build a power base separate from their party, but for a large majority, the power base is now the party."

Jacobson's insight provides a second potential reason for why our theory suggests we live in more partisan times than in the past. Later in the book, we show that members holding safer seats are more partisan. One reason for this behavior, we contend, is that they need to appeal to primary and reelection electorates who are animated by nationalized politics. This calculation is somewhat different than in the past. Even though the number of safe seats in Congress has not dramatically increased in the past 70 years, what plays well with voters in safe districts likely has changed. The move from local politics, which did not require that incumbents adopt a partisan persona to win reelection, to nationalized politics, where partisan team play is part of a typical campaign strategy, is a shift that has likely changed how legislators publicly present themselves. In other words, safe districts are not the culprit for more intense partisans on Capitol Hill per se. Safe districts mixed with nationalized politics are.

Again, our theory, data, and analysis focus on the contemporary Congress. But when we consider why members are displaying more or less partisan intensity these days and compare those reasons to how legislative politics used to operate, we can begin to at least speculate on why partisanship, and its determinants, has changed over time.

For the balance of the book, we turn our attention to the present to provide a novel explanation for why members differ in their partisanship and for this behavior's consequences. In chapter 2, we propose a theory of individual-level partisanship. In chapter 3, we define the concept as well as introduce and validate our measure of partisan intensity. Chapter 4 describes the tenor of members' partisan intensity by developing a partisan tone score, which we use to describe who bickers with the other party, cheerleads their own, or does both.

In chapter 5, we test hypotheses from chapter 2 that predict members' partisanship. Through a series of empirical tests, we show that legislators' partisan intensity is an amalgamation of their electoral circumstances and their personal ambitions. Chapters 6 and 7 consider the consequences of partisanship. In chapter 6, we assess whether excessive partisanship affects members' behavior and effectiveness in the legislative process. We show that partisan intensity is associated with fewer bipartisan cosponsorships, both by the member and by others on the legislator's bills, and increased partisan voting on the floor but does not affect a lawmaker's legislative effectiveness. In chapter 7, we show that voters may penalize legislators for being excessively partisan, but this lost vote share is manageable for most members and can be offset by adopting a more negative partisan tone. Finally, in chapter 8, we assess congressional partisanship during the first few years of Joe Biden's presidency and conclude by offering ways to lower the partisan temperature on Capitol Hill.

TWO

Why Partisanship?

People are concerned about partisanship. For many, there is too much of it. In 2023, the Pew Research Center reported that Americans had an "unrelentingly negative" view of politics, "with little hope of improvement on the horizon." For most of those surveyed, the main reason for their despondency was that far too much attention in the American political system was paid to partisan disagreements between Democrats and Republicans. Pew reported that "more than eight-in-ten Americans (86%) say the following is a good description of politics: 'Republicans and Democrats are more focused on fighting each other than on solving problems'" (Doherty et al. 2023).

Concerns about partisanship are not new. In "Federalist No. 10," Madison writes of the conventional wisdom in 1787 that "the public good is disregarded in the conflicts of rival parties" and "measures are too often decided by . . . an interested and over-bearing majority" (1787). In his presidential farewell address, George Washington argues that partisans misrepresent public opinion because they "render alien to each other those who ought to be bound together by fraternal affection" and "put, in place of the delegated will of the nation, the will of the party" (1796). Although Madison and Washington had no experience with the modern party system, their criticisms clearly resonate with many today. Congress is regularly derided for its partisanship and the numerous members who put their party's interests ahead of the country's.

Not everyone agrees with the dim assessments of Madison, Washington, and many modern Americans. Those who have experienced political moments with little to no disagreement between parties celebrate partisanship's importance. Writing in response to the founding generation's distrust of parties and criticizing the one-party Era of Good Feelings, Martin Van Buren argued that "party divisions and political organizations" are essential to managing conflict "when men are brought under one government who differ radically in opinion" (1867, 15–16).[1] In 1950, the American Political Science Association (APSA) famously called for more responsible parties. One of its main recommendations was more partisan loyalty, where only team players be allowed to "participat[e] in the common enterprise" of governing (American Political Science Association 1950, 2). Writing in the 1970s, David Broder (1971) argued that political power needed to be concentrated with party leaders and that party caucuses should be the ones who select every leader in Congress, from Speaker of the House down to the committee chair leading the least influential committee.

Looking back, these reformers seem to have got what they wanted, although perhaps not for the best. Sixty-three years after the first APSA report, a new one on negotiating compromise in Congress featured prominent scholars arguing that more partisanship was not needed and instead stood as a principal roadblock to lawmaking (Binder and Lee 2013). As we document throughout the book, Broder's proposed remedies, which were adopted in the 1970s, are a key driver of partisanship, and returning to a system where some members are empowered by entities other than party caucuses is an easy way to reduce its intensity.

These many arguments about partisanship, spanning centuries, highlight two important points. First, the seemingly obvious claim that partisanship is a problem that needs to be solved is not so obvious. Partisanship is an easy scapegoat in hyper-partisan times but becomes a missing ingredient in politics during moments when it has faded away. The answer to the philosophical question about what constitutes the "right" amount of partisanship depends on the time, and the question, while very important, is not one we will answer in this book.

Second, given that the debate about partisanship's role in government dates to the earliest American presidents, it would seem reasonable that researchers would have developed an account of why legislators adopt partisan behaviors. That is not the case. A good deal certainly has been written about it, especially legislative voting patterns, but without an underlying explanation of legislators' day-to-day partisan performances.

Indeed, rather than offering a comprehensive theory, research on this topic is piecemeal. Studies explore different factors, such as seat safety, the holding of leadership positions, insecure majorities, and differences between Demo-

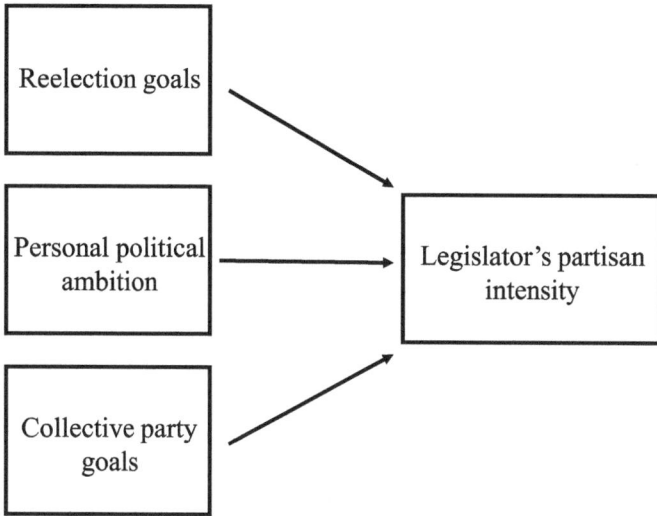

Fig. 2.1. Major Factors That Predict a Legislator's Partisan Intensity

crats and Republicans, among others, as contributing to legislative partisanship. In this chapter, we construct a more unified explanation for this behavior while acknowledging that political scientists have connected many factors to this concept. This means our discussion includes many components. So, before moving forward, we focus on our main points as a touchstone to return to as we introduce new ideas or complexities. Our argument is that partisan intensity varies among members for two main reasons: voter demand back home and differences in political ambition. We also contend that collective party goals are closely linked to these factors (e.g., being in the majority party affects one's political influence), and throughout this chapter, we note these connections.

Figure 2.1 is a simple visual representation of our argument. As we progress through the chapter, we will both introduce variables that capture each of these components and make the argument a bit more complex, especially in tying collective party goals to individual ones. Even as we do, everything we discuss either fits into one of Figure 2.1's three components or is a factor that others have proposed affects partisanship that we will later include as control variables in our statistical models. Our theory and analysis later in the book mostly examine members' reelection motivations and political ambition because they differ by member, but all three factors combine to form a legislator's partisan intensity.

Foundational Assumptions and Our Argument

This chapter offers a theory of members' partisanship. Its underlying assumptions are simple and include some of the most fundamental ideas in the study of congressional behavior. The first is that legislators have three goals: winning reelection, enacting good public policy, and gaining political influence.[2]

Second, legislators are goal oriented, meaning that the actions they take while in office are in pursuit of their goals. Although they work to make good policy and accrue influence, winning reelection is the goal they prioritize. Indeed, for most of their decisions, the first question they ask is, How will this affect me on Election Day? Only after answering that question do members consider how a certain action advances their policy goals or increases their political power.

Third, their public behavior on social media is easily observed by voters and their fellow legislators. This is not to say that everything they do is systematically tracked and cataloged by others (other than by researchers, of course) but simply that their public behavior is *public*.[3] That is, we assume that it is reasonably easy for the average voter to learn about a member's public behavior, especially because they publicize their actions.

An implicit assumption is that this public social media behavior reflects the legislator's views, preferences, and priorities. This raises the question of whether it is the legislator who is composing and sending social media posts or a staffer. Practically, the answer is that it depends. Some members, like Chuck Grassley and Dana Rohrabacher, are infamous for writing their own misspelling-filled tweets. Others probably only abstractly know what social media is. Most fall somewhere in between. For our purposes, we assume that these posts reflect lawmakers' genuine views and preferences. This is the approach political scientists adopt when studying any type of congressional communication, be it social media posts, newsletters, press releases, or speeches delivered on the floor or in committee. Members of Congress rarely, if ever, write any of these documents themselves. Moreover, we very reasonably assume that communications staffers are faithful agents when posting on behalf of the member. They strategize with their bosses when deciding what to post. Nothing gets someone fired faster than producing content that harms the lawmaker's reputation.

Fourth, legislators develop reputations among their voters and colleagues. In fact, they work hard to carefully cultivate their public images through their "presentations of self" (Fenno 1978, 54). Like actors, Fenno argues, lawmakers calculate their public appearances to get the optimal response from an audience. For legislators interacting with constituents, this means winning their vote. On Capitol Hill, they develop reputations based on their legislative styles. From these assumptions, we develop a theory of congressional partisanship that considers how this behavior helps lawmakers achieve their goals. In doing so, we revise conventional claims about what motivates partisanship and arrive at a series of theoretical expectations that we test in the subsequent chapters.

Our argument is twofold. First, we contend that legislators calibrate their partisan intensity to achieve two of their goals: win reelection and become more politically important. Partisanship helps incumbents appeal to copartisan voters and build a positive party brand. Those in safe seats display more partisan behavior as they appeal to an electorate of fellow party members, while those in competitive districts adjust their partisan behavior to gain support from a broad coalition of voters.

However, appealing to voters only partially explains why members cultivate partisan personas. Incumbents adopt more partisan behaviors as they try to become more politically influential. In the contemporary Congress, such ambitions as moving up the party leadership ranks, running a committee, or running for higher office require that legislators be good team players. The constituents who select people for these positions are their copartisan legislators or, in the case of elections, the extended party network. Their prerequisite for promoting members into these positions is that they are reliable partisans. Consequently, those running for and holding these roles display more partisan intensity as a signal that they can be trusted to support the party. As they strive to achieve their reelection and power-seeking goals, partisanship is adopted as a home style that is used to appeal to voters and a hill style that helps lawmakers become more politically influential.

The second part of our argument is that a member's partisan behavior comes with minimal, if any, negative consequences. Legislatively, we expect that it affects cosponsorship and floor voting. More partisan members may be less willing to cosponsor bills from the other party, and their ideas might also receive less opposition support early on. Regarding voting, we expect that they are more willing to vote with their party, especially when the president takes a stance on an issue. But overall we do not expect that more partisan intensity reduces a legislator's effectiveness. Instead, sometimes it can be a legislative asset. It helps lawmakers accrue power and institutional status. Opposition members may even see partisans as good partners who will prevent their issue from being politicized. No matter the mechanism, partisan intensity does not hobble members' legislating.

Similarly, we argue that members face few electoral consequences for acting too partisan. Although previous research suggests they are penalized for excessive partisanship, most incumbents are in safe enough seats that they can comfortably handle this vote share loss. In fact, lawmakers need to be just as concerned that not being partisan enough might attract a primary challenger. Even if a substantial penalty exists, they can compensate for it by changing their partisan tone. Except when members hold unsafe seats, being more combative can increase voter support by appealing to many of their constituents' affectively polarized attitudes.

Taken together, our theory paints a clear picture of partisanship in the contemporary Congress. Partisanship is used to appeal to voters to help incumbents win reelection and helps them show off as good team players, the prerequisite that convinces copartisans to promote them to powerful positions. Using partisanship to achieve these goals requires flexibility. Members need the option to strategically increase their partisan intensity as they seek more power. The minimal legislative and electoral consequences allow this. Members can become more partisan when they run for and hold leadership positions without worrying that doing so will cost them their seat. The result is a hyper-partisan Congress where members strategically use this behavior to achieve their goals without much downside.

The Conventional Story

Before we develop our theory, it is worth outlining the conventional explanation for members' partisanship and where it falls short. In the *home style* view, members strategically calibrate their partisanship to match their voters' preferences so they can win reelection. Those representing safe seats, which are dominated by one party, are intensely partisan. This appeals to the party base, which is motivated by animosity toward the opposition (Mason 2018; Abramowitz and Webster 2018; Doherty and Kiley 2016). For members in competitive districts, displaying less partisanship is smart politics, as it helps appeal to a wider range of voters. Not surprisingly, researchers consistently find an association between partisan behavior and a district's partisan lean (Carson et al. 2010; Gelman and Wilson 2021; Meinke 2009). Put differently, a conventional home style explanation is that each legislator develops a partisan persona that reflects their voters' preferences for this sort of behavior. Tailoring their partisanship builds trust and support among constituents, which helps the member win more votes on Election Day.

This argument, while tidy, is too simplistic. An important assumption underlying the home style argument is that a lawmaker's self-presentation constructs a personalized profile that helps voters evaluate them separate from their party. Yet, over the past few decades as politics have become more polarized, partisan, and nationalized, the importance of a member's personal brand has dissipated. Party line voting has reached record levels, ticket splitting is rare, and those in competitive seats have their electoral fates determined by nationalized trends in voting, not personal performance. Although some special cases come to mind, they are exceptions. As Jacobson (2017, 46) notes, "The growing dominance of state and district partisanship . . . and the declining impact of incumbency have made it increasingly difficult for congressional candidates to win and hold constituencies against the partisan grain." The result is "a diminished 'personal vote'" replaced with an electoral landscape where a lawmaker's political party is a more important factor than their carefully crafted persona.[4]

In addition, the connection between a member's seat safety and their partisan behavior is surprisingly weak. The correlation between these factors only hovers between 0.3 and 0.4.[5] Moreover, an individual's partisanship fluctuates over time. The within-member correlation between congressional terms is 0.53, and on average, a member's partisanship shifts 4 percent every two years even though their district's partisan lean remains much more stable. In some cases, these changes are drastic. Before Donald Trump's first election, Adam Schiff (D-CA) was a fairly partisan Democrat, ranking around the 75th percentile of his party. Yet, for the entirety of Trump's first term, he transformed into one of the most partisan members in Congress. His district did not change during these years, but his behavior did.

In the Senate, same-party senators representing the same state and facing the same voters also differ in their partisanship. Even though they both represented Kansas, during the six years we analyze, Jerry Moran (R-KS) was one of the least partisan senators, while Pat Roberts (R-KS) was more partisan than most.[6] These differences did not change when one of them was running for reelection. The Kansan senators are not anomalies. From New York and Rhode Island, Chuck Schumer (D-NY) and Sheldon Whitehouse (D-RI) are much more partisan than Kirsten Gillibrand (D-NY) and Jack Reed (D-RI). In fact, most states with senators from the same party have one who is much more partisan than the other.

We do not dispute that members adopt partisan behaviors to appeal to voters. Part of our theory suggests that electoral considerations play a role in how partisan they act. However, the idea that lawmakers simply calibrate their partisanship based on their district's partisan lean cannot entirely explain these between- or within-member differences. Rather, different assumptions about what underlies partisanship in the contemporary Congress provide a stronger foundation for understanding this behavior.

Complicating the Conventional Story

Our theory's starting point is based on how lawmakers conceptualize their electoral prospects. The standard view, derived from the idea that incumbents are single-minded reelection seekers, is that their public actions, including their calibrated partisan behavior, are used to increase their vote share. In other words, they try to maximize their winning margin on Election Day by building a personal reputation that appeals to voters. Their carefully tailored partisan personas are part of that reputation.

Yet, in the contemporary Congress, that view is not quite right for two reasons. First, as Fiorina (1974) argues, when members build comfortable enough electoral margins, they are willing to lose some vote share to pursue activities that help them achieve their other goals. Fiorina dubs these legislators "maintainers," a class of members that has expanded since he introduced this idea in the 1970s as districts have become even less competitive.[7]

Although this argument was published 50 years ago, the core insight is generalizable and applicable today. No matter the year, be it 1974 or 2024, an incumbent only needs 51 percent of the vote to guarantee reelection. That has not changed, and neither has lawmakers' goal of reaching an "aspirational level" of vote share that provides them a comfortable electoral cushion on Election Day.

Although these maintainers still worry about being reelected, they engage in a wider range of activities, some of which may lose votes. A smaller group is made up of maximizers, whose behavior is designed to build a larger electoral cushion. Representing competitive districts, they try to increase their vote share to an aspirational level that will make them feel electorally safe (Fiorina 1974). Their activities focus on maximizing votes, and they rarely act in ways that will reduce their Election Day vote total.

Fiorina explicitly cautions against assuming that a certain winning margin means an incumbent has achieved their aspiration level. He contends it varies by member. Even so, most incumbents hold safe seats and are most likely maintainers. For the six years we analyze, the average vote share for those running for reelection was 65 percent. A standardized measure of seat safety that accounts for legislators who choose not to run for reelection indicates the average district has a 10-point partisan lean toward the incumbent's party.[8] Put simply, most members are likely maintainers, not maximizers.

Second, these days, copartisans' electoral fates are often linked (Lee 2009; Jacobson 2017). Legislators are increasingly evaluated not on their individual performance but by their party's brand and actions (Jacobson 2015, 2019). This shift is what Arnold (1990) describes as voters relying on a "party performance rule" to evaluate candidates rather than an "individual performance rule." Knowing this, members are incentivized to maintain a positive party brand. Maximizers need it to help them win tough races. Maintainers want it because their party needs to win competitive districts in order to win majority status. This creates a collective esprit de corps, which is the glue that holds copartisans together in Congress (Lee 2009).

This idea of partisan-linked fate, which facilitates individual-level partisanship, has been well developed over the past few decades. The argument is straightforward: as voters increasingly support candidates based on their party affiliation, legislators work to build their partisan brand. However, brand building creates a collective action problem. Everyone benefits from a good public image, but lawmakers prefer that their colleagues do this work so they can focus their attention elsewhere. To solve this (and other) collective dilemmas, members elect party leaders who are charged with tending to and strengthening this collective image (Cox and McCubbins 2005).

In turn, leaders manage the brand and balance it against other competing concerns like advancing the party's policy agenda (Koger and Lebo 2017). As part of their roles, they develop messaging campaigns, control the legislative agenda to provide members with credit-claiming opportunities and protect them from bad votes, and prospect for chances to confront the opposition in order to score political points. Many of the rank and file readily adopt these partisan talking points, which allows them to focus their energies elsewhere, to be seen as a good team player, and to advance the party's collective image to their voters back home.

Partisanship as a Reelection Strategy

This more nuanced explanation of how members see their electoral fortunes provides a starting point for how their reelection concerns affect their partisan behavior. First and foremost, it suggests that a district's partisan lean should be associated with a member's partisan behavior. Maximizers in competitive seats carefully cultivate a weaker partisan persona to avoid losing voters who are not motivated by those sorts of appeals. Maintainers have more freedom in developing this part of their home style, but for many, an easy way to preserve their electoral cushion is to display more partisanship to remind their copartisans who dominate the electorate and are motivated by partisan appeals that they are on the same political team.

However, a district's partisan lean is not the only electoral factor that affects partisanship. Concerns about the party's brand motivate legislators to collectively shift their partisan behavior. Political scientists have shown that three institutional factors are associated with these changes. First, minority party status is associated with more partisan confrontation. The argument is that since the minority party is shut out of or has a reduced role in the legislative process, they spend their efforts attacking the majority party (Russell 2018; Lee 2016; Egar 2016).

Second, narrow majorities amplify everyone's partisan inclinations (Gelman 2020a; 2019; Lee 2016). When a majority's seat share is smaller, and every seat counts, improving the party brand can be the difference between winning enough seats to control the chamber or not.[9] In these situations, legislators' partisan intensities in both parties should increase as party brand building takes on even more significance.

Third, being in the party opposite the president is related to more partisan behavior. As the dominant figure in politics, the president serves as a lightning rod for partisan attacks (Gelman and Wilson 2021; Lee 2008). For his opponents in Congress, he is an easy target, as the president activates partisan animosity among the base and the administration is constantly in the news. Partisan attacks aimed at the president are a cheap and profitable way to score political points. Certainly, the president's copartisans defend him and often do so vigorously, but the opposition tends toward a unified front against the president's actions (Lee 2009).

Together, these factors point to how multiple electoral pressures contribute to a member's partisan persona. Yes, their district's partisan lean matters, but it is not deterministic. Rather, legislators' need for a positive partisan brand pushes them to collectively adopt more partisan behaviors in certain institutional settings. Table 2.1 summarizes our expectations about how lawmakers' reelection concerns affect their partisanship.

Partisanship and Power Seeking

So far, we have articulated how partisan behavior is driven by members' goals to win reelection and majority status. But even with this more nuanced expla-

TABLE 2.1. Reelection and Collective Party Goals Expectations

	Expected Effect	Hypothesis
Seat safety	+	*Members holding safer seats are more likely to display higher partisan intensities.*
Serving in the minority party	+	*Members in the minority party are more likely to display more partisan intensity.*
Narrow majorities	+	*Narrow majorities are associated with more partisan intensity.*
Party opposite the president	+	*Members in the party opposing the president are more likely to display more partisan intensity.*

nation, an election-based argument cannot explain many of the within-party differences in partisanship. Lawmakers in similar electoral situations, like the same-state senators we previously discussed or representatives in equally safe seats, still display varied partisan intensities. The institutional changes we identify as affecting this behavior, like being in the party opposite the president, impact everyone and create collective shifts in partisanship. Something else must also be incentivizing legislators to become good team players.

We argue that members strategically adopt partisan behaviors to achieve another of their goals—becoming more influential in politics. Once in Congress, lawmakers have two main avenues to increase their political influence. They can hold more powerful positions in their current chamber, or they can run for higher office.[10] The chances of success for both are enhanced by strengthening ties to the party by increasing their partisanship.

If higher partisan intensities help members become more politically influential, which we argue below, then it seems like a rational response from lawmakers is to always maximize this behavior. In other words, everyone should act as partisan as possible all the time. Although this seems reasonable, it is not how legislators present themselves. As Russell (2021) shows, being a good team player is only one activity members are engaged in. They are also claiming turf as issue experts, building ties to local organizations, and solving more parochial problems, among others. Even when messaging is very easy on social media, participating in partisan disputes takes time and effort and reveals a legislator's priorities. If their main concern is not becoming more politically influential, they will emphasize the sorts of messages that achieve the goal they are emphasizing, which may not be partisan in nature.

Moreover, if some members will do whatever it takes to be a good team player as they pursue more influence, they will always seek to exceed other members' partisan intensity. If that is the case, the rational response for someone who is not seeking promotion is to limit their partisan behavior to a level that satisfies their voters and builds the party's brand while focusing on achieving their reelection and policy goals. Put simply, for those whose primary goal is not to become more politically influential, it is not worth trying to match the partisan intensity of those who are desperately trying to show off as good team players.

Power-seeking legislators who want to become more powerful in their respective chambers can follow two main trajectories—they can join and move up the party leadership ranks or get ahead by becoming chair or a ranking member on a committee.[11] These opportunities, and the reasons lawmakers pursue them, are different. Those on the party leadership track are more interested in keeping up with daily political machinations, messaging, and helping the party succeed (Green and Harris 2019). Rising through the committee ranks to become a committee chair offers members the opportunity to affect public policy and have influence over other members who are interested in similar issue areas. Even if these positions offer different types of power and require different skills, those holding them must fulfill the same fundamental prerequisite: They need to be a good team player. The reason is simple: The constituents for a party or committee leader are their copartisans in the House or Senate. In this principal-agent relationship, the rank and file willingly delegate power to their elected leaders, with the understanding that the leaders will pursue the party's collective goals of winning a majority and negotiating legislation that is acceptable to the caucus (Cox and McCubbins 2005; Koger and Lebo 2017).[12]

This connection is clearest for the high-ranking party leaders who lead their caucuses. Prior to the start of a new Congress, the party meets and elects who will lead it. Members have different reasons for supporting certain candidates, but the most basic qualification for anyone being considered is that they will steadfastly support the party and its members. This willingness to solve the collective action problems associated with advancing the party's interests is why the caucus membership allows leaders to set the agenda, whip votes, and coordinate messaging campaigns. As a consequence, a potential candidate's minimum qualification for a top leadership position is that they are an enthusiastic team player.

For those trying to become or keep their jobs as lower-level party leaders, like conference secretary, the electoral dynamics are similar. Winning these positions requires support from a majority of the party caucus. When multiple people run for a spot, the rank and file consider a wide range of factors.

Some are concerned with ensuring descriptive representation or increasing the leadership's diversity. Others seek turnover to allow for fresh ideas and perspectives. Yet, no matter their other voting considerations, the underlying prerequisite for any candidate is whether they are a reliable partisan. Indeed, during leadership contests, legislators report perceiving that some members are more partisan than others, aspirants cultivate their brands as partisan fighters or not, and caucuses often select leaders based on these considerations (Green and Harris 2019; Mann and Ornstein 2012; Sinclair 2006).

For committee leaders in the House, this requirement of being a good team player is similar. At first, this might seem puzzling. After all, chairs and ranking members do not just parrot the party line but care about legislating on issues they have developed expertise on, want to build bipartisan relationships to advance legislation, and, in many cases, have worked with the other party's members for years on these policy topics.[13] Moreover, some legislators talk about the norm of seniority as important in deciding the next committee chair or ranking member. Although all of that may be true, committee leaders have the same constituents as party leaders—their caucus's members. In today's House, each party's steering committee nominates a slate of committee leaders for approval by the party's members. Often, the caucus affirms the steering committee's recommendations, but ultimately the decision of who leads the committees is up to the caucus.

Again, when contentious races for House committee leadership arise, members report weighing a variety of factors in who they will vote for. Some members cite the seniority norm as important, while others support candidates who are ideologically similar to them. But the foundational consideration is a candidate's partisan behavior and whether they reliably support the party. Take, for instance, the House Republican race to elect a new Transportation Committee leader in 2018. The determining factor in the race, between Sam Graves (R-MO) and Jeff Denham (R-CA), was that Denham was not a good team player (McPherson 2018).

If supporting the party is a prerequisite for moving up the party and committee ranks, then we expect current leaders and aspirants to show their ambition through increased partisan intensities. For those in leadership, keeping their position means adopting a hill style that is unwaveringly supportive of their party. They build the party brand by advancing bills that burnish their side's reputation, maintaining floor discipline to show party unity on controversial issues, and developing messaging campaigns that their backbenchers can use back home (Gelman 2020a; Pearson 2015; Lee 2016). More broadly, their public personas are intensely partisan as they willingly wade into, or create, partisan disputes in an effort to score political points (Russell 2018, 2021a). Those aspiring to a leadership role also increase their partisan behavior to show their copartisans that they will be good team players. The reasoning follows why Jeff Denham did not win his copartisans' support when they sought committee chairs. The prerequisite for representing the party is being a good teammate.

In the Senate, the link between leading committees and being a reliable partisan is less clear. The ratio of senators to chair and ranking positions is much higher than the ratio in the House, so it may not be possible for the caucus or conference to always find a good team player to lead the panel. More importantly, a committee leader's constituents are not necessarily their copartisans. Currently, Senate Republicans on a committee, not the entire conference, select their leader. Until recently, 2017, the Senate Democrats did not publish their own rules.[14] As of writing, the party's steering committee makes recommendations to the caucus, who then elect chairs and ranking members. However, by rule, every caucus member is guaranteed a chair or ranking member position on a committee or subcommittee ("Rules for the Democratic Conference" 2022). This disparity in how Senate committee leaders are selected, and their relative availability, provides us an opportunity. If these chairs' and ranking members' constituents are not their party members, then we should not observe the same partisanship patterns we see with party leaders and House committee leadership. Rather, we expect that their partisan intensity does not increase once they are elevated to these positions. This provides a good test of whether being elected to these leadership posts increases partisanship or whether simply serving in an important role drives this behavior.

For leadership elections decided by party members, journalistic and scholarly accounts point to the importance of partisanship in running for and winning them. The most common way this is discussed is in relation to money. When running for a position, candidates loosen their leadership political action committees' purse strings and donate generously to their copartisans. Shutt (2020) puts it best: "No race would be complete without substantial cash being committed to colleagues' reelection campaigns."

Yet money is only one very easily tracked measure of team play. When House Republicans shuffle their committee leaders due to their self-imposed term limits, new chairs are more likely to win not only if they gave more money to fellow members but also if they reliably voted with the team (Deering and Wahlbeck 2006). Congressional insiders often cite the importance of being allied with leadership or previous service to the party, like running the electioneering committee (Strong and Livingston 2012). The common element among all these activities is that leadership aspirants try to show that they are good team players and can be trusted with the authority they want delegated to them.

If becoming more powerful within the chamber demands that members increase their partisan intensity, then we expect to observe three behavioral patterns. First, those elected to party and House committee leadership positions should display more partisanship than the rank and file. This follows the adage that incumbents are reelection seekers but adapts it to a different setting. In this case, the election happens to be for a leadership spot and the constituents are their copartisans in the chamber.

Second, aspirants for these leadership roles should strategically increase their partisan behavior in order to show their copartisans that they are good team players. Third, after the leadership election occurs, we should observe a divergence in candidates' partisan intensities for two reasons. First, those who win, and enter the party leadership ranks or lead a committee, should keep their highly partisan style in an effort to keep their new position. The loser's partisan behavior, assuming they choose not to run for a leadership office again, should decrease, as they no longer have a reason to display outsize party loyalty. Second, those holding leadership positions benefit the most from their party winning majority status. The difference in power between the Speaker of the House and the minority party leader is vast. Serving as the committee chair rather than the ranking member means controlling the committee's agenda. As such, those in powerful roles should work hardest to build the party brand since winning majority status is especially valuable.

Besides winning leadership races, lawmakers have a second way of becoming more influential in politics: They can serve in a higher office. Research on progressive ambition emphasizes that seeking higher office changes member behavior as they try to maximize the chances that they win the more coveted position (Victor 2011; Hibbing 1986; Treul 2009). We expect that one of these behavioral changes is increased partisan intensity.

In an era of nationalized elections, legislators rely on their good relationships and support from the national party and the extended party network. This support matters early in the election cycle when ambitious members jockey to win a primary nomination. Indeed, members are more successful at running for higher office when they are better connected to the party (Hassell 2016). Beyond winning the primary election, Jenkins, Crespin, and Carson (2005) argue, "higher office seekers . . . endeavor to maintain good relations with the national party hierarchy for a variety of campaign related reasons

TABLE 2.2. Power Seeking's Expected Effect on Partisanship

	Expected Effect	Hypothesis
Current party and House committee leaders	+	*Party and House committee leaders are more likely to have higher partisan intensities than rank-and-file legislators.*
Senate committee leaders	Null	*Senate committee leaders are not more likely to have higher partisan intensities than rank-and-file senators.*
Candidates for leadership roles	+	*Candidates for leadership roles are more likely to have higher partisan intensities than other rank-and-file members.*
Winners and losers of leadership races	+ for winners – for losers	*Leadership race winners are more likely to maintain higher partisan intensities while losers become less partisan.*
Candidates for higher office	+	*Candidates for higher office are more likely to have higher partisan intensities.*

and strive to send signals that they are loyal party members" (370). To that end, those running for a new position show more partisan loyalty than other members (Jenkins, Crespin, and Carson 2005; Treul 2009a). In addition to winning the support from the national extended party network, statewide or presidential races often include contentious primaries and tough general elections. This increased competition demands more partisan behavior from candidates, both to win the nomination and to engage in the bitter campaigning that is associated with these top-of-the-ticket races. Table 2.2 summarizes our expectations about how legislators change their partisan behavior as they try to become more politically influential.

Other Explanations

In addition to these individual and collective factors, political scientists argue that certain subgroups of members are more predisposed to partisanship. One claim is that some lawmakers' personal qualities, which got them to Washington, DC, in the first place, affect their partisan behavior. The most prominent version of this is the cohort hypothesis—the idea that members elected during a wave election often bring a hard-edge partisan demeanor with them to Congress. Theriault (2013) shows that "Gingrich Senators," Republican members elected to the House after 1978 who eventually became senators, played

TABLE 2.3. Personal Factors' Expected Effect on Partisanship

	Expected Effect	Hypothesis
Members elected during wave cohorts	+	*Members elected during wave elections are more likely to have higher partisan intensities than other legislators.*
Republicans	+	*Republicans are more likely to have higher partisan intensities than Democrats.*

an outsize role in producing the more partisan contemporary Senate. This is related to a different argument that certain freshman cohorts—progressives in the late 1950s, Watergate babies in the 1970s, Tea Party Republicans in the 2010s—bring more partisan politics to shake up a staid legislature (Lawrence 2018; Ragusa 2016; Sinclair 2006).[15]

A second argument is that Republicans are more partisan because their home style demands are different than those of Democrats. In this view, the parties differ in their underlying composition, and Republicans, who prize cohesiveness and unity, reward partisan behavior more than interest group–centric Democrats, who are more interested in concrete results (Grossmann and Hopkins 2015). Both qualitative and quantitative research finds a partisan asymmetry, with Republicans emphasizing partisanship more than Democrats (Russell 2018; Mann and Ornstein 2012).

The specter hanging over any theory of partisanship is ideological extremity's role in creating partisan behavior. Some argue that it causes partisanship (Russell 2021a), some contend that partisanship and ideology are connected in complex ways (Koger and Lebo 2017), and others treat them as independent (Gelman 2020b). Our study falls into the second category, but as we discuss in the next chapter, disentangling these concepts in the contemporary Congress is often impossible. To that end, we take a conservative route in our analysis by usually treating ideology and partisanship as independent in our statistical tests. In doing so, we assess partisanship's effects after accounting for ideological extremity even though measures like DW-NOMINATE conflate these concepts in complicated ways, especially during the time period we are examining (Aldrich, Montgomery, and Sparks 2014). As Everson et al. (2016, 106) argue, since the 1970s, "the war of ideas" that ideological scores attempt to measure "is not the sole or primary determinant of combat."

We do not hypothesize that ideological extremity increases partisan intensity, as any result may be due to a genuine relationship, the complex interplay of these factors, or measurement error in how political scientists measure ideology and distinguish it from partisanship. Regardless, by including an ideology-based control variable that may also measure some partisan teamsmanship, we are stacking the deck against our hypotheses.

Partisanship's Negative Consequences

So far, we have developed an explanation for why members adopt partisan behaviors. We contend that these personas help them achieve multiple goals—winning reelection, becoming more politically influential, and helping their party win and maintain majority status. This behavior, which they use to appeal to constituents, copartisans in Congress, and the extended party network, is public. People back home and in Congress are watching these partisan displays and deciding whether they want to reward or punish this behavior. In this section, we theorize about its legislative and electoral consequences. Our main contention is that any penalty from excessive partisan behavior is minimal and, for most members, can generally be ignored. Rather, legislators have a nearly free hand to act as partisan as they want.

Legislative Consequences

Earlier in the chapter, we argued that a member's copartisan lawmakers are an audience paying attention to the member's partisan demeanor. However, the other party's legislators are also watching these public displays of teamsmanship and evaluating whether that member will be a good legislative partner. This across-the-aisle vetting is important. Even in a polarized, partisan Congress, most legislation passes with bipartisan support (Curry and Lee 2020). Members build credibility and support for their ideas by securing support from opposition legislators when they propose their ideas. This signals to party leaders, committee chairs, and other members that the bill could survive a legislative process that requires support from both Democrats and Republicans.

This cooperation happens early when bills are being written or are ready for introduction. Members seek out others to collaborate with in developing legislation (Craig 2021), strategically work with odd bedfellows (Kirkland 2011), and build large bipartisan coalitions (Harbridge 2015) to signal how widespread the support is for their idea. When a bill is introduced, bipartisan cosponsor coalitions can increase the chance the bill will be considered, although it depends on institutional factors and party leaders' political calculations (Gelman 2020a; Harbridge 2015).

Lawmakers regularly argue that this search for legislative partners from the other party is an important step in the bill development process. French Hill (R-AR) is explicit that Republican members believe that "to move a bill, you better have a Democratic sponsor" (Wiseman, Volden, and Hill 2020). Joe Neguse (D-CO) explains that, in developing these relationships, a great deal of effort goes into "identify[ing] partners whom I can work with to try to solve problems" (Wiseman and Neguse 2021).

A legislator's partisan demeanor, and the bills they introduce to signal their partisan bona fides, affects this relationship building. The bills that strong partisans introduce are more likely to burnish their reputations as good team players rather than serve as genuine attempts at policymaking. They want to politicize an issue and use messaging legislation as a way to do so. Moreover, strong partisans are less likely to cosponsor bills proposed by members from the other party. Their interest is in preventing the other party from securing policy wins and building a record to run on. Withholding support early in the legislative process is an easy decision for strong partisans. The fewer the bipartisan cosponsors, the weaker the signal to leadership about the bill's widespread support. By not supporting the legislation, strong partisans have the opportunity to politicize the idea by framing it in partisan terms, stop it from advancing, and deny the other party's members a policy win.

When voting, a member's partisanship affects their willingness to support the party. Ambitious members, who are looking to get ahead by advancing in the chamber or running for higher office, need to build a public record of party fidelity (Treul 2009). We argue this should produce two empirical patterns. First, partisanship should be associated with a higher likelihood of supporting the party's position on important votes, even after controlling for a legislator's ideology. Second, strong partisans are more likely to support the president's position when he comes from their party and to oppose him when he is from the opposite party. Voting for or against the president, the most prominent partisan figure in Washington, DC, is an easy, high-profile display of one's partisan bona fides.

Even if partisanship affects members' cosponsorship and voting decisions, the outstanding question is whether it makes them less effective legislators. Normatively, this seems like an attractive proposition. Those who choose to politicize issues should pay the price of being less effective at getting their ideas enacted. They should not be able to play it both ways, where they can bicker with the other party, pivot, and have their bills seriously debated.

If this sort of legislative penalty happens, it potentially operates through two mechanisms. First, it might be due to agenda setting. In this scenario, as members become more partisan, they emphasize messaging legislation that tries to score political points. Since these measures are not supposed to become law, we would observe stronger partisans as less effective lawmakers and a direct, negative correlation between a member's partisan intensity and their legislative effectiveness.

A second potential mechanism is that more partisan members are ostracized and punished by the other party in the legislative process. Since partisan behavior is public, those in the other party may be less inclined to help advance ideas sponsored by those who constantly bicker with them. This effect would likely be most felt by minority party members, whose measures only move forward at the majority's discretion. If this is happening, we would expect that members' legislative success is affected by their partisan reputations and that any effect is more pronounced for minority party legislators who are punished by majority party agenda setters.

Both of these ideas seem appealing, but we are skeptical of any lawmaking penalty, as there is very little empirical evidence that partisan behavior affects individual legislative success. Some studies link bipartisan collaboration early in the legislative process with helping ideas move through Congress (Craig 2021). Others suggest that acting more bipartisan when cosponsoring bills is linked to more legislative success (Harbridge-Yong, Volden, and Wiseman 2023). Yet, seriously working together in the legislative process is often driven by shared issue interests, not partisan considerations (Bratton and Rouse 2011; Kirkland 2011). When complaining about strong partisans, members do not cite their inability to move legislation as the problem. Rather, their unwillingness to break from the party when voting and their eagerness to politicize issues are the more common concerns (Dingell 2014). In fact, legislators usually say they are willing to work with anyone if they happen to have shared interests.[16]

Effective lawmaking often stems from institutional factors, like being a committee chair who has some agenda-setting power and a larger staff of experts who can help write bills (Volden and Wiseman 2014; Lewallen 2020). Yet, these same members who are trying to move up the congressional ranks also need to be good team players. Consequently, more partisan members often have more of the institutional resources that increase their legislative effectiveness.

In addition, even if partisanship is linked with proposing messaging bills that are intended to score political points, those measures are not the only ones legislators introduce. Rather, most legislators fashion themselves as engaged policymakers who, no matter their partisan demeanors, are working

TABLE 2.4. Partisanship's Hypothesized Effect on Legislative Effectiveness

	Expected Effect	Hypothesis
Attracting cosponsors from the other party	–	*As member's partisan intensity increases, their bills attract few cosponsors from the other party.*
Cosponsoring bills proposed by members from the other party	–	*As a member's partisan intensity increases, they are less likely to cosponsor bills proposed by those in the other party.*
Supporting the party's position	+	*As a member's partisan intensity increases, they are more likely to vote with their party.*
Supporting the president's position, if he is from your party	+	*As a member's partisan intensity increases, they are more likely to vote with a copartisan president.*
Opposing the president's position, if he is from the other party	+	*As a member's partisan intensity increases, they are more likely to vote against a president from the other party.*
Legislative effectiveness	Null	*A member's partisan intensity does not affect their ability to get their ideas considered and enacted.*

to change policy (Russell 2021b). Put differently, their public personas signal not only their partisan intensity but also their expertise on issues.

This helps explain why those in one party do not punish opposition members with partisan reputations. Those reputations are only part of their legislative makeup, and in their search for partners to work with across the aisle, shared interests or areas of expertise on a particular topic are likely more important. In fact, it is possible that, when they are not messaging, those who are more partisan are sought-after collaborators in writing bipartisan legislation. Getting a highly partisan member from the other party to support your bill signals to other members that this issue is not ripe for politicization but rather offers a real chance to change the law.

Even though the opposition may not *like* the strong partisans from one party, those partisans are not the legislators the other party tries to punish or ostracize. Instead, the other party tries to deny credit-claiming opportunities to those in electorally vulnerable districts. If, as we hypothesize above, seat safety and partisan intensity are correlated, then being more partisan is not associated with the other party deliberately withholding support for a member's ideas. If anything, we should see the opposite—that weak partisans in unsafe seats are the ones sidelined by the opposition.

Electoral Consequences

Political scientists have theorized and found evidence that more partisanship is linked to an electoral penalty. The main argument, laid out in studies by Koger, Lebo, and colleagues, is that voters are more likely to punish lawmakers whom they see as more partisan (Koger and Lebo 2017; Carson et al. 2010). This contrasts with early work that argues members pay an electoral penalty for being too ideologically extreme (Canes-Wrone, Brady, and Cogan 2002). The evidence for the partisanship penalty comes from studying how voters respond to members' votes. In Koger and Lebo's (2017) experiments, respondents are presented with a vote framed as either partisan or ideological. They find that respondents are less likely to say they will support an incumbent who voted in a partisan way compared to one who voted ideologically. Counterintuitively, they also find that respondents who identify as strong partisans are the most likely to punish legislators who vote in lockstep with the party.

Observational evidence from Koger, Lebo, and colleagues shows that members who vote with the party more often receive a lower vote share after taking into account their seat safety and ideology (Carson et al. 2010; Koger and Lebo 2017). They estimate that a 10-percentage-point increase in a lawmaker's party unity score, which is quite large, translates into a 1 percentage point penalty on Election Day. However, when disaggregated by seat safety, this effect is greatest for those in marginal districts. Those holding seats in districts won by the president in the other party pay a significant penalty for their party unity voting on Election Day. Members in toss-up districts or in those that slightly lean toward their party pay little to no penalty, and those in safe seats receive a vote share bonus for voting with their party (Koger and Lebo 2017).

Harbridge-Yong's research presents a somewhat different picture. In a series of studies with her coauthors, she finds that strong partisan voters do not prefer legislators framed as bipartisan compromisers and that voters reward partisan conflict as long as it ends in a victory for their side (Flynn and Harbridge 2016; Harbridge and Malhotra 2011).

Yet, if partisanship is about appealing to both voters back home and copartisans on Capitol Hill, as we argue, then legislators need a somewhat free hand to change their partisan demeanors. If the penalty for being a good team player is swift and substantial, then only those in the safest seats might take the electoral risk required to get promoted in Congress or to run for higher office. Moreover, the linked partisan fate that promotes cooperation and teamsmanship should fray much more easily than it does if the price for it is high. This creates a bit of a paradox. If partisanship is motivated by factors besides what voters back home want, why would legislators be willing to incur an Election Day penalty? How can members manage their political ambitions, which require partisan displays, while staying in office?

We contend that most lawmakers are able to effectively manage any negative electoral consequences. Recall that most of them are maintainers, not maximizers. They are willing to take actions that reduce their vote share because they have enough of an electoral cushion to manage the risk to a point. A maintainer who wants to move up the party leadership ranks, run a committee, or run for higher office can comfortably increase their partisan intensity. In doing so, they are trading between their goals of winning reelection and becoming politically influential. For them, the small decrease in vote share is worth the opportunity to become more important.

Maximizers are more constrained. They cannot forfeit votes to pursue promotions. That being the case, we would expect that these members rarely act in partisan ways that could hurt their reelection chances. Yet, that is not the case. One of Koger and Lebo's (2017) key insights is that maximizers are pushed into situations where their partisanship exceeds what voters will tolerate. They may be forced by leadership to take partisan stances that are penalized. If a penalty does exist, it is reasonable to assume all members face it. Maximizers are not able to hide from important partisan disputes, while maintainers do not mind them much. This argument produces a nuanced expectation. We anticipate that an electoral penalty exists but that its substantive effects are not large enough to bother most members.

Weak Partisans and Being Primaried

The argument that excessive partisanship creates a backlash on Election Day opens the door to the opposite situation: that members who are not partisan enough are more likely to be primaried. Incumbents cultivating a partisan persona need to worry not only about winning their general election but also about winning their party's nomination. This means appealing to a party base of engaged voters who are motivated by negative partisanship and affective polarization (Iyengar, Sood, and Lelkes 2012; Westwood, Peterson, and Lelkes 2019; Huddy, Mason, and Aaroe 2015).[17] For most members, this is not a problem. The day-to-day teamsmanship on Capitol Hill serves as a constant reminder to primary voters that the incumbent is on their team. However, weak partisans, those who avoid bickering with the other party or cheerleading their own, might face accusations back home of not being a good team player. This provides an opening to ambitious primary challengers, who can argue that they will better support the party's interests.

Research on congressional primaries focuses on ideology, not partisanship, in explaining why challengers run against incumbents (Boatright 2004; Jewitt and Treul 2019). However, in his careful coding of primary challenges, Boatright (2013) shows that many are not ideologically driven and that those classified as such are described as the officeholder being "too moderate or insufficiently partisan" (67). Similarly, Jewitt and Treul (2019) use descriptions from the *Almanac of American Politics* to code why members are primaried. It only includes ideology, not partisanship, as an explanation.

In contemporary politics, the emphasis on ideology is reasonable. Tea Party challengers to Republican incumbents in the 2010s were ideologically motivated. Similarly, prominent Democrats who have been recently primaried, like Joe Crowley (D-NY), Eliot Engel (D-NY), and Michael Capuano (D-MA), were good team players who were defeated by ideologues. On the other hand, anecdotes also suggest that partisan considerations might motivate challengers. The six House Republicans who voted for Donald Trump's second impeachment all attracted primary challenges. Mark Sanford (R-SC) lost his primary after criticizing Trump. In a primary rematch, Mark Harris (R-NC) unseated Robert Pittenger (R-NC) largely based on the former's platform of unflinching support for the president (and perhaps through some election fraud). Meyer (2021) provides more systematic evidence that links partisanship with primary behavior. He shows that primaried senators vote often with party leaders, not their ideologically extreme colleagues, in an effort to ward off quality challengers.

Although we have anecdotes and some evidence about primary challengers being motivated by partisanship, the question of whether ideology, partisan intensity, or both motivate primary challenges is rarely tested. In contemporary politics, we expect that both matter. Political scientists have repeatedly shown that ideological moderates are more likely to attract a challenger. But, especially in an age of hyper-partisanship, weak partisans who do not show enough party fidelity are likely to as well.

The Consequences of Partisan Tone

Research on partisanship and election outcomes almost exclusively analyzes votes. The studies that reveal the Election Day penalty use party unity scores (Carson et al. 2010; Koger and Lebo 2017), which are based on important floor votes, to proxy for partisan behavior. The survey experiments that try to identify which voters are reacting to partisanship provide vignettes based on lawmakers' votes on a bill or their broader voting record (Dancey and Sheagley 2018; Harbridge and Malhotra 2011).

This focus on votes presents two problems. First, as we reiterate throughout the book, so much partisan behavior is never voted on. As such, members might be partially evaluated on their partisan performances that fall outside the official roll call record. Second, and more importantly, voting obscures the tone that legislators use when being a good team player. Take, for instance, Republican senators' partisan actions at the end of Brett Kavanaugh's highly partisan and controversial Supreme Court confirmation.[18] With one exception, they all voted yea. A vote-based measure would count them as all acting the same. Their rhetoric suggests otherwise. Some were cheerleaders who applauded their party for confirming Kavanaugh and touted his conservative credentials. Their partisan tones were positive and cheerful. Others fumed at Senate Democrats and spent most of their time using a negative, combative tone even as their party won the political fight.

Just as a partisan voting or rhetorical record is strategic, the tone members adopt when acting partisan is strategic too. Politicians have encouraged and received the message that many voters are motivated by dislike for the other party, not necessarily support for their side (Iyengar et al. 2019). Combative, negative partisan tones are common in Congress, and adopting one has a clear goal: to motivate the partisan voters who are the foundation of most members' reelection constituencies. Doing so offers another way that partisanship can increase vote share. Rather than joining every partisan dispute, lawmakers can use a caustic tone when they do choose to join the fray. This behavior shows constituents that even if lawmakers are not involved in constant bickering, they are still on the same team and share their animus toward the opposition. As Election Day approaches, this provides weaker partisans political cover. They can point to memorable, highly combative moments to build their partisan bona fides. If this is the case, then a negative partisan tone should be associated with members winning a higher vote share.

Yet, if a negative partisan tone is so profitable, then why doesn't everyone engage in this behavior all the time? The reason is simple: Those in less safe seats do not benefit from the negativity. In more marginal districts, incumbents need to build a coalition beyond the party base. Constantly bickering with the other party does not motivate the independents who dislike political brawling or the opposition moderates they need to win. That being the case, the effect of partisan tone is conditional. For those in safer seats, a negative one is politically profitable. We expect it is correlated with winning more votes. For

TABLE 2.5. Partisanship's Expected Electoral Consequences

Decreased general election vote share:
- *as partisanship increases.*
- *as partisan tone becomes more negative and incumbent holds competitive seat.*

Increased general election vote share:
- *as partisan tone becomes more negative and incumbent holds a safe seat.*

Attracting a primary challenger is more likely as partisanship decreases.

the maximizers holding marginal seats, negativity hinders them, and it should reduce their Election Day performance.

Taken together, our expectations about partisanship's electoral consequences suggest members likely have a free hand to act as partisan as they want. Even if a general election penalty exists, it is one most maintainers can afford. To ward off primary challengers, incumbents need to show at least some respectable level of partisan fidelity, but the typical day-to-day partisan bickering is likely enough. Finally, most legislators can strategically adopt negative partisan tones to compensate for any electoral damage created by their unwillingness to consistently join the partisan fray. We outline these expectations in table 2.5.

Conclusion

In this chapter, we present a theory of congressional members' partisanship. We argue that this behavior serves multiple goals: winning reelection, becoming more politically influential, and helping the party achieve and maintain majority status. In analyzing how partisan behavior helps lawmakers achieve their goals, we depart from the conventional story that it is just a presentational style used to appeal to voters. Rather, it is shaped by a variety of factors as they try to win reelection, improve their party's image, and seek promotions in Washington, DC.

Based on our argument, we propose a number of empirical predictions that should be consistent with partisanship being both a home style and a hill style. Seat safety should be associated with a member's partisan intensity, but so should institutional factors like narrow majorities and membership in the party opposite the president. Additionally, we expect party and committee leaders, and those seeking promotions to these roles, to act more partisan than other legislators. Finally, we contend that partisanship's consequences are fairly mild. We expect that it affects cosponsorship and voting patterns but otherwise does not reduce lawmakers' legislative effectiveness. Similarly, it may produce a small electoral penalty, but one that most members can afford to incur. In the following chapters, we develop and validate measures of legislators' partisan intensity and their partisan tones. In chapters 5, 6, and 7, we test our theoretical expectations.

THREE

Moving Beyond Votes

Defining and Measuring Partisan Intensity

Few documents reveal a person's essential qualities like an obituary. These remembrances emphasize important traits—a person's professional achievements, their personal accomplishments, and their positive qualities or, because politeness dictates so, dressed-up negative ones. Obituaries not only record a life's details but also reveal which qualities matter and are worth reporting.

What traits do obituaries suggest define a lawmaker's career? Certainly their legislative successes and issue advocacy are remembered. But so is their partisan behavior, or lack thereof. Members are often lionized for their lack of partisanship and their willingness to work across the aisle. Thad Cochran was remembered as a "throwback from a more genteel era of American politics, rarely engaging the brutal fights and pitched partisanship of today's modern-day Senate" (Everett 2019). Bob Michel was a "genial conciliator" (Clymer 2017). Elijah Cummings, who ended his career as a partisan brawler as the ranking Democrat on the House Oversight Committee, was memorialized for his fierce support for his party and his private, bipartisan friendships (Berman 2019). Even strong partisans are remembered for their unyielding styles. Alcee Hastings was not celebrated for his lawmaking skills, as he "never sponsored major legislation" (Seelye 2021).[1] Rather, his pointed partisanship was a defining trait: Hastings's obituary writer politely described him as someone who "could be counted on to express himself freely. He had a particular loathing for President Donald J. Trump, whom he once called a 'sentient pile of excrement'" (Seelye 2021).

Much of Hastings's partisan persona that was so notable to his obituary writer can be seen through his Twitter posts. During his final two years in office, 42 percent of his messaging was partisan in nature. Some of it touted the House Democrats' work on the Rules Committee, which he served on, but most of it attacked the Trump administration. In 2019, he started the year excoriating the president over the government shutdown. He regularly posted using the hashtag #TrumpShutdown while still finding the time to post about the Mueller investigation and Trump's relationship with Vladimir Putin.

By the summer of 2020, Hastings's Twitter timeline was a mix of messaging about how to get COVID aid, hurricane updates, standard PR about various bill introductions, and a near constant criticism of prominent Republicans. He angrily posted about Trump's attempts to end the census count early, Senate Majority Leader Mitch McConnell's refusal to bring up a police reform bill in response to George Floyd's murder, and Governor Ron DeSantis's decision to lift COVID restrictions on Floridians gathering in public places. Representative Hastings saw a lot going wrong in the United States and argued that Republicans were to blame for most, if not all, of it.

Hastings passed away in 2021. His obituary writer had a lot of material to work with. After all, few politicians have the résumé of being an impeached federal judge who was then elected to Congress 15 times. But even a cursory glance through Hastings's Twitter posts, especially during Trump's first term, reveals a deeply committed Democratic team player. The writer would have missed an essential aspect of Hastings's priorities without reflecting on this part of his political style.

More broadly, memorializing members' partisan demeanors suggests that this trait is important and that it varies among lawmakers. If everyone was a genial, bipartisan compromiser or a hard-edged partisan, no one would comment on this quality. Instead, for many members, their partisan behavior is a defining feature of their time in office. Yet, as a concept, partisanship has become a catchall term to describe a wide range of members' behaviors, whether appropriate or not.

Understanding partisanship, and its consequences, requires a careful definition and measure, which are the tasks we take up in this chapter. In the following pages, we define partisanship, what it is and what it is not, as well as introduce a measure of lawmakers' partisan intensity using their Twitter posts. The idea underlying our measure is straightforward. Lawmakers vary in how often they use explicitly partisan language. We assume that this rhetoric reflects their underlying partisan intensity, that is, their willingness to devote time and effort to support their party (Hall 1996).

As we discuss throughout the chapter, partisanship takes many forms and can be measured in different ways. The most common way it is operationalized uses roll call votes or bill cosponsorships. Our approach differs and offers more advantages in capturing the concept. Social media posts include more partisan disputes than the roll call record or bill introductions. Moreover, votes and cosponsorships are limited by selection effects and are confounded by ideology and pressure from leadership. Twitter posts reflect "the largely voluntaristic" and deliberate decisions members make when building their partisan brands (Lee 2009, 18). Indeed, an important distinguishing factor between these standard measures and ours is that most other ones are preference based. They assess, for instance, if a member supported a bill. This treats very different partisan situations the same. By measuring a legislator's intensity, we can assess who was involved in a partisan situation and how active they were in vocalizing that partisanship.

We measure individual-level partisanship by training a neural network to identify partisan tweets from the over three million posted from 2015 through 2020 (the 114th through 116th Congresses) and validate our results in multiple ways. We show that out-of-sample official party Twitter accounts reveal high levels of partisanship. We find that highly partisan events produce more partisan intensity than other, less divisive moments and that our measure captures a different dimension of political conflict than ideological polarization.

What Is Partisanship?

As a concept, partisanship is used to define all sorts of congressional behavior. Sometimes it is a synonym for ideological polarization. It is often deployed as a pejorative, where being "partisan" is used as shorthand for something that has gone wrong or is illegitimate. It is linked or conflated with other concepts as well, like divisive behavior, incivility, or bad faith. Even when it is defined more precisely, as members engaging in team play that helps their party, the term can be difficult to pin down because partisanship is not limited to one situation or activity. It happens in various congressional venues and can be measured in many ways. Voting, bill cosponsorships, floor speeches, social events, social media posts, and congressional trips have all been used to study the concept.

When describing partisanship, the common thread among congressional observers and members themselves is the conclusion that today's Congress and its members are hyper-partisan. Whether it is their voting records, rhetoric, or personal interactions, the general consensus is that partisanship is prevalent and consequential. Yet, because the term is used as a catchall to describe a wide range of legislative behaviors and activities, it is important to be precise in exactly what we mean when we discuss partisanship.

A Definition of Partisanship

Partisanship is when legislators support their party or oppose the other party. It arises due to "competing political interests" (Lee 2009, 3) and manifests when members seek to gain advantage for their side, usually at the expense of the opposition. Members are being partisan when their actions benefit their party at the expense of the other party.[2]

Political scientists often describe modern congressional parties as teams, who work together to beat the other party electorally and on policy issues (Koger and Lebo 2017; Lee 2009). If Democrats and Republicans are teams, then members are the players and partisan activities help the team advance its goals. Like any team, teammates vary in their commitment to the group's cause. Some are eager supporters, helping their copartisans, fighting with the opposition, and advancing their party's messages. Others are more reluctant, only joining the fray when necessary. Thus, in the simplest terms, we understand partisanship as a member's willingness to help their team.

This concept is one of four mutually exclusive and exhaustive categories that describe how a member's behavior intersects with their partisan identity. Bipartisanship is when politicians from opposite parties work together. Crosspartisanship occurs when members of the same party fight with one another. Nonpartisan behavior describes situations that have no partisan content. Wishing your constituents a "Happy National Lobster Day" is one appetizing example. These categories are mutually exclusive, and any sort of legislative behavior or rhetoric can be placed in one of them (Rhodes and Albert 2017).

Defining individual-level partisanship this way reveals three of its important features. First, a member's decision to engage in partisan behaviors is "largely voluntaristic" (Lee 2009, 18). Certainly, in some venues, lawmakers are coerced to act in a partisan manner. Party leaders can pressure members to support the party on a roll call vote. Members might be asked to carry the president's water on Capitol Hill or make a statement to display party unity on an important issue. Yet, as we discuss in the next chapter, these situations are the exception, not the norm, in the day-to-day partisanship that defines congressional politics. Even in the face of this pressure, and in some cases severe consequences, the decision to act in a partisan way is up to the member.

Second, as we argued in chapter 2, legislators are deliberate in the partisan styles and reputations they develop. Every day, they are confronted with potential partisan disputes that they can engage in or avoid. When speaking publicly and engaging with constituents, they decide whether to frame what is going on in Washington, DC, and their behavior, as partisan or not. In cultivating a personal legislative style on the Hill, nearly 40 percent of legislators are best described as party soldiers or party builders, who work to advance partisan goals and generally avoid bipartisanship (Bernhard and Sulkin 2018). Just as members carefully tend to other parts of their images, they also cultivate the partisan aspect of their brands.

Third, partisanship varies in its tone. Political scientists pay a great deal of attention to negatively toned partisanship and partisan warriors, the members who traffic in hard-edged, inflammatory activities and who refuse to compromise with the other party (Theriault 2015). Yet, it does not need to be negative. It can be effusively positive as legislators work to cast their party in the best possible light. Near constant partisan credit claiming is a way legislators try to improve their side's brand and provides an affirmative case for why voters should support them and their party. A common version of what we call partisan cheerleading is when legislators argue that their party is responsible for a strong economy. When low unemployment numbers are released, strong partisans argue the same jobs report happened because of the "Obama economy" or GOP tax cuts.

Both types of partisanship—positive and negative—are important to include in any study of this concept. Take, for instance, lawmakers' behavior during the Trump presidency. Without question, partisan bickering was a regular occurrence. However, Republican cheerleading of Trump was an important dynamic in Washington, DC. Anytime the president did something controversial or objectionable, the immediate question was who in the Republican Party would support him or remain quiet.[3] Tracking who would provide cover for the president quickly became a litmus test for which strong partisans defend their party leader's actions and who would stay out of the fray.

This version of cheerleading, while taking on unusual significance during the Trump era, is not new. It follows the Eleventh Commandment, popularized by Ronald Reagan, that "thou shalt not speak ill of any fellow Republican" (1990). In the modern Congress, members closely hew to Reagan's adage. Within-party public fighting is rare. Instead, when legislators talk about their party, they do so in an overwhelmingly positive way.[4]

The Many Faces of Partisan Behavior

Importantly, partisanship is not limited to one activity or situation. Rather, it happens in many venues and takes many forms. It includes the confrontational, ugly politics people commonly associate with the concept. Hardball tactics that split the parties, like locking the door so your opponents cannot join a conference committee negotiation (Sinclair 2006), are one version of partisanship. It also includes other, tamer behaviors that arise from the common day-to-day business on Capitol Hill, like taking a partisan tact in media interviews.

The most studied type of partisanship is how often members vote with their party. Research on party voting examines why lawmakers support their party on the floor (Cox and McCubbins 1991; Patterson and Caldeira 1988), the influence party leaders having in twisting members' arms to back the leadership's position (Snyder and Groseclose 2000; Ansolabehere, Snyder, and Stewart 2001), agenda-setting effects on party unity (Crespin, Rohde, and Vander Wielen 2011), and the consequences of lawmakers' partisan voting records (Carson et al. 2010). A second research area uses bill cosponsorship patterns. This version assesses who is willing to work across the aisle early on in the legislative process or who endorses only their copartisans' bills (Harbridge 2015; Kirkland 2011; Rippere 2016).

Members can act as partisans (or not) in other ways. They regularly travel together on fact-finding congressional delegations, or CODELS, some of which are bipartisan (Alduncin, Parker, and Theriault 2017). On Capitol Hill, they arrange social events, like seersucker day or potlucks (Lawless, Theriault, and Guthrie 2018). Some members join the fun, no matter the organizers' party, while others avoid participating in building the institution's bipartisan social fabric. Researchers have even examined who is more partisan in who they mingle with on the House and Senate floors (Dietrich 2021).

Beyond legislators' activities in Washington, DC, and who they travel with, their partisanship is reflected by their rhetoric. One of their main daily tasks, especially in the age of social media, is to explain their actions to voters, activists, and donors. This can involve partisan framing, and members differ in how often they use such rhetoric in their floor speeches and on social media (Maltzmann and Sigelman 1996; Morris 2001; Russell 2018).

No matter the venue, partisan behavior occurs on a spectrum and is not fixed. Some politicians are strong partisans, who are motivated by having their side win at the expense of the opposition. Others are not. Yet, as we show throughout the book, lawmakers strategically increase or decrease their partisan intensities as they pursue their goals of winning reelection and becoming more politically influential.

To summarize, we define partisanship as supporting one's political side or opposing the other party. For individual legislators, the extent to which they engage in this behavior is voluntaristic and deliberate. Yet, as we note above, partisan behavior happens in all sorts of ways. This creates confusion, as many concepts are conflated with partisanship. Thus, before we present our partisan intensity measure, we will next distinguish partisanship from what it is *not*.

Partisan Warfare, Bickering, and Fighting Are Types of Partisanship

A common convention political scientists employ in describing congressional partisanship is to use the term adjectivally. Members might be engaging in partisan *warfare*, partisan *bickering*, partisan *fighting*, or some other noun. Although these terms are sometimes used interchangeably, researchers have been careful in defining them. For instance, Lee (2009, 193) describes partisan bickering as "when partisans impeach one another's motives, question one another's ethics and competence, engage in reflexive partisanship, and—when it is politically useful to do so—exploit and deepen divisions rather than seeking common ground." Theriault (2013, 11) argues that partisan warfare is similar but more extreme. It involves "strategies that go beyond defeating your opponents into humiliating them . . . go beyond fighting the good legislative fight to destroying the institution and the legislative process." In chapter 4, we use our own modifiers–bickerers, opportunists, and cheerleaders—based on members' partisan tone.

No matter the specific vocabulary used, these terms are descriptions of different types of partisanship. "Warfare" and "bickering" are negative versions that differ in their extremity and tactics. A more general term like "partisan fighting" describes when legislators attack one another and encompasses ideas like warfare and bickering (Gelman 2020b).

Our goal is not to split hairs but to point out that these sorts of terms capture specific types of behavior. Partisan warfare is different than partisan cheerleading, where members of the same party credit claim for their collective successes, but both are dimensions of partisanship. We broadly explore this concept and include all these dimensions in our study.

Partisanship Is Not Polarization

Partisanship is often used synonymously with ideological or partisan polarization, but importantly, these concepts are different (McCarty 2019). Ideological polarization is "a separation of politics into liberal and conservative camps" (McCarty, Poole, and Rosenthal 2016, 4). That is, it is policy based. "Partisan polarization," the term most commonly conflated with "partisanship," is a type of ideological polarization in which Democrats and Republicans disagree on policy issues. Polarization does not need to be based on partisanship.[5] For instance, age, race, and class polarization are all possible types of polarization and do not necessarily involve being a Democrat or Republican. Put differently, ideology is a "belief system" made up of ideas, attitudes, and issue positions (Converse 1964). Partisanship is a type of group conflict and reflects a willingness to support the party.

These concepts are blurred because they are not mutually exclusive. In the modern Congress, many political disagreements are both ideological *and* partisan. When an issue splits the parties, lawmakers not only want their preferred policy but also want a political win from the situation. Sometimes, they do not even try to make policy but use a polarizing issue to make their party look good or to embarrass the other side (Gelman 2020a; Egar 2016; Lee 2016). Consider the following examples that help distinguish what is partisan, ideological, or both.

During the first Trump presidency, many of the most consequential issues Congress dealt with were purely partisan. Most notable were the president's two impeachments. Asking a foreign leader for dirt on a political opponent and inciting an insurrection are not ideological stances. Rather, the issues were partisan as one party tried to hold the other party's leader accountable. In the end, most lawmakers voted in a partisan way, supporting their team's dominant position.[6] Other Trump-related fights, like House Democrats subpoenaing his tax returns and demanding transcripts of his conversations with Vladimir Putin after their Helsinki conference, were partisan but not ideological. Similarly, the Republican-led Benghazi hearings, and subsequent attacks related to Hillary Clinton's private email server, were pure partisan politics.

More rarely, issues can feature ideological but not partisan conflict. During the "Textbook Congress," this sort of dispute was more visible when northern and southern Democrats openly disagreed on civil rights issues. Today, ideological fights still happen: Bills can pass the House or Senate with bipartisan majorities without the support of the extreme wings of one of the parties. For instance, in late 2020, Congress passed a temporary continuing resolution to keep the government open. It passed the House overwhelmingly, with only the most extreme conservatives voting no.[7]

The reason why polarization and partisanship are used interchangeably is that so much conflict includes both. Not only are hot-button topics, like abortion, gun control, climate change, taxes, and electoral reform, issue-based disputes, but they also split the parties. Although within-party views are not monolithic, almost all congressional Democrats are more liberal than Republicans (and vice versa) on these and many other topics. As a result, the issue often gets wielded for political gain: merging ideological methods with partisan motivations. Additionally, engaged citizens often graft an ideological dimension onto purely partisan disputes. For example, Republican activists viewed their congressional copartisans as more conservative if they supported Donald Trump during the purely partisan disputes we discussed above (Hopkins and Noel 2022).

Perhaps the best encapsulation of this intertwining is Supreme Court nominations. Senators openly discuss the ideological implications of certain nominees. These are also political disputes that are deeply partisan. Republicans' refusal to vote on Merrick Garland's nomination, their nuking of the filibuster to confirm Neil Gorsuch,[8] and their handling of sexual assault allegations against Brett Kavanaugh were partisan, not ideological, issues. Yet, without question, these partisan moves are used to confirm liberal or conservative justices to the Supreme Court. It is easy to see how polarization and partisanship become blurred.

Members' rhetoric reflects the way ideology and partisanship can intertwine as they strategically portray issues as ideological, partisan, or both. When Senator Bernie Sanders (I-VT, 2018) tweeted that "the repeal of #Net-Neutrality hands the internet over to a handful of corporations while people of color, low-income families, disabled communities and rural towns get pushed offline," he was making an issue-based, ideological claim about net neutrality. Nothing in his post mentions Democrats or Republicans or invokes any sort of partisan consideration.

Other messages on the same topic show how the issue can move from a purely ideological debate to a partisan one. Senator Catherine Cortez Masto (D-NV, 2018) framed the situation as unified Democrats trying to peel off one GOP vote to preserve net neutrality:

> Today is the day. @SenateDems are officially filing the petition that allows us to force a vote on the Senate floor to save #NetNeutrality. But we still need #OneMoreVote to get it done. If you want to protect a free, open internet, make your voices heard before it's too late!

Representative Kathy Castor (D-FL, 2018) took a different partisan approach by highlighting this as a partisan fight and critiquing Republicans, including President Trump, Speaker Paul Ryan, the House Republican Conference, and the entire Republican Party:

> Trump/GOP repeal of #NetNeutrality goes into effect today even though most Americans support free, open internet. This will hurt

small businesses & consumers! @SpeakerRyan @HouseGOP blocking
@USRepMikeDoyle resolution to #SavetheInternet even after Senate
voted to do so!

In a polarized political environment, the differences between these concepts might seem pedantic. But the difference is important. As strategic communicators, lawmakers are careful and purposive when they politicize a situation by framing it as a partisan issue. Some lawmakers follow Senator Sanders's
strategy and avoid partisan rhetoric. Others constantly talk about politics in
partisan terms.

A perfect example of these strategies, and their consequences, is the 2018
North Dakota Senate race. The incumbent Democrat, Heidi Heitkamp, was
defending her seat in a deep red state against Congressman Kevin Cramer.
Heitkamp had a near impossible task. North Dakotans strongly supported
President Trump, and he actively campaigned for Cramer. She had to run a
campaign that highlighted her popular issue positions, while carefully avoid-
ing partisan rhetoric that reminded North Dakotans she was a Democrat or
criticized the president. Heitkamp's solution was to avoid directly criticizing Trump but mentioning him to tout her bipartisan accomplishments. Her
social media posts, like the one below, used him as a credit-claiming device to
burnish her bipartisan bona fides.

In May, the President signed my bipartisan #Relief4MainStreet bill into
law which included provisions I fought for to help boost investments
in #smallbiz & startups in ND & rural America by eliminating unnecessary red tape. Read more @emergingprairie. (Heitkamp 2018b)

When talking about issues, Heitkamp spoke in ideological terms, portraying herself as a moderate with sensible issue positions that any reasonable
North Dakotan could support. Her messaging on net neutrality avoided any
partisan language, tried to appeal to moderates and conservatives, but still
adopted a common Democratic slogan, #SaveTheInternet, without mentioning the party itself:

@FCC North Dakota businesses are worried about higher online business costs, & many working families & millennials are anxious about
rising internet rates & limited access. Let's #SaveTheInternet & allow
North Dakotans to thrive. (Heitkamp 2018a)

In contrast, Kevin Cramer campaigned as a partisan. He constantly invoked Trump and told North Dakotans he would reliably support the president. To be fair, Cramer also ran on a conservative platform, but the purest distillation of his campaign was that he backed Trump and Trump backed him. In the end, Cramer won, but the moral of the story is not that one type of campaigning is more effective than another. Rather, it is that ideology and partisanship are not synonymous, and politicians strategically mix and match them. As such, we should pay close attention to when they use partisan language. That choice is intentional and, as we show throughout the book, consequential.

In distinguishing ideology and partisanship as distinct but interrelated concepts, we see the serious measurement challenges created by their overlap. When an issue is both partisan and ideological, we cannot disentangle the concepts from one another. However, any reasonable evaluation of partisanship also needs to account for ideology. As a result, we are faced with two options. The first is to find a set of purely partisan situations and measure which legislators participated the most in them. Lee (2009) takes a similar approach in showing that parties regularly work as teams on issues that are not ideological. The problem is that if we are interested in comprehensively measuring and assessing partisanship, we would exclude most of the cases. Furthermore, as Hopkins and Noel (2022) show, what we might argue is purely partisan might be viewed as ideological by voters and activists.

The second option is to use the standard measures of political ideology, like DW-NOMINATE, which also partially measure partisan teamsmanship (Aldrich, Montgomery, and Sparks 2014). In doing so, we will underestimate the effect of partisanship, as some of the variation is being captured by the ideology measure. We adopt this approach, which allows us to more comprehensively evaluate partisanship, with the caveat that we may be underestimating its effects when we control for ideology.

Partisanship Is Not Incivility (and Incivility Is Not Necessarily Partisan)

Besides ideology, partisanship is often conflated with incivility. Of course, many vitriolic attacks are overtly partisan. Extreme examples, like Mo Brooks (R-AL) equating Democrats to Nazis on the House floor,[9] stand out as instances that tie these concepts together. Beyond the sensational, political scientists have documented for decades how uncivil behavior intersects with hard-edged partisanship, with regular updates that include new players like the Tea Party or the Freedom Caucus (Gervais 2019; Gervais and Morris 2018; Uslaner 1993; Dodd and Schraufnagel 2013).

Partisan behavior can be uncivil, but it can also be polite or even downright cheerful. A good deal of partisanship comes from politicians touting their party's and copartisans' achievements. Credit claiming, for a good economy or popular policies, is a hallmark of this rhetoric. None of it is uncivil. Even negative partisan messaging can remain civil. For example, when Senator Tom Carper (D-DE, 2017) tweeted "RT @EPWDems: Senate Democrats call on Republican leaders to postpone final vote on nomination of Scott Pruitt to lead the EPA," he created a partisan frame for the reader, portrayed the other party's decision as wrong, and remained civil. Moreover, sometimes incivility can be cross-partisan. Donald Trump reserved special animus for members who criticized him, like when he called Mitt Romney a "pompous ass" (Foran 2019). Incivility and partisanship sometimes go hand in hand on Capitol Hill. It is reasonable to pay close attention to this type of rhetoric and the toxic environment it creates. However, these concepts are distinct.

Bad Faith Arguments, Trolling, Ad Hominem Attacks, and Lies Are Not Necessarily Partisan

Some legislators, especially on social media, like to gain attention by making outrageous claims. Often doing so includes name-calling, bad faith arguments, and emotionally charged language. The targets for this internet trolling can be partisan. While in office, Dana Rohrabacher (R-CA) maintained a unique social media presence, as he would often post controversial content and then argue with those who responded. Some of his attacks were partisan, like calling Barack Obama a fascist. Other targets, like "global warming alarmists," scientists, and critics of his pro-Russian views, were not (Goldmacher 2013).

This sort of bad etiquette is not limited to unique characters like Rohrabacher. Members defy rhetorical norms to make headlines, raise campaign donations, influence a policy debate, and show that they can drive a media narrative. Their comments can be profoundly distasteful, but they are only partisan if their idea is couched in a partisan frame.

Partisanship Is Not Necessarily Bad or a Sign That Something Has Gone Wrong

Partisanship is regularly used as a pejorative, describing how a particular situation, or Congress more generally, has gone wrong. Legislators like to complain that bills are written or investigations are conducted in a partisan manner, without input from their side. Journalists regularly cite partisanship as standing in the way of compromise. Even political scientists point the finger at hard-edged partisans for much of the worst behavior on Capitol Hill and consistently show that bipartisanship is the key to achieving legislative results. In fact, an entire literature examines what makes members more bipartisan, with the underlying assumption that working across the aisle is normatively good.

Without question, partisanship can be problematic, especially in lawmaking. Researchers have no shortage of anecdotes and data that show it inhibits legislating in a political system with numerous veto points (Curry and Lee 2020; Harbridge-Yong, Volden, and Wiseman 2023). Yet it is essential to other congressional functions and representative government more broadly. It can fuel public oversight of the executive branch (Kriner and Schwartz 2008; Parker and Dull 2009; McGrath 2013). In multiparty political systems with free and fair elections, parties need to compete for office, and in doing so, they need to make an electoral case for their side. That requires partisanship.

Moreover, depending on one's political affiliations, the behavior from some of the strongest partisans in Congress can be very popular. Democratic voters surely saw Adam Schiff, their lead impeachment manager during Trump's two impeachments, as doing important work that held the president to account. By our measure, he was the most partisan legislator during that time. Similarly, Republican voters showed no qualms with the way that Mitch McConnell, the most partisan senator, pursued a partisan approach to approving scores of conservative judges while Trump was president.

Partisanship plays an essential role in legislative politics and cannot be branded as an unalloyed good or bad feature. Some versions can harm the institution's functioning, but others are what incentivize Democrats and Republicans to hold one another accountable for their actions. Its reputation as a problem, one that has made it a pejorative synonymous with dysfunction, is overly simplistic.

Operationalizing Congressional Partisanship

Since partisanship is not defined as one activity, it has been measured in many ways. Vote-based measures assess a legislator's partisan loyalty (Theriault 2008; Carson et al. 2010; Ansolabehere, Snyder, and Stewart 2001).[10] Cosponsorship data is used to measure bipartisanship by calculating how often members cosponsor legislation with opposition lawmakers ("Bipartisan Index" 2021; Harbridge 2015; Fowler 2006; Lawless, Theriault, and Guthrie 2018).[11]

Researchers have also analyzed how often legislators voluntarily cooperate

TABLE 3.1. Votes and Cosponsorship Opportunities for 12 Partisan Events

	Event	# of Votes	# of Bills / Resolutions
114th Congress	Merrick Garland's Supreme Court nomination	0	0
	House Democrats' sit-in to protest GOP inaction on gun legislation	0	1
	Hillary Clinton's use of a private e-mail server	0	3
	Conclusion of Benghazi investigation	0	0
115th Congress	Brett Kavanaugh's Supreme Court nomination	2	0
	Steve Bannon's appointment to the National Security Council	0	1
	Condemning President Trump's remarks after white supremacist rally in Charlottesville, VA	2	2
	President Trump's firing of FBI Director James Comey	0	8
116th Congress	Conclusion of Mueller investigation	1	1
	President Trump ordering that Lafayette Square be cleared of protestors	0	1
	Nancy Pelosi tearing Trump's State of the Union Address	0	1
	House Republicans disrupting House Intelligence hearings related to Trump's presidency in a Capitol sensitive compartmented information facility	0	0

in less formal settings. Such situations as who travels together to foreign countries on official business (a CODEL), who attends one another's social events in the Capitol, or who speaks to one another on chamber floors show disparities in who is collegial and cooperative in these less visible, off-the-record settings (Dietrich 2021; Alduncin, Parker, and Theriault 2017; Lawless, Theriault, and Guthrie 2018). More in line with our approach, some have examined partisan rhetoric, often by analyzing speeches and statements submitted into the congressional record and, more recently, social media (Maltzmann and Sigelman 1996; Morris 2001; Russell 2018, 2021b).[12]

Although these measures provide important insights, many of them suffer from measurement error. The most commonly used ones, votes and cosponsorships, present three main problems. First, many partisan disputes do not produce voting or cosponsorship data. For example, judicial confirmations, one of the most contentious issues in the modern Senate, are not cosponsored.

Similarly, party leaders control the floor agenda to determine which partisan fights receive a vote (Gelman 2020a).[13] As table 3.1 shows, during the six-year period we analyze, contentious partisan disputes produced very few, if any, votes or cosponsorship opportunities.

Second, bills and vote-based measures are confounded by ideology and agenda-setting effects. Cosponsorships reflect both a legislator's willingness to work with the other side and also their support for the proposed policy (Kirkland 2011). Votes are generated from a censored agenda determined by party leaders. Moreover, when voting, members' decision-making is also influenced by their policy preferences and pressure from leadership, not just partisan considerations (Krehbiel 1993). As we show in later chapters, both of these measures are poor proxies for measuring partisanship, as they are associated with *both* lawmakers' partisan intensity and their ideology.

Third, votes and cosponsorships, and other non-rhetoric-based approaches, measure a legislator's revealed partisan preferences, that is, their willingness to take a partisan position (Hall 1996). However, preference-based measures treat very different disputes in the same way. High-profile battles, like a Supreme Court nomination, count the same as less important fights, such as confirming a district court judge. Rather, a better measure is members' "revealed intensities" for partisanship, the "time and . . . effort [they] devote" to partisan activities (Hall 1996). An intensity-based approach captures not only whether a legislator took a partisan position, and their preference, but how involved they were in the particular situation.

To understand how this difference is important, consider how each approach would measure the partisan behavior surrounding Donald Trump's first impeachment. Using preference-based measures, almost all House Democrats and Republicans would have been measured identically. The impeachment resolution was not cosponsored, and all Democrats, except for three, voted to impeach and all Republicans voted not to impeach.[14] The bluntness of the proxy yields a nearly complete lack of variance.

In contrast, an intensity-based approach would show substantial differences in members' partisan behavior. House Judiciary committee members publicly argued for nearly a week over whether Trump's behavior was impeachable. After the House impeached him, the Democratic impeachment managers argued for Trump's conviction before the Senate. During the Senate trial, some representatives devoted all of their public messaging to talking about it, while others were much quieter. At the end of the ordeal, even though almost all of them voted in a partisan way, their behavior during those two months varied drastically. Our intensity-based measure captures these differences. A preference-based one does not.

The Promise of a Social Media–Based, Rhetoric Measure

Rhetoric-based approaches can measure a legislator's partisan intensity. However, many are limited. A commonly used data source are speeches delivered in the congressional record (Morris 2001; Maltzmann and Sigelman 1996). Yet, like votes and cosponsorships, it does not comprehensively cover partisan disputes. For example, during the 114th Congress, House Republicans created a select committee to investigate a terrorist attack on the US consulate in Benghazi, Libya. The committee was viewed as a partisan exercise to politically damage Hillary Clinton, the Democratic nominee for president. Representative Trey Gowdy (R-SC), the committee chair, did not make any statements that were recorded into the congressional record about the investigation.

The House's rules restrict members' remarks to the topic being considered. Unrestricted floor time allows for more rhetorical freedom but is limited. Additionally, nothing is entered into the record when Congress is not in session, which includes nearly half of the days in a congressional term. Consequently, partisan behavior that arises when members are back home, and especially on the campaign trail, is not included in this data. Press releases and newsletters allow for more unconstrained rhetoric, but they are used much less frequently than social media.

Twitter's ubiquitous use among members of Congress, particularly during the years we study, offers a new opportunity to measure partisanship and is well suited for this task. Lawmakers use social media in ways similar to other mediums, both in their broadcast communication style (Jungherr 2016) and in their message content (Golbeck, Grimes, and Rogers 2010; Straus et al. 2013). They post much more frequently on social media on a wider range of topics than through other mediums. For example, during the 115th Congress, lawmakers sent over 1.2 million tweets, with the median lawmaker posting 1,628 messages. During the same time, the congressional record included about 37,000 total entries, many of which do not include members' statements (e.g., entries that report on committee activities or that record bill introductions). To put the sheer size of social media data in perspective, the average congressional record for a Congress runs to approximately 30,000 print pages, while the tweets of members would run to over 170,000 pages if printed out equivalently. Other communication modes are used less often. Members send about 500 press releases and 100 newsletters per congressional term (Grimmer 2013). As with other mediums, legislators used Twitter to position take, credit claim, and advertise. They simply did much more of it on this platform.

In that vein, Twitter posts from this time offer a more comprehensive record of legislators' communications. Not only did members post unique messages, but they also linked to their floor speeches, press releases, media interviews, and other items they want their supporters to view. In fact, Twitter was often the only place members responded to the issues of the day or fast-moving news stories. In that political environment, tweeting became the predominant venue for legislators' unrestricted rhetoric and was often viewed as a type of "digital homestyle" (Gervais and Morris 2018). As a low-cost tool, legislators could tweet from anywhere at any time, so their posts included their reactions to contemporaneous issues that other forms of communication often miss.

Researchers have recognized Twitter as a valuable data source and have used it to study a wide range of congressional behavior, including how congressional candidates campaign online (Jungherr 2016), how that campaigning is gendered (Mechkova and Wilson 2021), legislators' ideology (Barberá 2015), presidential support (Miras 2019), issue attention and agenda setting (Russell 2021b; Barbera et al. 2019), substantive representation (Dancey and Masand 2017; Gervais and Wilson 2017), and incivility (Gervais and Morris 2018). Similar to our work, Russell (2018, 2020) uses tweets to study positive and negative partisan rhetoric in the Senate.

Anyone who spends their time reading legislators' social media posts will notice a pattern. Some are written by the members themselves. The informal style, many spelling errors, and idiosyncratic content choices are hallmarks of self-written content. Most posts are polished, on message, and clearly written by communications staffers. As we note early in chapter 2, we adopt the same assumption that decades of research on congressional communications follow: Communication from a legislator, whether written by them or staff, which describes almost all social media posts, floor speeches, newsletters, oversight questions, or any other material not directly said by the member off the top of their head, reflects their perspective on that topic.[15]

Although promising, social media data presents limitations. Unlike other partisanship measures, such as votes or floor speeches, tweets are not part of the formal record and may be a less costly way to display this behavior. Ill-advised posts can be deleted.[16] The remaining tweets may show more partisan intensity than other communication modes, as Twitter users are more politically engaged and partisan than the general public (Wojcik and Hughes 2019). If that is the case, we might overestimate Congress's partisan tenor. Yet, legislators differ in their partisan intensity and do so in predictable ways. This suggests that even though the proximate audience for these tweets is politically engaged, members are still carefully crafting their public messages.

Additionally, partisanship displayed on Twitter does not capture all the various ways this concept arises in Congress. We are not examining private partisan behaviors that arise through interpersonal interactions. Even as partisanship can have multiple dimensions, our approach is more comprehensive, as a social media–based measure captures many more partisan events than other approaches and is not censored by agenda-setting effects. Simply, our measure includes all of the partisan situations lawmakers wish to discuss. Like any legislative speech, posting decisions are strategic, and as we show throughout the book, these carefully cultivated personas are not showmanship.

Measuring Partisan Intensity on Twitter

In classifying tweets, we are interested in partisan rhetoric, which are statements that support one's political party or disparage the opposition party. In contrast, bipartisan rhetoric supports working with the other party. Cross-party rhetoric, or intraparty fighting, is communication in which copartisans disparage each other or their own party. Finally, nonpartisan rhetoric does not discuss political parties or their members. Usually, these messages are entirely apolitical (e.g., wishing followers a happy new year).

Our data includes tweets sent by members of Congress during the 114th through 116th Congresses (2015 through 2020).[17] Most maintain more than one Twitter account, usually an official one and a campaign one. A few members also tweet from personal ones, while a minority also have a dedicated press account separate from their others. Although legislators use these accounts for different purposes, and the chambers have rules for what official accounts can be used for,[18] we collected tweets from every account. In our research, we treat all statements on Twitter as equivalent, regardless of the nominal role of the particular account. That is, we treat a partisan message sent from a personal, campaign, or press account the same as one from the member's "official" account. In total, our data includes 3,743,909 tweets gathered from 1,291 distinct Twitter accounts.

To measure a member's partisan intensity, we developed a coding scheme that classifies a tweet as partisan or not. Our approach is based on a single underlying principle: Is the legislator posting content that creates a partisan frame for the reader? In applying this standard, we do not assume people necessarily make these partisan connections or that a social media audience needs to have some level of political knowledge to detect partisan language. Instead, we focus on the lawmaker's content decision: Are they framing their message in a partisan way?

TABLE 3.2. Partisan Tweet Coding Rules

Rule	Examples
Explicitly using party labels	Democrats, D's, Dems, Democrat Party, Republicans, GOP, R's, Reps
Mentioning the president, administration, or prominent presidential appointees	@POTUS, Trump, Obama, Mike Pence, Betsy DeVos, Kellyanne Conway, Gina McCarthy
Mentioning party leaders or partisan groups	Mitch McConnell, Paul Ryan, Nancy Pelosi, Tea Party, Freedom Caucus, Blue Dogs
Partisan issues related to good governance, scandals, or corruption	Russia investigation, Benghazi, Hillary Clinton's e-mails, Trump's golfing
Partisan issues related to congressional procedure or a party's handling of an issue	Merrick Garland's nomination, House Democrats gun violence sit-in
Discussing policy issues using partisan monikers	#GOPTaxScam, Obamacare, #TrumpBudget
Retweeting a partisan or party leader	@realdonaldtrump, @SenateDems
Explicitly attacking a member of the other party	Committee chairs/ranking members criticizing one another by name or Twitter handle
Campaign tweets that encourage voters to support a candidate, including vote, donation, and volunteering appeals, endorsements, and attacks on their opponent	#VoteBlue, #VoteThemOut

For example, members of Congress strategically talk about bureaucratic implementation. Weak partisans discuss their interactions with the agency itself, a nonpartisan, technocratic frame. Their posts mention the Department of Justice or the Environmental Protection Agency (EPA). Strong partisans like to invoke political actors and use partisan frames in their messaging. The "Department of Justice" becomes the "Obama administration's Department of Justice," or an "EPA decision" is "Scott Pruitt's decision." Unlike the weak partisan, the strong partisan is trying to create a partisan frame and wants their audience to attribute some government action to the presidential administration or a political appointee. Even if the audience is not always consciously picking up on the framing, the politician is making a deliberate choice to portray an issue in a partisan way.

Our coding rules reflect these linguistic choices, and many posts are easy to classify as partisan or not. Mentioning the parties themselves or the president or explicitly attacking a member of the opposition party is straightforward, partisan language. Tweets that use partisan policy labels (e.g., Obamacare

TABLE 3.3. Example Tweets About Donald Trump

Tweet	Legislator	Rhetoric Type
Grateful to the Dreamers who have stood up repeatedly to make their voices heard, and for Leader Pelosi for holding the floor of the House to defend Dreamers from Trump's attempts to deport them. Let's pass the #DreamActNow.	Raul Grijalva (D-AZ)	Partisan
3.7 million jobs have been created since Nov. 2016. Americans are thriving under the Trump Administration's business forward economic policies. Do you agree? #MAGA	Roger Williams (R-TX)	Partisan
The deadline to request tickets from my office to the inauguration of Donald Trump is TODAY at noon.	Stephanie Murphy (D-FL)	Nonpartisan
RT @rareliberty: Donald Trump being president is making very clear who is principled and who is just partisan.	Justin Amash (R-MI)	Cross-partisan
The House approved the most far-reaching overhaul of the criminal justice system in a generation Thursday, sending bipartisan legislation to President Trump. I supported this bill, and look forward to its positive effects on our society.	Don Bacon (R-NE)	Bipartisan

Note: Justin Amash subsequently left the Republican Party. At the time he sent this tweet, he still identified as a Republican.

or #TrumpBudget) constitute partisan rhetoric. Similar posts that use non-partisan phrases, such as the "Affordable Care Act" or the "budget proposal," do not.[19] Table 3.2 includes the nine categories we counted as constituting partisan language.[20]

Of course, a tweet's partisan nature is contextual. A post attacking President Trump sent by a Democrat is partisan. The same tweet sent from a Republican is cross-partisan. Similarly, a Democratic tweet supporting President Trump is classified as bipartisan, while a supportive Republican one is partisan. As such, we cannot simply develop a partisan dictionary that includes words like "Trump." To highlight why this is the case, table 3.3 includes tweets that mention the word "Trump" and shows how a post is dependent on both language and context.

To test our hypotheses, we require all congressional tweets to be classified as partisan or not. However, the sheer scale of this task is beyond manual hand coding, and so we turned to natural language processing tools for use on large quantities of text in order to make the classification problem tractable.

We trained a convolutional neural network to recognize partisan tweets. As a first step, for each Congress in our study, we hand coded 20,000 tweets as partisan or not based on our coding scheme from table 3.2.[21] These 60,000 tweets constituted our training data. We then trained a neural net to classify tweets as partisan based on that training data (with a random sample reserved as an out-of-sample test). After evaluating that the performance of the neural net on the out-of-sample test set was highly accurate, we applied the neural net model to the entire dataset of congressional tweets, classifying each tweet as partisan or not.

The neural network is built to perform a text classification task such that it takes as an input the text of a tweet and provides as an output what category of a predetermined list that tweet most closely belongs in. The neural network framework we used was SMaBERTa, which is a variant of the Bidirectional Encoder Representations from Transformers (BERT) model that has been specially trained on social media content.[22] This is important because while the baseline models are trained on patterns in the English language in general (using the full text of English-language Wikipedia as a corpus), the SMaBERTa framework adds additional layers trained on tweets. Because tweets are systematically different from general English-language texts—shorter, more colloquial, less formalized grammar, more slang and abbreviations—this additional layer provides the neural net with far greater nuance for classifying the patterns it finds in tweets. Thus, our neural net had effectively three layers integrated for this classification task: the general layer of the English language, the specific layer of English-language tweets, and our trained layer of partisanship.

We additionally customized the neural network's algorithm in two ways. First, we triple weighted mentions (e.g., @realdonaldtrump) by duplicating them when present at the end of the text of the tweet. Since partisan tweets are often classified based on whom they target or retweet, we use this overweighting technique to signal to the neural net that these particular words likely have higher semantic significance, all else being equal.[23]

Second, most tweets include links, some of which simply connect to embedded tweets but many of which link to websites other than Twitter.[24] In iterative testing of the neural net models, we found that one initial source of systemic error involved tweets with minimal neutral text (such as "look at this") but with a link to a highly partisan article being misclassified as "not partisan." As a result, in early runs, our model would systematically produce false negatives. To handle this issue, we examined the links present in our false negatives to manually develop lists of partisan Twitter accounts and keywords

TABLE 3.4. Out-of-Sample Performance of Neural Network

114th Congress		Hand-Coded			
		Partisan	Not Partisan	*Accuracy:*	95.0%
Model Prediction	Partisan	186	29	*Precision:*	86.5%
	Not Partisan	22	784	*Recall:*	89.4%
115th Congress		Hand-Coded			
		Partisan	Not Partisan	*Accuracy:*	94.0%
Model Prediction	Partisan	302	31	*Precision:*	90.7%
	Not Partisan	29	638	*Recall:*	91.2%
116th Congress		Hand-Coded			
		Partisan	Not Partisan	*Accuracy:*	96.3%
Model Prediction	Partisan	304	31	*Precision:*	90.8%
	Not Partisan	6	659	*Recall:*	98.1%
114th–116th Congresses		Hand-Coded			
		Partisan	Not Partisan	*Accuracy:*	95.1%
Model Prediction	Partisan	792	91	*Precision:*	89.7%
	Not Partisan	57	2,081	*Recall:*	93.3%

in external URLs that universally identify a link as partisan. If a partisan link is included, we reclassified the tweet as partisan.[25] The supplementary materials in our earlier work where we developed this method include our account and keyword lists (Gelman and Wilson 2022). These reclassified tweets constitute 10 percent of the partisan messages in our data. Overall, including each customization, the triple weighting and the URL logic, improved the model's performance by three percentage points.

We evaluated whether the neural network was effective by taking a random sample of 1,000 hand-coded tweets from each of the three Congresses and using them as a stratified out-of-sample test. We trained the algorithm on the other 57,000 hand-coded tweets in order to classify tweets as partisan or not, utilizing the algorithm discussed above. The neural network performs well, accurately classifying 95.1 percent of the out-of-sample test tweets, with 89.7 percent precision and 93.3 percent recall. These are summarized in table 3.4, both in total and stratified by Congress in order to evaluate whether there were any systemic differences in performance per Congress. In each Congress, and overall, the neural network exhibited high performance on all metrics, and thus we considered it usable for the remaining congressional tweets.[26]

Results and Measurement Validation

How much partisan content are legislators posting? And how much do they vary in their partisan intensities? The answer to both questions is a lot. Of the over 3.7 million tweets we collected, 31 percent (over 1.1 million) are partisan. Not surprisingly, as table 3.5 shows, the Congresses during Donald Trump's presidency produced more overall partisanship. The 115th Congress, covering Trump's first two years in office, produced the highest proportion of partisan tweets. On the face of it, this is a bit surprising, as the 116th term included two presidential impeachments and was an election year. In fact, members sent nearly 75,000 more partisan tweets during the 116th Congress. The difference is that lawmakers also tweeted more during those two years, which lowered the share devoted to partisanship.

We measure intensity in two ways. First, most of our analyses use the proportion of a legislator's tweets devoted to partisanship. This approach captures intensity by assessing who, when choosing to talk, frames more of their rhetoric in a partisan way. However, members differ in their social media activity, with some posting substantially more than others. That being the case, a second measure of intensity is the number of partisan posts they send. This captures who speaks in a partisan way most often. In describing partisan intensity, we mostly use the first measure, as it is easily compared between lawmakers. Later in the book, when we explore the causes and consequences of this behavior, we use both.

Descriptive Statistics

Although Congress is often described as a partisan institution, as figure 3.1 shows, members differ a great deal in their partisan intensities. The average legislator devotes 28 percent of their posts to partisan rhetoric, equivalent to 653 tweets per Congress (a little less than one partisan tweet per day). Others largely avoid or embrace party-based messaging. About 10 percent spend less than 10 percent of their tweets discussing Democrats and Republicans. In contrast, those above the 95th percentile dedicate over 55 percent of their public messages to partisan posts.

Figure 3.2 shows how individual members vary in their partisan intensity. Party leaders, like Nancy Pelosi (D-CA) and Mitch McConnell (R-KY), consistently displayed high partisan intensities in all three Congresses. In contrast, moderate senators, like Susan Collins (R-ME) and Joe Manchin (D-WV), did

TABLE 3.5. Total Tweets, by Congress

Congress	Total Tweets	Partisan Tweets	Proportion of Partisan Tweets
114th (2015–16)	916,594	211,608	0.23
115th (2017–18)	1,268,184	430,592	0.35
116th (2019–20)	1,543,757	506,000	0.33

not emphasize partisan rhetoric. Ted Cruz (R-TX) shows volatility in his intensity over these six years. In the 114th Congress, while running for president, he was an outlier. After losing the Republican nomination and returning to the Senate, his partisanship stabilized as somewhat middling.

The outliers at the top of these distributions were members in important investigatory or messaging roles. For instance, Adam Schiff (D-CA) was one of the strongest partisans during the Trump presidency. In the 115th Congress, he was the ranking member of the House Intelligence Committee, which hotly debated Russia's role in supporting the Trump campaign in the 2016 election. In the 116th Congress, he was the lead impeachment manager during the president's first impeachment. In fact, only three people, all Republicans, showed more partisan intensity than Schiff. Mark Meadows, who eventually became President Trump's chief of staff, was the most partisan member in this Congress. He was trailed by Mitch McConnell, the Senate majority leader, and John Ratcliffe, who was controversially appointed as director of national intelligence in what was viewed as an attempt to politicize the agency (Barnes, Fandos, and Goldman 2019).

Our measure seems to be capturing partisan intensity, but we validate it in three ways. First, we use our training set to predict the partisan intensity of nine out-of-sample Twitter accounts: President Trump, the House and Senate Republicans, the House and Senate Democrats, and each congressional party's campaign account (the National Republican Congressional Committee, National Republican Senatorial Committee, Democratic Congressional Campaign Committee, and Democratic Senatorial Campaign Committee). President Trump regularly invoked partisan language on Twitter, praising Republicans and disparaging Democrats. The party accounts are used to advance partisan online messaging campaigns. As such, we expect our model to rate each account as highly partisan. Table 3.5 lists these scores and their within-Congress percentile.

Not surprisingly, these accounts, especially the parties' electioneering arms, emphasize partisan rhetoric much more often than the average member

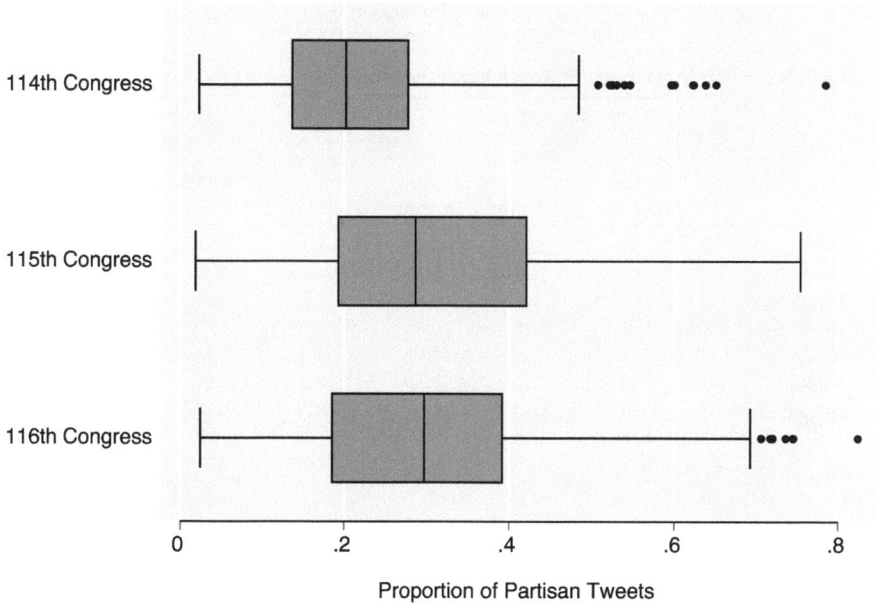

Fig. 3.1. Distribution of Legislators' Partisan Intensity

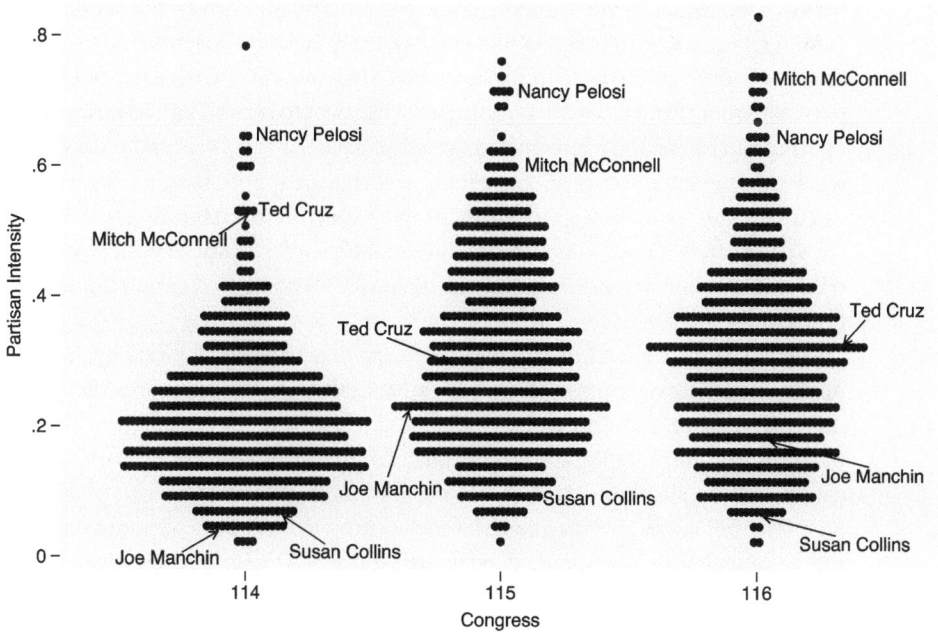

Fig. 3.2. Dot Plot of Legislators' Partisan Intensity

TABLE 3.6. Party Accounts' Partisan Intensity Scores

	114th Congress (2015–16)		115th Congress (2017–18)		116th Congress (2019–20)	
	Partisan Intensity	Percentile	Partisan Intensity	Percentile	Partisan Intensity	Percentile
DCCC	0.75	99th	0.73	99th	0.70	98th
DSCC	0.83	99th	0.76	99th	0.76	99th
House Dems	0.53	97th	0.68	98th	0.56	94th
House GOP	0.60	98th	0.54	92nd	0.70	98th
NRCC	0.82	99th	0.61	97th	0.71	98th
NRSC	0.76	99th	0.82	99th	0.69	98th
Donald Trump	0.76	99th	0.54	92nd	0.59	96th
Senate Dems	0.60	99th	0.64	98th	0.69	98th
Senate GOP	0.54	97th	0.51	89th	0.50	89th

of Congress. The parties themselves and President Trump also display high levels of partisan intensity and consistently rate as posting the highest proportion of partisan messages within their parties.

As a second validation check, we assess whether our measure captures the partisan intensity surrounding some particularly bitter disputes between Democrats and Republicans. When events largely viewed as partisan arise, we should observe an increase in partisanship. To assess this, we use the twelve partisan events from table 3.1 as moments we expect to see spikes in interparty fighting and calculated aggregate congressional partisanship scores during the week those events occurred. For events that spanned more than a week, we calculated the score during the moments we expect partisan fighting to peak. As we expected, a one-tailed t-test shows that legislators displayed more partisan intensity during these high-profile fights (0.34) compared to more docile times (0.29, $p < 0.0001$).

Finally, we examine how similar our measure is to political ideology. One possibility is that our approach simply captures the same liberal-conservative dimension others have previously calculated. However, our results show that partisanship and ideology are different. To measure their correlation, we calculated the absolute distance between a member's first-dimension DW-NOMINATE score and the median score during this six-year period, which reflects a legislator's ideological extremity. Table 3.7 includes their bivariate correlations by party and chamber.

Unlike other measures of ideology, whose correlation with DW-NOMINATE hovers around 0.9 (Bonica 2014), we are capturing a different

TABLE 3.7. Partisan Intensity and Ideology Correlations

Total	0.32
House	0.31
Senate	0.32
Democrats	0.39
Republicans	0.29

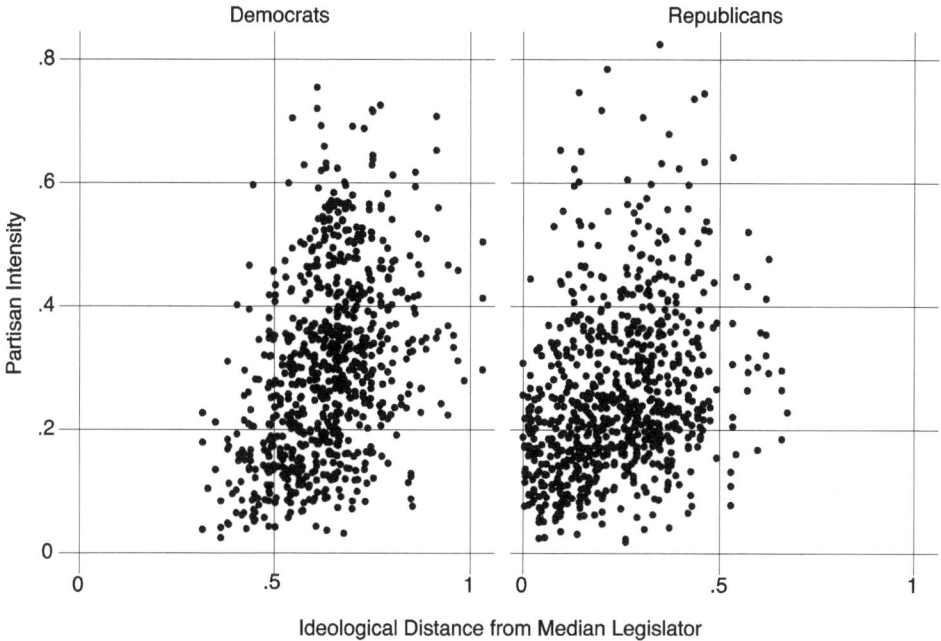

Fig. 3.3. Scatter Plot of Partisan Intensity and Ideology Measures

dimension of political conflict. Put differently, members' partisan intensity, measured using their Twitter posts, is weakly related to their ideological voting patterns. To better display this relationship, or lack thereof, we plot these measures against each other, by party, in figure 3.3. If moderates were always weak partisans, we would see clusters of dots near the graphs' origins. Those clusters do not exist. Rather, moderates vary in their partisanship. Although many employ this rhetoric sparingly, others devote 20 or 30 percent of their Twitter posts to explicitly partisan messages. Interestingly, the most ideological members display middling levels of partisan intensity. The most variation comes from the more ideologically typical.[27]

Taken together, these validation checks offer evidence that we are measur-

ing partisanship. As we expect, party leaders are much stronger partisans than
the rank and file. Our model rates out-of-sample party accounts and President
Trump as highly partisan. Events that we expect to produce significantly more
partisan intensity than more banal, day-to-day disputes did so. Finally, our
approach does not simply remeasure political ideology.

Conclusion

In this chapter we take on two simple but important tasks: defining and measuring partisanship. We distinguish it from other concepts, like ideology, but
note that in Congress it manifests in many ways. Our measurement approach
uses the millions of tweets that sitting members of Congress posted during
the 114th, 115th, and 116th Congresses in order to directly measure partisan
intensity. We accomplished this task by using a combination of hand coding
and sophisticated neural networks to classify this total corpus of text many
times larger than the congressional record. The resultant models were highly
accurate in out-of-sample tests and, in substantive terms, can be demonstrated
to produce a more comprehensive and nuanced quantification of partisan
behavior than has existed in prior literature. In the next chapter, we classify
the tone of these partisan tweets to understand how lawmakers use negative
and positive rhetoric in conjunction with partisanship.

FOUR

Bickering or Cheerleading

The Tone of Congressional Team Play

A good partisanship story has a few common elements. First, it has a compelling villain, preferably a hypocrite. Second, it has moral clarity, with distinctly right and wrong sides. Third, the partisan behavior speaks to something bigger about Congress or the politics of the time, usually with the lesson that the villain is contributing to some unfortunate demise of norms, productivity, or civility in the Capitol's hallowed halls.

Former President Barack Obama's and former Senator Olympia Snowe's (R-ME) versions of how the Affordable Care Act (ACA), a bill that passed on partisan lines, was written and passed are great partisanship stories. In Obama's telling, a few good-willed Republican senators really wanted to help write the legislation, but villains like Mitch McConnell and more hard-line members stood in their way. Jim DeMint (R-SC) famously said that the ACA would be Obama's "Waterloo. It will break him" (Obama 2020, 399). The former president suspected that even the most moderate Republicans pulled out of negotiations once McConnell, minority leader at the time, threatened to strip them of their committee posts.

Snowe saw it differently. As the last Republican senator who negotiated with the Democrats on the ACA, her perspective was that Nancy Pelosi and Harry Reid, the Speaker of the House and the Senate majority leader, respectively, were the villains. Instead of waiting for the bipartisan Group of Six senators to do their job, they undermined the entire process by using partisan maneuvers to write and pass a bill without Republican input while publicly insulting Republicans who sought compromise along the way.

For readers, both accounts offer the same conclusion: Even on tough issues, some politicians genuinely want to solve problems through bipartisan cooperation; unfortunately, partisan bickerers, whose only concern is having their party win, get in the way. In their tellings, Obama and Snowe were just two people, who happened to be the president and a pivotal senator, whose choices were limited by the partisan bickerers who prevent any sort of compromising. For Obama, it was the McConnells and DeMints of the world who would never have allowed any Senate Republicans to break ranks. For Snowe, Pelosi and Reid were never going to allow a bipartisan bill to pass. She and Obama tried, but the partisans won.

No matter how we view Obama's and Snowe's versions, they follow a standard narrative that reflects how partisanship is usually discussed. At its core, it involves divisiveness and conflict. Terms like "partisan warrior," "bickering," "confrontation," and "fighting" are common. More extreme versions are described as ugly politics and partisan warfare (Theriault 2015). In short, partisanship's tone and resulting actions are usually portrayed as negative.[1]

This focus on partisan bickering is not the whole story. Just as Snowe and her fellow Republicans mercilessly attacked Democrats for the ACA, Democrats spent years trying to construct and sell a *positive* partisan message about the law. More generally, besides trying to make the other side look bad, legislators work to make their side look good. They expend energy and effort building a positive party brand, extolling any good outcome that can be associated with their party. This demands positive partisan messaging and credit claiming, or what we call partisan cheerleading.

In this chapter, we measure the tone of congressional partisanship to assess how much bickering and cheerleading is happening. To do so, we use a neural network to classify the tone of the partisan tweets we identified in chapter 3. With this data, we report two findings. First, we show that most partisan rhetoric, 60 percent, is negatively toned, although members still send tens of thousands of positive messages.

Second, we categorize strong partisans into three categories—the bickerers who most emphasize negative rhetoric, the cheerleaders whose tone is more positive, and the opportunists who mix the tone of their partisanship strategically. After identifying these groups, we assess the factors associated with members who stir up partisan trouble relative to those who prefer cheerleading their side. We find that negative partisan tones are mainly associated with the reelection-seeking factors we identify in chapter 2, not the promotion-seeking ones. In particular, members holding safer seats and in the party opposite the president are much more likely to engage in negative partisan talk. Bickerers, who we define as the most partisan lawmakers with the most negative tones, hail from very safe seats and are almost always in the party opposing the president. Alternatively, with the exception of legislators running for higher office who consistently use more positive rhetoric, promotion-seeking factors are not related to any tonal differences.

This distinction in which factors relate to negative partisan rhetoric reflects different demands for partisan displays. Voters, especially in safer districts, *want* combative bickering. For many, it reflects how they want their member to represent them. On the other hand, copartisans on the Hill just want their colleagues to be good team players. They do not care as much about the tone. Cheerleaders are fine as long as they back the party. Consequently, partisan promotion seeking and tone are not tied together.

Does Partisanship's Tone Matter?

Before examining differences in partisan tone and who the bickerers and cheerleaders are, it is worth considering whether the tone of partisan rhetoric matters.[2] Research on the link between elite discourse and citizens' opinion formation shows it does. As we discussed in chapter 1, a main reason congressional partisanship matters is it influences how voters see the political world. Issues become politicized and compromise becomes more difficult when they become wrapped up in partisan identities. Yet, the consequences of portraying politics this way partially depend on its tone. Political scientists have shown behavioral differences in the public who hear the message that "my side is great" compared to those who hear that "the other side is terrible."

The main concern about partisan rhetoric is that bickering, in which members adopt a negative tone that often attacks the opposition, contributes to voters' dislike of those in the other party and undermines their support for compromise. The research on this topic is wide-ranging and the results are decidedly mixed as social scientists explore different concepts (e.g., emotional language, affective polarization, partisan animus) and reasons (e.g., media consumption, local political context) for why partisan voters' aversion toward the opposition has increased over the past few decades.[3]

However, researchers have produced consistent evidence that the tone of elite partisan rhetoric affects the public. Negative campaigning increases dislike for the other party (Iyengar, Sood, and Lelkes 2012), elite incivility reduces outgroup trust (Gervais 2017, 2019), and as elites have displayed more dislike for the other party, partisan voters have followed suit (Banda and Cluverius 2018). Studies on emotion show that politicians strategically use affective rhetoric, especially negative emotions like anger, which engages and rallies copartisan voters (Stapleton and Dawkins 2021; Valentino et al. 2011). Less research considers how partisan cheerleading affects the public's views on the party, but studies on positivity, often expressed through emotions like enthusiasm, signal that "things are going well and our goals are being met" (Albertson, Dun, and Gadarian 2020). Others examine how parties build their collective brands through policy appeals and individual members' personal credit claiming (Woon and Pope 2008; Grimmer, Messing, and Westwood 2012; Egan 2013). The goal of a positive tone is to motivate supporters, increase their interest, and maintain their support (Albertson, Dun, and Gadarian 2020).

Besides affecting voters, partisan bickering has consequences for congressional operations and productivity. As we have noted throughout the book, compromising members regularly blame strong partisans who traffic in negative rhetoric for politicizing issues and torpedoing compromises. Political scientists have corroborated this view, showing that members who prefer partisan warfare make bipartisan negotiations difficult, if not impossible, and use brinkmanship tactics that have serious public policy repercussions (Theriault 2013; Mann and Ornstein 2012; Lee 2009). The roll call record, which researchers use to measure legislative polarization, is heavily influenced by partisan bickerers as lawmakers force votes to embarrass the other side (Egar 2016; Gelman 2020a; Lee 2016). Indeed, partisanship's tone, and its assumed negativity, is generally viewed as problematic and worthy of more attention.

Measuring Cheerleading and Bickering

In evaluating the partisan tone in Congress, we explore two features that generate the most interest from congressional observers. First, we assess how members differ in their partisan tones. Second, we define three groups of strong partisans based on their relative negativity. We distinguish who is a bickerer (those who adopt the most extreme negative tones) from cheerleaders (whose rhetoric is the most positive) and opportunists (who mix their tones).

Concerns about partisanship focus on bickerers, who are also called partisan warriors, as a problem. These are uncompromising members who constantly attack the opposition. Although bickerers are widely acknowledged as important in Congress, researchers have not clearly defined this group, defined how they differ from other strong partisans, and determined if they are different than ideologues. As such, one of our goals in this chapter is to evaluate how strong partisans vary their tones and to use this variation to appropriately categorize them. Doing so means we can study what is motivating bickerers, as well as cheerleaders and opportunists.

The first step in classifying these partisan types is to measure a tweet's tone. We use a neural network to do so, which is a similar approach to how we classify tweets as partisan or not. We use the Stanford CoreNLP project, which is a sophisticated set of linguistic analysis tools that use sentence- and word-level context in addition to a vast training library on English-language grammar and syntax (Manning et al. 2014; Socher et al. 2013). This set of tools provides an estimate of positive or negative sentiment at the sentence level, making it ideal for evaluating positive or negative tone in tweets, which are typically roughly sentence length. This algorithm significantly outperforms similar such algorithms that operate simply at a word frequency level (i.e., using a dictionary that flags certain words as always positive or always negative regardless of context). Thus, for every tweet, not only do we classify whether it is partisan or not, we also track whether its tone is positive or negative (with a residual of tweets that the CoreNLP sentiment classifier evaluates as neither negative nor positive). Table 4.1 includes examples with varying tones.

As a first step, we evaluate whether lawmakers' partisan and nonpartisan tones differ. To do so, we calculated the percentage of negative partisan tweets ((# *of Negative Partisan Tweets*)/(# *of Partisan Tweets*)), positive partisan tweets, negative nonpartisan tweets, and positive nonpartisan tweets sent by lawmakers.[4] On average, 60 percent of a legislator's partisan posts are negatively toned. Only 19 percent are positive. The remainder are classified by the neural network as neutrally toned. Tweets that do not include partisan language follow a similar but less extreme pattern. Of those posts, 47 percent include a negative tone and 29 percent are positive.[5] Legislators' messaging tends to be negative, but their partisan rhetoric is pointedly so.

To put this level of negative versus positive speech in perspective, we took a random sample of all tweets from the United States during this time period, in addition to a random sample of tweets containing verbiage about American politics.[6] We then applied the same Stanford CoreNLP polarity process to those random tweets (10,000 of each set). American tweets in general were 17 percent positive and 21 percent negative, while American tweets about *politics* were 13 percent positive and 34 percent negative, with the balance in each set neutral. While exploring the tweets of the public in depth is beyond the

TABLE 4.1. Tone and Partisanship Example Tweets

Tweet	Legislator	Tone and Partisanship
To trump and his shameless lackeys a titanic public health crisis is a threat not to the American public but to trump's political standing. That's what they're focused on.	Bill Pascrell (D-NJ)	Negative and partisan
Looking forward to being sworn into the 116th Congress today as Democrats take control of the House of Representatives. I'm ready to get to work to push forward a positive agenda that will benefit North Carolina's First Congressional District and the American people. #NC01 #NCPol	G.K. Butterfield (D-NC)	Positive and partisan
Remember Google's motto used to be "Don't be evil." They no longer have that motto. Instead, they now have a monopoly with 90% of online searches.	Kevin McCarthy (R-CA)	Negative and nonpartisan
I had a fantastic time celebrating and honoring our veterans at the 6th Annual Lucedale Veterans Day Parade. As we head into Veterans Day, please take a moment to reflect on the sacrifices made by those who have fought for and defended our freedoms.	Steven Palazzo (R-MS)	Positive and nonpartisan
Shameless Selfie with the "fightin 51st" precinct. The Knox County GOP is reorganizing during the flood.	Tim Burchett (R-TN)	Neutral and partisan
@HouseJudiciary Markup Hearing on H.R. 35, the Emmett Till Antilynching Act and others.	Sheila Jackson Lee (D-TX)	Neutral and nonpartisan

scope of this book, it gives us an interesting perspective on just how positive and negative congressional tweets are: substantially more positive *and* negative than either general tweets from America or even specific tweets about American politics.

On the one hand, legislators' emphasis on bickering follows the conventional view that partisanship tends to be negative. On the other hand, legislators are still engaging in a good deal of cheerleading, to the tune of over 218,000 positively toned partisan tweets during this six-year period. Moreover, these aggregate percentages mask substantial tonal differences among lawmakers. Some exclusively bicker while others avoid fights and orient their rhetoric toward cheerleading.

To measure a legislator's partisan tone, we created a partisan tone score. We assigned negative tweets a value of -1, neutral ones a 0, and positive tweets a 1. We summed these values for members' partisan tweets and divided that value by the number of partisan tweets they sent ((Σ *Partisan Tweets Senti-*

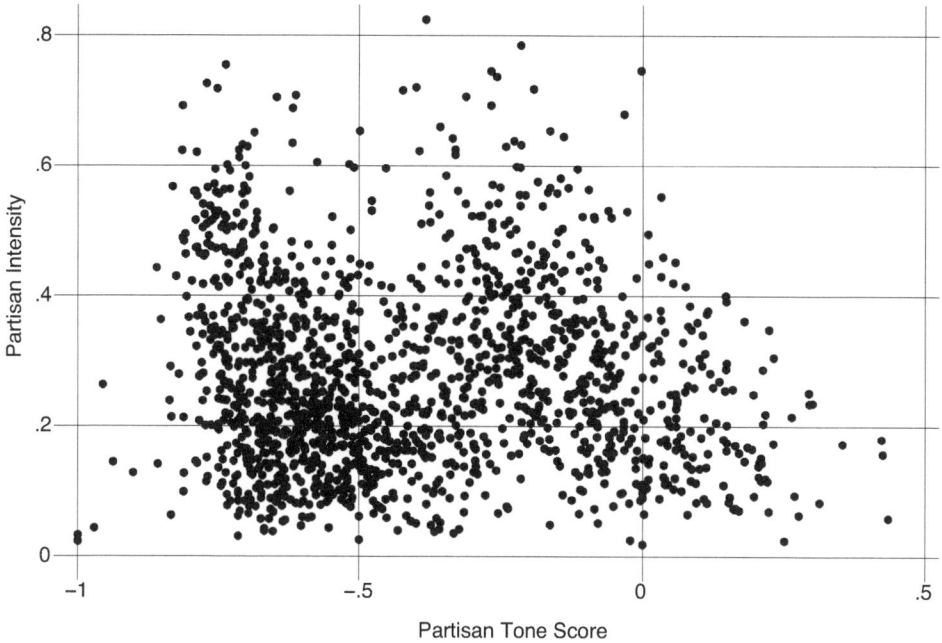

Fig. 4.1. Legislators' Partisan Intensity and Tone

ment)/(# of Partisan Tweets)). The result is a score that ranges from −1 (only bickers) to 1 (only cheerleads). A score of 0 means a member perfectly balances their partisan bickering and cheerleading.[7] To get a sense of the differences in members' tones and how it relates to partisan intensity, we graph lawmakers' tone scores against their partisan intensity in figure 4.1.[8]

The plot's most notable feature is the lack of relationship between partisan intensity and tone. The correlation between the two variables is −0.08. Put differently, strong partisans' overall tone is not oriented more toward bickering than their colleagues. Rather, most members' partisan tone is negative, but to varying degrees. Only a few legislators emphasize cheerleading more than bickering, and those who do tend to be weak partisans. However, since the partisan tone score is a ratio that accounts for how often members send partisan messages, strong partisans are still posting more negatively toned tweets. In fact, the correlation between a lawmaker's partisan intensity and their raw partisan sentiment, the number of negatively toned tweets they post, is −0.48. Thus, strong partisans may bicker more because they are sending more partisan posts, but many of them are also cheerleading as well.

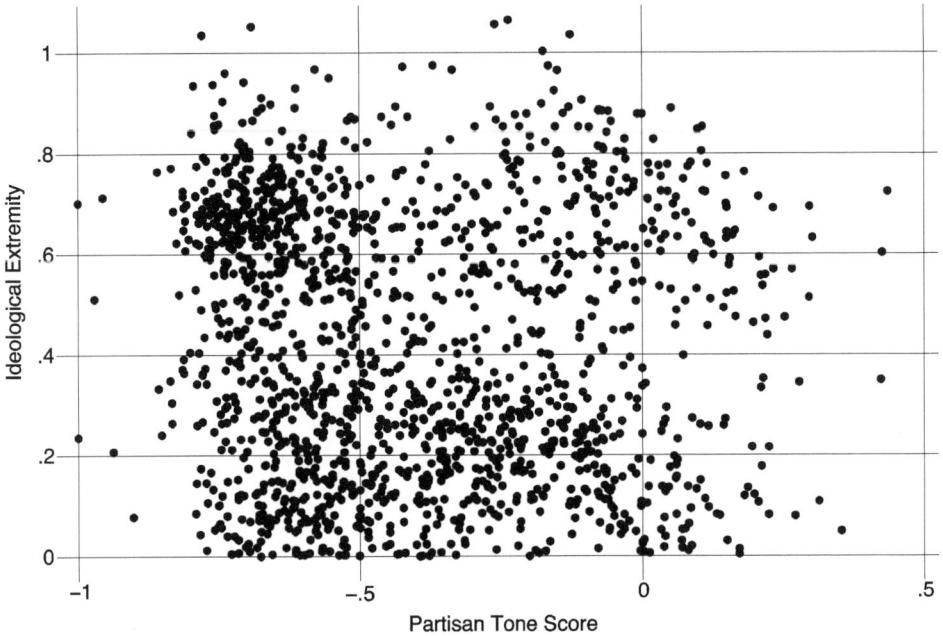

Fig. 4.2. Legislators' Ideological Extremity and Tone

The relationship between ideological extremity and partisan tone is also weak. In figure 4.2, we plot a member's partisan tone score against their ideological extremity, measured as their ideological distance from the chamber median. These variables' correlation is only −0.1, which indicates that a simple story of ideologues driving partisan bickering is not what is going on.

Identifying Partisan Bickerers, Cheerleaders, and Opportunists

These differences in strong partisans' tones suggest they are adopting different partisan approaches. The most negative are fulfilling the partisan warrior stereotype. However, some are tonally quite balanced, as they sprinkle more positive messages along with their attacks. Others are much more positive, although in the aggregate still posting slightly more negative messages. In explaining what motivates strong partisans' behavior, distinguishing between these different rhetorical approaches is important. As strategic communicators, members are choosing to emphasize a certain tone when cultivating their partisan personas. Categorizing them in this way will help explain the most extreme partisan behavior on Capitol Hill.

To define groups of strong partisans by their tone, we begin by considering what political observers mean when they talk about partisan warriors or, as we call them, bickerers. These members constantly pick fights with and attack the other party. In our terms, they have high partisan intensities with a tone that is overwhelmingly negative. Cheerleaders, on the other hand, are the masters of spin. They look for any positive news about their party and broadcast it widely. In their opponents' eyes, they are the sycophants who are unable to marshal a bad word toward their copartisans under any circumstance. In the middle are the opportunists whose partisan rhetoric mixes the positive and negative.

Moreover, when thinking about who is a bickerer, opportunist, or cheerleader, these categories are not based on some absolute threshold. Instead, they are relative based on the partisanship level in a particular Congress. Bickerers are the members who focused most on attacking the other side in a given term. By this definition, only the most extreme members fall into this category, and not everyone can be a bickerer no matter their partisan intensity or tone.

To identify these three groups, we defined strong partisans as legislators whose partisan intensity was at or above the 75th percentile in a given congressional term.[9] Among these members, bickerers are those whose partisan tone was at or above the 75th percentile in negativity. Cheerleaders are at or below the 25th percentile in negative tone, and opportunists are those whose fall in the middle 50th percentile. Of course, these cutoffs are arbitrary, but we contend that they capture the essence of what it means to be a bickerer, cheerleader, or opportunist and allow us to explore the different motivations for adopting these partisan approaches.[10] Later in the chapter, we also examine partisan tone as a continuous variable, among both strong partisans and all legislators. For now, we focus on the tone of highly partisan members, and based on our categorization scheme, table 4.2 includes counts for how many Democrats and Republicans are in each group during the three Congresses we analyze.

For those who followed Congress during these years, each category includes familiar names, and some members always are categorized in the same way. Adam Schiff (D-CA), the lead Democrat on the House Intelligence Committee and the impeachment manager, was a bickerer in all three terms. Paul Ryan (R-OH), the House Budget Committee chair and then the Speaker of the House, was an opportunist. Cheerleaders adopted a positive partisan persona for different reasons. In 2015 and 2016, the 114th Congress included Nancy Pelosi (D-CA), the Democratic Speaker of the House, and Mick Mul-

TABLE 4.2. Number and Percentage of Strong Partisan Types, by Congress

	Definition	Party	114th Cong. (2015–16)	115th Cong. (2017–18)	116th Cong. (2019–20)
Bickerer	Top 25% in partisan intensity; top 25% in negative partisan tone	Democrat	18 (11%)	72 (50%)	53 (25%)
		Republican	28 (13%)	1 (<1%)	16 (8%)
Opportunist	Top 25% in partisan intensity; middle 50% in negative partisan tone	Democrat	26 (15%)	29 (20%)	17 (8%)
		Republican	29 (14%)	19 (7%)	41 (22%)
Cheerleader	Top 25% in partisan intensity; bottom 25% in negative partisan tone	Democrat	19 (11%)	2 (1%)	3 (1%)
		Republican	14 (5%)	26 (10%)	11 (6%)

Note: Percentages are the number of strong partisan types divided by the total number of party members serving during that Congress.

vaney (R-SC), a Freedom Caucus backbencher. Pelosi posted about Democrats' Obama-era accomplishments. Mulvaney regularly lauded Republican party presidential candidates, especially Trump in 2016, in what seemed to be a promotion-seeking bid.[11]

Highly partisan legislators did not always stay in one category. Rather, as Obama left office and was replaced with Trump, they changed their tones. For example, Republican leaders like Mitch McConnell (R-KY) and Kevin McCarthy (R-CA) shifted from bickerers during the Obama years to opportunists during Trump's term. Indeed, the most striking feature from table 4.2 is the clear effect Donald Trump's election had on legislators' tones. A substantial number of Democrats shifted to much more partisan and negative rhetoric in 2017 and 2018, relative to the final two years of the Obama administration. In fact, half of all Democrats rated as bickerers those two years. In a stark contrast, the most partisan Republicans became cheerleaders with positive tones once Trump was in office. This reflects a common feature of those years that no matter what Trump did, many Republican legislators cheered him on. These trends toward the most partisan Democrats using a negative tone and Republicans adopting a positive one persisted but at lower levels in 2019 and 2020. As the presidential election became a focal point and Democrats became the House majority, more Republicans became opportunists and bickerers, not cheerleaders. Similarly, the extraordinary number of Democrats classified as bickerers decreased as other politicians, like Joe Biden and the other Democratic presidential hopefuls, took some attention away from Trump.

Clearly, who was president, at least during these six years, affected who was a bickerer, opportunist, or cheerleader. But the changes from the 115th and 116th Congresses, when Trump was president the whole time, suggest other factors affect when members adopt very partisan rhetoric and the tones they use. Indeed, the partisan tone a member adopts between Congresses is not strongly correlated. The correlation between a member's partisan tone score in the 114th Congress and the 115th is only 0.24. Between the 114th and 116th Congress, it is even lower: 0.12. When only looking at the within-member correlation during the Trump presidency (the 115th and 116th terms), it increases to 0.5. This indicates that lawmakers' partisan tones are not particularly stable and are likely affected by their political circumstances.

What Is Associated with Negative Partisan Tones?

To the extent that bickering is cause for concern and that members' partisan tones regularly shift, the natural question is, What motivates this behavior? We approach this question in two ways. First, we assess what factors are associated with overall changes in partisan tone. In other words, we analyze the partisan tone score we introduce above as a continuous variable. Second, we consider what factors differentiate partisan warriors, opportunists, and cheerleaders from each other and other members. In this case, we break Congress into four discrete groups (three groups of strong partisans based on their tone and then everyone else).

Although we do not hypothesize about what affects a member's partisan tone in chapter 2, our theory provides some guidance. Recall that our argument is that partisan behavior is aimed at two audiences, voters and copartisans in Congress. Research on voters, especially copartisans, indicates they often prefer and react to negatively toned rhetoric (Iyengar, Sood, and Lelkes 2012). They want to see their representatives show partisan fidelity, and in their view, this often means bickering with the other side. For their part, copartisan legislators want to see their leaders as reliable team players. This can mean picking fights with the other party, but it also means building and boosting a positive party brand that the rank and file use to run on back home.

In both cases, partisan voters and copartisans on the Hill are looking for partisan behavior. But the type they want varies. That being the case, we expect that the reelection-related factors that affect members' partisan intensity also affect their tone. In particular, as their seat safety increases, their messaging should become more negative. This reflects that more of their constituents are the partisans who prefer a more combative tone. We also expect the collective factors that move lawmakers' overall partisan behavior to also affect their tone. Serving in the minority party, the party opposite of the president, and having narrow majorities in a chamber are cited as factors that increase partisan acrimony and should be associated with more negativity (Lee 2016; Russell 2021a; Lee 2009).

In contrast, we expect that for those members appealing to their colleagues, namely, those holding leadership positions, either they display more positivity or their institutional roles do not affect their tones. On the one hand, leaders look to cheerlead their party's achievements, but on the other hand, they are eager to be combative and to support their side during a partisan dispute. Whatever their tonal choices, unlike voters who generally prefer negativity, their copartisans mostly care that their teamsmanship is reliable. As such, depending on their eagerness to cheerlead, this can produce more positive tones or a wide range of tonal approaches that do not produce any strong pattern. Regardless, we do not expect them to display significantly more negative tones than the rank and file.

Beyond members appealing to these constituents at home and in Washington, DC, political scientists have argued that, like partisan intensity, other factors affect partisanship's tone. Russell (2021a) argues Republicans tend to use more negative partisan rhetoric than Democrats, but as we saw in table 4.2, this finding might be an artifact based on who is sitting in the Oval Office. Representatives and senators might differ in their tones, as the Senate is generally viewed as the more deliberative, conciliatory chamber. Finally, newer members are often associated with bringing harder-edged styles to Congress. They replace moderates, and new show horses whose goal is to seek attention often captivate the media with their new antics and seemingly outrageous behavior.

To explore what factors are associated with negative partisan tones, we specified a regression model that includes the factors listed in table 4.3 and two additional control variables: a legislator's ideological extremity, measured as their ideological distance from the chamber median using DW-NOMINATE scores, and congressional term fixed effects. Our model is an ordinary least squares (OLS) regression with robust standard errors clustered by member. In figure 4.3, we present the coefficients from the model, which reflect how much a variable makes a member's partisan tone more positive or negative.[12] The regression table is in the chapter's appendix.

The results indicate that tone is affected by members' reelection concerns, including their seat safety and factors related to party brand-building activities, not by becoming more politically influential. Seat safety, being a presi-

TABLE 4.3. Measurement of Factors Used to Predict Partisan Tone

Variable	Expected Effect	Measure
Seat Safety	–	Avg. of member's party's presidential vote share over last two elections
Majority Party	+	Dichotomous
Majority Party Size	+	% of seats held by majority party
President's Party	+	Dichotomous
High-Ranking Party Leader	+ or null	Dichotomous (1 if top 3 leadership positions in House; top 2 in Senate)
Low-Ranking Party Leader	+ or null	Dichotomous (1 if not top leader but in leadership ranks)
Committee Leader	+ or null	Dichotomous (1 if chair or ranking member)
Running for Higher Office	+ or null	Dichotomous (1 if representative running for Senate/statewide office or senators running for president)
Republican	–	Dichotomous
Senate	+	Dichotomous
Terms Served	+	Count of completed terms served

dential copartisan, serving in the majority party, and the majority's size are all associated with changes in tone. Moreover, all are in the expected direction, except for the majority party variable, and generally follow other research that finds these factors are associated with more confrontational politics over a long time period (Lee 2009; 2016). In contrast to previous research, our results indicate that being in the majority produces more negativity (Russell 2021a). The only power-seeking factor that is correlated with tone is running for higher office. Legislators running for a more prestigious position tend to adopt more positive partisan tones than those staying in their seat. Second, our results contrast with previous findings about which members contribute to the partisan bickering on Capitol Hill. Unlike Russell (2021a), we find that Republicans adopt more positive partisan tones. Again, we suspect that these divergent results are driven by the time periods that different studies analyze. Additionally, newer members are not using more negative tones. In fact, longer-serving legislators are associated with more negativity.

Indeed, many of the factors in figure 4.3 have a substantial predicted effect on a member's partisan tone. Supporting a copartisan chief executive increases positivity 8 percent. Those in the safest seats have partisan tone scores that

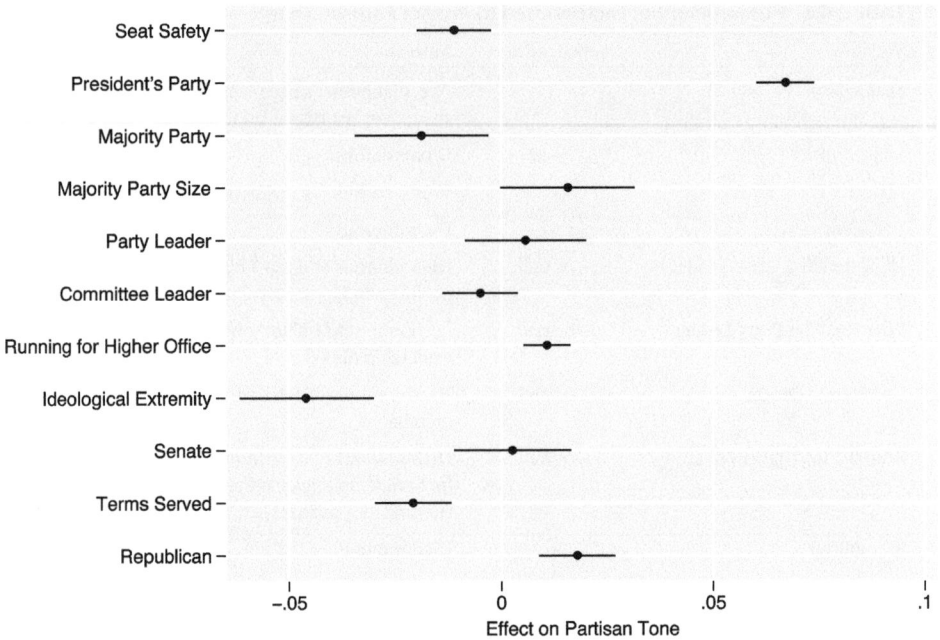

Fig. 4.3. Factors That Affect a Member's Partisan Tone

are 3 percent more negative than those in the most marginal districts, and compared to the chamber median, the most ideologically extreme lawmakers' partisan tone score is 12 percent more negative.

What Distinguishes Bickerers, Opportunists, and Cheerleaders?

Although our previous analysis provides insight into what factors affect partisan tone, a more pressing concern is what motivates strong partisans to adopt caustic or more conciliatory ones. After all, the concerns we outline above about partisan negativity are not about weak partisans who sometimes use combative language. Most commentators worry about the bickerers, whose main goal is to constantly politicize issues by using negative partisan rhetoric. To analyze what factors are associated with high partisan intensity and different tones, we split the lawmakers in our data into four groups. The first three groups are the bickerers, opportunists, and cheerleaders, defined in table 4.2. Recall that these are members who rate in the 75th percentile and above in partisan intensity, with each group displaying different degrees of negativity in their tones. The baseline group are weaker partisans who display less partisan intensity. Our goal in this analysis is to identify factors that distinguish certain types of strong partisans from one another as well as from the rest of Congress who display less partisanship.

What distinguishes bickerers, an active partisan with a caustic tone, from the less intensely partisan lawmakers? In chapter 2, we hypothesize that partisan activity comes from reelection and promotion-seeking behavior. Above, we contend that negativity is principally used to appeal to voters. Thus, we expect that bickerers are more likely to hold safe seats because their reelection constituents mainly include party members. Bickerers do not need to appeal to moderates, independents, or voters from the other party. Unlike the other reelection-related factors we identify, which affect copartisans collectively, members in safe districts have the latitude and incentive to use combative rhetoric to appeal to their party base, who dominates the electorate.

In contrast, we do not expect that seat safety distinguishes cheerleaders from most other legislators. These more cheerful partisans are showing off as good team players, but not using a tone that appeals to constituents who prefer negativity. Opportunists, whose tone falls in the middle 50 percent but is still mostly negative, are also likely to represent safer seats than less partisan members. Their mixing of positive and negative partisan rhetoric suggests some of their behavior is targeted at partisan voters, even as they mix in more conciliatory language.

Based on the descriptive statistics from table 4.2, we expect that being in the same party as the president is associated with being a cheerleader and opportunist, not a bickerer. Since the president's copartisans seek to tout his accomplishments, their tones should shift more positive. Like before, we do not expect that most of the promotion-seeking factors will distinguish between these three categories. Our only expectation is that seeking higher office, which requires building enthusiasm among voters and was strongly associated with more positive partisan rhetoric in table 4.4, will be correlated with being a cheerleader and opportunist rather than a bickerer.

To examine differences between these three types of strong partisans, we use a multinomial logistic regression. The dependent variable is a member's partisan type, defined as being a bickerer, opportunist, or cheerleader or in the baseline category of lawmakers whose partisan intensities fall below the 75th percentile. We include the same independent variables outlined in table 4.3. The coefficients in a multinomial logistic regression compare a category to the baseline. In our case, this means the results in the table analyze whether a bickerer is statistically distinguishable from a weaker partisan who falls below the 75th percentile in partisan intensity.[13]

TABLE 4.4. Factors That Differentiate Strong Partisans Based on Tone

More (less) likely to be a . . .	than a . . .	
Bickerer	Cheerleader	Seat Safety (+)
		President's Party (−)
		Running for Higher Office (−)
		Ideological Extremity (+)
		Republican (−)
Bickerer	Opportunist	President's Party (−)
		Running for Higher Office (−)
Opportunist	Cheerleader	President's Party (−)
		Running for Higher Office (−)
		Ideological Extremity (+)

Although we are interested in what separates these different strong partisan types from the rest of Congress, our main interest is understanding why those with high partisan intensities choose more or less negative tones. To evaluate this question, we compare which coefficients are statistically different ($p < 0.05$) between these three groups—bickerers, opportunists, and cheerleaders—based on the statistical models whose full results are in the chapter's appendix.[14] In table 4.4 we list which factors differentiate these partisan types. A positive sign next to the variable indicates that it is associated with the "more likely" category in that row.

Substantively, the most consistent factor that differentiates these groups of strong partisans is whether they are in the same party as the president. Being a presidential copartisan makes it more likely a highly partisan lawmaker adopts a more cheerful tone. The probability that someone is a cheerleader increases 0.03 if they are in the same party as the president. In contrast, opportunists are 3 percent less likely to be in the president's party. For bickerers, that value is 16 percent. Put differently, sharing a partisan label with the president helps a good deal in explaining gradations in strong partisans' rhetoric.

Seat safety is also associated with more negative partisan rhetoric. Compared to members in the most competitive districts, those in the safest seats are 10 percent more likely to be bickerers. The effect is nearly identical for opportunists.[15] Interestingly, seat safety does not have a statistically significant effect on a strong partisan being a cheerleader.

The final factor that consistently differentiates these groups is whether a member is running for higher office. In chapter 2, we discussed how this promotion-seeking behavior is aimed at other officeholders and the extended party networks whose endorsement and support are valuable assets. The tonal approach that strong partisans take, as they run for positions like senator or president, is to speak more positively about their party. A cheerleader is 23 percent more likely to be running for higher office than not. An opportunist is 16 percent more likely. Bickerers are very unlikely to be running for higher office—the predicted probability they are doing so is only 0.01. This consistent association between running for higher office and having a positive tone follows research on enthusiasm that emphasizes that candidates are trying to motivate supporters and boost interest in their campaigns (Albertson, Dun, and Gadarian 2020; Gelman, Wilson, and Petrarca 2021).

What Is Motivating the Partisan Fighters on Capitol Hill?

At the outset of the chapter, we outlined what is viewed as a serious problem in Congress: the constant, negative partisan bickering that inhibits the legislature from doing its job. In that vein, we investigated members' partisan tones and the factors associated with differences in their relative negativity. Our analysis uncovers three important results. First, the average partisan tone is more negative than positive. Only a handful of members, most of whom do not use much partisan rhetoric, post more positive partisan messages on social media than negative ones. The perception that when lawmakers discuss the parties they are bickering with one another is well founded.

Second, two factors consistently are associated with differences in partisan tone. The president's party has an outsize effect on how members talk. His copartisans adopt more positive tones, albeit most are still mostly negative, as they cheerlead his administration's accomplishments. Those in the other party embrace tones that are much more negative as they look for any opportunity to attack the most prominent politician in American government. Given the time period we are examining, particularly the four years Donald Trump was president, this dynamic makes sense as Republicans dutifully applauded his every move while Democrats were merciless in their criticism. Additionally, seat safety is consistently associated with more negative partisan tones. Members holding safer seats use more negative partisan rhetoric, and bickerers, the most intensely partisan and negative members, are more likely to come from uncompetitive districts or states.

Third, our analysis revises some common claims about who is perpetuating the partisan animosity on Capitol Hill. New legislators, on average, are not using more negativity than longer-serving ones, even after we control for seat safety. In fact, it is the opposite. Moreover, for this time period, we do not find that Republicans adopt more negative partisan tones. Rather, our results point to larger structural factors as being associated with more combative tones. Who is in the White House, a district's partisan lean, whether lawmakers are in the majority party, and their party's seat share at the time all are more strongly related to lawmakers' rhetorical tenor than how long they have been in Congress or their political party.

Stepping back, we show that partisan rhetoric is not constantly negative. Instead, different factors are motivating different tones. In particular, reelection-seeking factors, not influence-seeking variables, are more associated with shifts in tone. This provides evidence that tonal changes are more about appealing to voters and building the party brand than about displaying good teamsmanship to colleagues.

Appendix

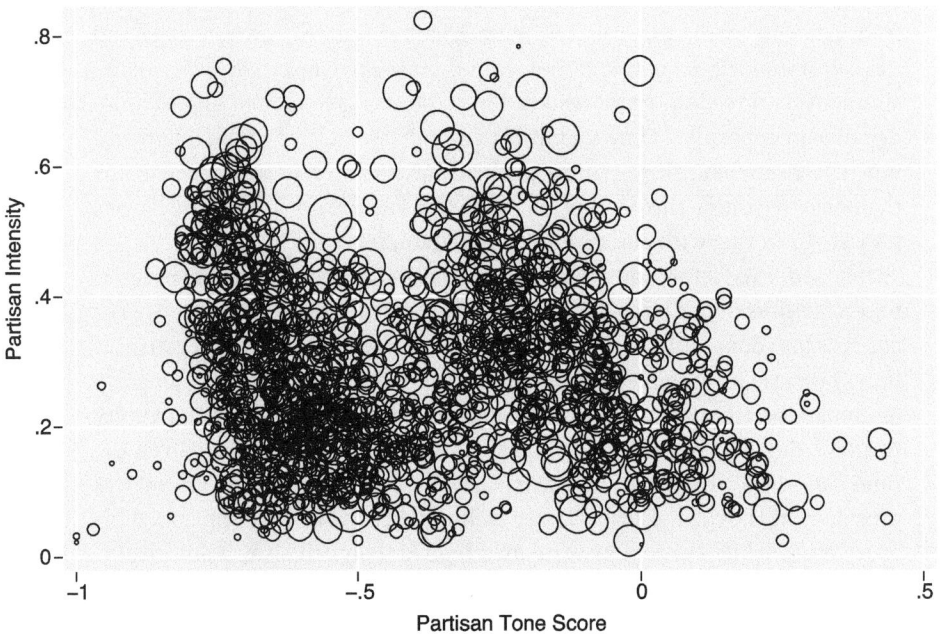

Fig. 4.4. Legislators' Partisan Intensity and Tone, by Total Number of Tweets

TABLE 4.5. Determinants of a Legislator's Partisan Tone

Seat Safety	-0.01^*
	(0.01)
President's Party	0.13^{**}
	(0.01)
Majority Party	-0.04^*
	(0.02)
Majority Size	1.05^*
	(0.52)
Party Leader	0.04
	(0.05)
Committee Leader	-0.01
	(0.01)
Running for Higher Office	0.06^{**}
	(0.02)
Ideological Extremity	-0.18^{**}
	(0.03)
Senate	0.01
	(0.02)
Terms Served	-0.01^{**}
	(0.01)
Republican	0.04^{**}
	(0.01)
Constant	-1.13^{**}
	(0.29)
N	1,566
Pseudo R^2	0.770

TABLE 4.6. Determinants of Strong Partisans' Tone

	Bickerer		Opportunist		Cheerleader	
	(1)	(2)	(1)	(2)	(1)	(2)
Seat Safety	0.02*	0.03*	0.03*	0.02*	−0.01	0.01
	(0.01)	(0.01)	(0.01)	(0.01)	(0.02)	(0.02)
President's Party	−0.35	−0.39*	−0.30	−0.19	0.24	0.20
	(0.20)	(0.19)	(0.19)	(0.22)	(0.23)	(0.26)
Majority Party	1.41**	1.41**	1.47**	1.54**	0.74	1.07
	(0.42)	(0.40)	(0.38)	(0.41)	(0.70)	(0.79)
Majority Size	−20.05	−16.58	−4.70	−5.78	−0.79	10.21
	(13.27)	(12.61)	(13.75)	(13.85)	(29.84)	(30.04)
Party Leader	2.76**	2.75**	2.26**	2.38**	2.12*	2.77**
	(0.82)	(0.82)	(0.80)	(0.81)	(0.97)	(0.97)
Committee Leader	1.27**	1.14**	0.49	0.65*	0.10	0.12
	(0.28)	(0.28)	(0.28)	(0.30)	(0.44)	(0.47)
Running for Higher Office	−0.43	−0.24	1.73**	1.52**	2.66**	2.84**
	(0.77)	(0.64)	(0.37)	(0.41)	(0.42)	(0.41)
Ideological Extremity	4.45**	4.38**	3.37**	3.47**	1.15	2.72*
	(0.87)	(0.81)	(0.73)	(0.80)	(1.25)	(1.26)
Senate	−0.72	−0.59	−0.38	−0.37	−0.40	0.58
	(0.44)	(0.42)	(0.48)	(0.51)	(0.94)	(0.88)
Terms Served	0.04	0.03	0.04	0.04	0.09**	0.02
	(0.03)	(0.02)	(0.02)	(0.02)	(0.03)	(0.03)
Republican	0.26	0.22	0.26	0.11	0.78	0.56
	(0.24)	(0.23)	(0.24)	(0.26)	(0.47)	(0.61)
Constant	5.73	3.94	−2.25	−2.01	−3.56	−10.96
	(7.53)	(7.15)	(7.81)	(7.85)	(16.97)	(17.13)

Model 1 N = 1,604; Model 2 N = 1,604
Model 1 R^2 = 0.11; Model 2 R^2 = 0.11

Note: Model 1 is based on the cutoffs for each type of partisan listed in table 4.2. Model 2 includes opportunists making up the middle 40 percent, not 50 percent, of strong partisans. The baseline category are legislators whose partisan intensity falls below the 75th percentile in a given Congress. Coefficients are estimated from a multinomial logistic regression with robust standard errors clustered by legislator.

FIVE

The Determinants of Congressional Partisanship

Lindsey Graham, South Carolina's senior senator, had become a sycophant. At least according to his critics. From the day Donald Trump was first inaugurated, Graham had a seemingly limitless well of unending and unconditional support for the president. For many, including some disaffected Republicans who had closely followed Graham's career, the change was an unwelcome surprise. During the 2016 presidential campaign, Graham had reserved special criticism for Trump. In May of that year, he tweeted that "if we nominate Trump, we will get destroyed . . . and we will deserve it" and called him "a 'nutjob' and a loser," as well as a "race-baiting, xenophobic, religious bigot" (Sykes 2019). In the 2016 election, he voted for Evan McMullin, a third-party candidate (Wang 2016). Yet, in early 2017, Graham resumed being a Republican team player, which meant supporting Trump. In fact, during the next four years, no Republican other than Senate Majority Leader Mitch McConnell displayed more partisan intensity than Graham.

Graham's partisan record during the Trump years is remarkable. When the Republicans' Obamacare repeal was faltering, he tried to rally the Senate GOP conference around one final version. When Brett Kavanaugh's Supreme Court nomination was flagging due to sexual assault allegations, Graham used his speaking time during the Senate Judiciary Committee hearing to accuse Democrats of "destroying [Kavanaugh's] life [in order to] hold this seat open and hope you win in 2020" and told his "Republican colleagues, if you vote no, you're legitimizing the most despicable thing I have seen in my time in politics" (Kirby 2018). Among conservatives, Graham is widely credited for saving

Kavanaugh's nomination (Wulfsohn 2018). As Senate Judiciary Committee chair, he bulldozed through Democratic complaints to confirm Trump's judicial nominees, including Amy Coney Barrett right before the 2020 election. He accused Democrats of having "Trump derangement syndrome,"[1] and after Trump lost to Joe Biden, he called the Georgia secretary of state to ask how signature matching for ballots worked in the state and if the secretary of state could throw out certain ballots (Kelly and Raju 2020; Caldera 2020).[2]

For his efforts, Graham became a deeply divisive figure in national politics. Democrats regularly pointed to his flip-flopping for partisan gain (Van Pykeren 2021), with President Obama describing him as "the guy who double crosses everyone to save his own skin" (Obama 2020, 505). Charles Sykes, a self-styled "Never Trumper," described Graham's transformation as turning from being "John McCain's best friend in the Senate . . . into Trump's shinebox" (2019).

In Republican circles, Graham was rewarded for his consistent team play. South Carolinians generally approved of his performance and reelected him by 10 points in 2020 ("Morning Consult Senator Rankings" 2019). In 2019, he became chair of the Senate Judiciary Committee and oversaw the vetting of scores of conservative judges during the last two years of the Trump presidency.[3] He was a constant presence on political television shows, especially on Fox News, being mentioned more often during the Trump years than figures like Mitch McConnell and Ted Cruz (Hong et al. 2021). Even if Democrats thought he was a sycophant, in Republican circles, Graham's partisanship paid dividends.

What explains Graham's behavior? The Occam's razor assessment is that Graham adopted a home style that fit his state. South Carolina Republicans, who dominate the state's electorate, loved Donald Trump, so a savvy politician like Graham embraced the president whole-heartedly. Certainly electoral considerations played a role, but it cannot be the whole story. Tim Scott, the other Republican senator from the state, represents the same voters but was not nearly as intensely partisan. Perhaps Graham's background as a "Gingrich Senator," a Republican elected to the House after 1978 who eventually joined the Senate, explains his strong partisanship (Theriault 2013). Yet, other Gingrich Senators like Richard Burr (R-NC) were reliable team players, but not to Graham's extent. Or maybe his role in leading a particular partisan committee required that he be a good team player. Indeed, we can point to many factors that may explain Graham's behavior, all of which have found some support in previous political science research. With so many possible reasons, it is difficult to know which factors are most important in explaining why some legislators like Graham adopt such partisan personas and others do not.

In this chapter, we describe why members of Congress vary in their partisan intensities and test various explanations for this behavior against one another. Our argument is that a member's partisanship is shaped by their goals to win reelection and become influential in Washington, DC. To achieve their reelection goals, members develop a partisan home style that reflects voter demand and promotes the party's collective brand (Fenno 1978). Their intensity reflects local voters' preferences as well as power dynamics in Washington, DC. Those in the majority party raise their intensity to cheerlead their accomplishments and defend against opposition attacks. Those in the party opposite the president attack the White House to score political points. These factors, used to burnish a member and their party's image among voters, are reliably associated with their partisanship.

Yet, a lawmaker's partisan intensity not only reflects how they want to be viewed at home. It is also a hill style that promotion-seeking, ambitious members cultivate to show copartisans that they are good team players. By proving their partisan mettle, they hope to win, and retain, powerful leadership roles or receive support as they run for higher office. As we show throughout the chapter, lawmakers increase their partisan intensity when they seek promotions to committee leadership or within the party leadership structure and when they run for higher office. Those who have been promoted to these roles maintain high intensities but after serving in them reduce their partisan behaviors.

We also assess other explanations for congressional partisanship and find mixed results. Republicans are more partisan than Democrats, as are representatives compared to senators. However, legislators elected during wave elections are not more intense partisans. Moreover, partisanship is not being driven by new, divisive lawmakers. Long-serving members, even after controlling for their powerful leadership roles and their relative seat safety, are, on average, more partisan. Our results show that while members' partisanship is associated with a number of factors, it can be understood as a predictable strategy that helps them stay in office and become more politically influential. As a result, an individual's partisan intensity can best be understood as a mosaic, created from their unique personal circumstances and career goals in Congress.

What Do We Know About Partisanship?

In chapter 2, we reviewed the previous research that examines why legislators act as partisans. While we will not rehash that entire discussion, it is worth briefly recapping both others' findings as well as our argument to contextualize our statistical analyses. Given the acrimony on Capitol Hill, political scientists have shown increasing interest in why Democrats and Republicans constantly engage in partisan bickering. One fruitful line of research examines parties as the unit of analysis. These studies show that many legislative disagreements are partisan in nature (Lee 2016, 2009) and that interparty fighting affects legislative organization (Koger and Lebo 2017). Other approaches examine how legislative cohorts contribute to a more partisan Congress (Theriault 2013; Sinclair 2006; Ragusa 2016) or use case studies to track how important events have increased partisanship over time (Mann and Ornstein 2012; Sinclair 2006; Smith 2014). A second literature considers individual-level partisan behavior, what we are studying, and examines different patterns in voting or bill cosponsorships ("Bipartisan Index" 2021; Lawless, Theriault, and Guthrie 2018; Harbridge 2015; Theriault 2013; Carson et al. 2010).

Together, these studies have developed a wide range of explanations for why partisanship has increased and predominates in the contemporary Congress. Research on parties emphasizes that collective goals—such as building a positive party brand and winning majority status–incentivize partisanship. In turn, legislative parties develop rules, institutions, and strategies that encourage team play. One consequence of this argument is that party leaders, who are charged by their copartisans with tending to the party's brand, should act like strong partisans (Cox and McCubbins 2005; Gelman and Wilson 2021; Russell 2018).

Others argue that partisanship is driven by a member's individual goal of winning reelection. In this view, partisan behavior is part of a legislator's home style that appeals to voters. Political scientists consistently find support for this claim as well, as seat safety is correlated with partisanship (Russell 2021b; Gelman and Wilson 2021). Yet, as we showed in chapters 3 and 4, partisan intensity differs among members from similar districts who are in the same party and share the same collective goals.

As such, other explanations abound. Treul (2009) provides evidence that progressive ambition, specifically when senators run for president, increases partisan voting. Russell (2018, 2020) and Theriault (2013) argue that Republicans display more negatively toned partisanship than Democrats. Ideology is often linked with partisanship, although as we previously discussed, this relationship is not surprising since measures like DW-NOMINATE conflate these concepts in complicated ways. These varying research approaches present a complex picture of partisanship. Political scientists have argued it is motivated by a wide range of goals, which in turn produce a multitude of explanations for this behavior. Moreover, researchers measure partisanship in different ways and do not test many of these claims directly against one another. This makes it difficult to assess which factors matter most in determining a member's partisan intensity.

Our Argument and What We Expect to Find

These previous studies suggest that no single factor causes partisanship; instead, it arises due to a variety of political circumstances. We agree, and rather than adding to these various explanations, we have developed a theory that clarifies why some factors affect a member's partisan intensity and others do not. Earlier in the book, we argued that a member's partisan intensity helps them achieve two goals: winning reelection and becoming more politically influential. As a home style, they cultivate a partisan persona that is acceptable to their voters and builds their party's brand, which supports their reelection efforts. Partisanship is also a hill style that lawmakers use to become more politically influential. They act as team players to signal to their copartisans that they can be trusted with leadership roles or will be good team players if elected to higher office. Together, the ways that members strategically increase or decrease their partisan intensity to achieve these goals explain substantial differences in how lawmakers portray themselves.

In chapter 2, we hypothesized that a number of factors should be associated with this behavior. As a strategy to win reelection, the partisan lean of a legislator's district as well as factors related to the party's collective image should increase their intensity. These include serving in the minority party, serving in a chamber with a small majority party, and being in the party opposite the president. Partisanship also changes as lawmakers seek political power. Running for committee and party leadership positions requires winning their copartisans' votes in the House or Senate.[4] Being a good team player is a prerequisite to being elected to these roles and keeping these positions. As such, we expect that those currently in leadership display more partisan intensity, as do legislators who plan on running for these positions. Previous research suggests that other factors also explain this behavior. Some have argued that Republicans outpace Democrats in their partisanship or that specific cohorts are to blame for the bickering on Capitol Hill. Others point the finger at new, attention-seeking members.[5]

For the remainder of the chapter, we test our expectations that partisanship comes from reelection and promotion-seeking factors and other explanations against one another using a suite of statistical tests. The results present a clear picture that reelection and promotion-seeking factors play an important role in dictating members' partisan intensity.

Testing Claims against One Another

To evaluate differences in partisan intensity, we begin by including all of the proposed explanations we discuss above in a single statistical model. Although political scientists have examined many of these factors individually, to our knowledge, these factors have never been tested together. The dependent variables are our two measures of partisan intensity we introduced in chapter 3: the proportion of partisan tweets and the number of partisan tweets a member posts. Table 5.1 summarizes the independent variables, our expected findings we outlined in chapter 2, and how we operationalized each covariate. Before presenting our results, the table includes some features worth highlighting.

First, the home style variables are commonly used to evaluate members' individual reelection goals (e.g., their seat safety), as well as what factors change their collective partisan goals (e.g., majority party status and serving in the president's party). Second, although previous studies examine how holding leadership positions affects partisanship, we examine this connection in a much more nuanced way. Usually, researchers will create variables for high-ranking party and committee leaders (Gelman and Wilson 2021; Russell 2021a). We include the standard *High-Ranking Party Leader* variable but specify four additional variables.

We split the traditional committee leader measure by chamber, creating *House Committee Leader* and *Senate Committee Leader* measures because Senate committee chairs and ranking members are not necessarily selected by the party caucus/conference. As such, we do not expect that Senate committee leaders need to show the same party fidelity as House committee leaders to retain their roles. In fact, this difference is a tidy test of whether promotion seeking is driving partisan intensity or whether simply holding an important role like committee leader is doing so.

Additionally, we create a dichotomous measure for *Low-Ranking Party Leader*, such as caucus chair or conference secretary. Our expectation is that these members need to display higher levels of partisan intensity to maintain these positions and to move up the leadership ranks when new positions open. However, the amount of partisanship that high- and low-ranking party leaders show likely differs. The Speaker of the House, for instance, is likely more intensely partisan than the caucus vice chair. By splitting them, we ensure that

TABLE 5.1. Potential Explanations for Legislators' Partisanship

Variable	Coding	Expected Effect
Reelection-seeking variables		
Seat Safety	Presidential vote share from member's party in most recent election	+
Majority Party	1 if in majority, 0 otherwise	−
Majority Party Size	% of seats held by majority party	−
President's Party	1 if presidential copartisan, 0 otherwise	−
Promotion-seeking variables		
High-Ranking Party Leader	Coded as 1 if top 3 party leader in House or top 2 party leader in Senate, 0 otherwise	+
Low-Ranking Party Leader	Coded as 1 if part of the party leadership but not a high-ranking leader, 0 otherwise	+
House Committee Leader	Coded as 1 if House committee chair or ranking member, 0 otherwise	+
Senate Committee Leader	Coded as 1 if Senate committee chair or ranking member, 0 otherwise	Null
Running for Leadership Position	Coded as 1 if running for a leadership position, including committee leader, 0 otherwise	+
Running for Higher Office	Coded as 1 if running for higher office, 0 otherwise	+
Other Explanations		
Terms Served	Count of number of congressional terms served	−
Senate	Coded 1 if senator, 0 if representative	−
Republican Party	Coded 1 if Republican, 0 otherwise	+
Ideological Extremity	Absolute ideological distance from chamber median (using DW-NOMINATE scores)	+
Partisan Cohorts	Individual dummy variables for Republicans elected in 1994, Republicans elected in 2010, Democrats elected in 2006, Democrats elected in 2008, and Democrats elected in 2018	+
Total tweets	Natural log of number of tweets legislator posted during a congressional term	+

extremely partisan, high-ranking leaders do not obfuscate whether these less important positions also correlate with this behavior.

Our argument that partisanship is motivated by promotion seeking means that aspirants for leadership positions, not just those holding them, should also show more partisan intensity. That being the case, we created a *Running for Leadership Position* dichotomous variable. These positions include all party leadership roles as well as the House committee chair and ranking member roles.[6] Members are coded as running for a committee or party leadership position in two ways. First, those currently holding a leadership position and continuing in that role in the next Congress are recorded as aspirants. Second, we collected data on legislators who are not in these leadership positions but who ran for them. The way this works is that at the end of a congressional term, a party caucus meets to (re)elect their leaders. Although these votes happen behind closed doors, they become public contests because those running announce their candidacies to their copartisans, leak this information to the press, and campaign for their fellow members' support.

The data on who ran for leadership positions comes from publications that closely cover party and committee leadership races, namely, *Roll Call*, *The Hill*, and *Politico*. In particular, *Roll Call* often includes summary articles that list everyone contesting a race either right before or after leadership elections occur. Although this reporting should be comprehensive, it is possible that this variable includes some measurement error due to unreported candidacies. However, since serious campaigns are run so publicly, the more realistic concern is that some legislators considered running, which raised their partisan intensities, but then chose not to after realizing they had no chance of winning. Those latent candidacies never receive news coverage and are coded as someone not running, which means we are most likely underestimating the effect that running for a leadership position has on partisanship.[7]

Importantly, this measurement is not just a proxy for leaders running to keep their current roles. For instance, candidates for party leadership positions are split evenly (59 each) between rank-and-file legislators who want to join the leadership ranks and those who already hold a position and are running for the same position or a new role. In total, we identified 118 candidates campaigning for a leadership role who did not hold one of these positions when announcing their candidacy and 179 members who retained leadership roles in the next Congress.

The *Running for Higher Office* measure includes representatives running for president, Senate, and statewide office as well as senators who ran for president.[8] We counted someone as running for president if they participated in a televised presidential primary debate. For candidates for other offices (e.g., a House member running for Senate), we coded them as running if they ran in the general election or entered a primary but did not receive their party's nomination.

Finally, we add variables that test the other common claims about what motivates partisanship—being a Republican, elected during a specific cohort, serving in the House—as well as how much a member posts on Twitter (partisan or not). We note that our measure for ideological extremity uses DW-NOMINATE scores, which are based on roll call votes. This would be problematic if our goal was to disentangle partisanship from ideology, but that is not our aim. Lee (2009) has persuasively argued that the roll call record and consequently DW-NOMINATE scores are a mix of ideological and partisan votes. In times of high partisan polarization, it is difficult to discern whether these measures show differences in policy views or coordinated teamsmanship (Aldrich, Montgomery, and Sparks 2014). Other measures that claim to measure ideology suffer from the same issues. For instance, CFScores are based on campaign donations (Bonica 2014), which may result from policy-based giving or be based on whom donors see as a good team player.

As we discuss in chapter 2, it may be possible to identify some purely partisan issues in Congress, but most contentious ideological issues these days are also partisan. Thus, finding a "pure" measure of ideology in a time of high partisan polarization is unrealistic. To the extent that our *Ideological Extremity* measure also captures some element of partisanship, then the best interpretation of that variable is that we are measuring what affects partisan intensity after controlling for a member's voting behavior. Again, the consequence is that we are underestimating how other factors affect partisan intensity because some of that variation is included in this measure.

Table 5.2 reports the results from two statistical models. The first, whose dependent variable is our proportional partisan intensity measure, is an OLS regression with robust standard errors clustered by legislator and includes congressional term fixed effects. The second, whose dependent variable is a count of partisan tweets, is a negative binomial regression model that uses a member's total tweets as an exposure term and includes the same robust, clustered standard errors.[9]

The results from table 5.2 are broadly in line with our expectations. All of the reelection-seeking variables are in the expected direction and statistically significant, with the exception of the *Majority Party* one. Its direction is reversed, indicating that majority party members display more partisan intensity than those in the minority. The promotion-seeking variables follow a similar pattern. All are in the expected direction and significant, except the low-ranking party leader variable.[10] Interestingly, as we argued, committee leaders in the Senate, who are not elected by their party members, do not show heightened partisan intensity, while those in the House do.

Our results both revise and support previous explanations of partisan intensity. In line with Russell (2018, 2020) and Theriault's (2013) work, we find that Republicans display more partisanship than Democrats. However,

TABLE 5.2. Determinants of Congressional Partisanship

	Expected Effect	(1) Proportional DV	(2) Count DV
Seat Safety	+	0.002***	0.009***
		(0.001)	(0.002)
Majority Party	−	0.044***	0.249***
		(0.016)	(0.064)
Majority Party Size	−	−0.843**	−3.895***
		(0.346)	(1.314)
President's Party	−	−0.070***	−0.250***
		(0.005)	(0.022)
High-Ranking Party Leader	+	0.140***	0.437***
		(0.040)	(0.110)
Low-Ranking Party Leader	+	0.024	0.088
		(0.017)	(0.057)
House Committee Leader	+	0.069***	0.207***
		(0.015)	(0.044)
Senate Committee Leader	Null	−0.063***	−0.158**
		(0.021)	(0.074)
Running for Leadership Position	+	0.019**	0.067*
		(0.009)	(0.034)
Running for Higher Office	+	0.065***	0.325***
		(0.022)	(0.074)
Terms Served	−	0.002**	0.006
		(0.001)	(0.004)
Senate	−	−0.033**	−0.104*
		(0.015)	(0.059)
Republican	+	0.025***	0.056
		(0.009)	(0.036)
Ideological Extremity	+	0.247***	1.028***
		(0.033)	(0.131)
Democrat 2006	+	0.024	0.089
		(0.020)	(0.067)
Democrat 2008	+	0.035	0.125
		(0.023)	(0.083)
Democrat 2018	+	−0.050***	−0.194***
		(0.014)	(0.063)
Republican 1994	+	−0.014	−0.107
		(0.029)	(0.124)
Republican 2010	+	0.011	0.052
		(0.014)	(0.057)
Total Tweets		0.022***	
		(0.005)	
Constant		0.444**	0.232
		(0.193)	(0.718)
N		1,566	1,566
R^2		0.40	0.032
α			0.182***

Note: Model 1 includes our proportional measure of partisan intensity and is an OLS regression with robust standard errors clustered by member with Congress fixed effects. Model 2's DV is a count of partisan tweets and is a negative binomial regression with total tweets as the exposure term and the same cluster robust errors as model 1.
*$p < 0.05$, **$p < 0.01$.

TABLE 5.3. Common Explanations for Legislators' Partisanship

Variable	Expected Effect	% Change in Partisan Intensity
Reelection-seeking variables		
Seat Safety	+	13.3%
Majority Party	+	4.4%
Majority Party Size	−	−4.1%
President's Party	−	−7%
Promotion-seeking variables		
High-Ranking Party Leader	+	14%
House Committee Leader	+	6.3%
Running for Higher Office	+	6.5%
Running for Leadership Position	+	1.9%
Other Explanations		
Terms Served	−	5.6%
Republican Party	+	2.5%
Senate	−	−4.2%
Ideological Extremity	+	25.3%

Note: % change in partisan intensity is the predicted average change in a member's partisan behavior as the listed variable moves from the minimum to maximum observed values.

new members are not the more intense partisans. On average, longer-serving lawmakers are the more active team players. We do not find support for the cohort hypothesis, as none are associated with higher intensities.

Although table 5.2 shows that lawmakers' partisan behavior is responding to reelection and promotion-seeking incentives, the more important question is how much these factors matter. In table 5.3, we take the statistically significant results from the previous table and list the average percentage change in a legislator's partisan intensity as a variable moves from its minimum to maximum observed values.

The striking feature of table 5.3 is the many factors that have substantively large effects on a lawmaker's partisan intensity. Not surprisingly, and for reasons we have already discussed about its relationship to partisanship, the *Ideological Extremity* variable's effect is very large. A one standard deviation increase in ideological extremity is associated with a 9 percent increase in partisan intensity.[11] However, even after taking the variable into account, our reelection and promotion-seeking explanations are related to large shifts in member behavior. All else being equal, the difference from serving in an unsafe seat to a very safe one is equivalent to moving from the 30th percentile in partisan intensity to the 70th.[12] Being elected a high-ranking party leader has a similar effect.

Although they produce smaller effects, changes in Washington, DC's political environment, like who the president is or which parties are in the majority, can substantially change a member's communication style. The median number of tweets a legislator posts in our data is 1,662. When their party loses the White House, we estimate that members will post 116 more partisan tweets, or about one extra partisan tweet every week of the congressional term, than if their party's candidate had won. Given that these factors operate in concert, shifting combinations of which party is in power, a member's role in the chamber, and personal factors can produce changes in partisan messaging equivalent to a dozen or more posts per week.

House and Senate Differences

Although our results support our expectations, it is possible they mask differences between the House and Senate. In particular, partisan behavior used for promotion seeking is likely different between the two chambers for reasons that are institutional and unique to the time we are studying. We have previously discussed the institutional difference. Unlike those in the House, committee leaders in the Senate during this time were not selected in a way that demanded partisan fidelity. As our theory predicts and table 5.2 shows, these different selection rules differentially affect House and Senate committee leaders' partisanship.

Additionally, during the six years we analyze, the Senate party leadership structure was remarkably stable. With the exception of Harry Reid's (D-NV) retirement and John Thune's (R-SD) selection as majority whip to replace John Cornyn (R-TX), the top party leaders remained the same and no public leadership fights occurred. Even the lower-level party ranks were stable. The main changes featured junior senators chairing the parties' campaign arms and Democrats adding some minor leadership roles in 2019 for progressives and moderates to project a unified front. Most senators never held or sought a leadership role.[13] Public accounts suggest that these changes were rarely acrimonious and that when someone felt slighted, a new leadership position was created for them.[14] Consequently, our data includes very little variation in the *Party Leader* and *Running for Leadership Position* variables. Unlike the House, it is likely we will not find an association between leadership seeking and partisan intensity in the Senate.[15]

Put differently, given differences in how committee leaders are selected during this time and the stability in the Senate parties' leadership ranks, we

TABLE 5.4. Determinants of Partisanship, by Chamber

Variable	Expected Effect	% Change for Representatives	% Change for Senators
Reelection-seeking variables			
Seat Safety	+	11.6%**	19.4%**
Majority Party	+	5.9%**	5.4%
Majority Party Size	−	−17%**	−19%**
President's Party	−	−6.4%**	−7.7%**
Promotion-seeking variables			
High-Ranking Party Leader	+	9.4%*	15.1%**
Low-Ranking Party Leader	+	4.5%*	3.8%
Committee Leader	+	6.7%**	−1.6%
Running for Higher Office	+	8.9%**	4.3%
Running for Leadership Position	+	3.3%**	−3.3%

Note: $+p < 0.1$, $*p < 0.05$, $**p < 0.01$. Effects are calculated as the predicted change from the minimum to maximum observed values for a variable from the results reported in model 1 in table 5.6 in the chapter's appendix.

expect that most of the promotion-seeking variables for the Senate will not show a significant relationship with partisan intensity. However, we still expect that party leaders and those running for president increase their partisan behavior. We evaluated chamber differences by estimating the same statistical models from table 5.2 but divided the data by chamber.[16] Table 5.4 includes the size of our main variables' effects on partisan intensity and if they are statistically significant. The full models are in the chapter's appendix.

Reelection-seeking factors animate partisanship in the House and Senate, albeit to different degrees. However, in the House, and unlike in the Senate, promotion seeking is more strongly associated with partisan intensity, with the exception of serving as a top-ranking party leader. We suspect this difference relates to differences in the chambers' structures and the importance of these positions for House members. In the Senate, leadership positions, for committees and low-ranking party roles, are not necessarily doled out based on party fidelity. Moreover, the chamber's small size allows senators to gain influence without these more formal roles by positioning themselves as lead negotiators on important issues or being the pivotal voters to break filibusters, among other actions. At first, the weaker finding that senators running for president ($p = 0.11$) are not more partisan than House members running for higher office is puzzling. Yet, that variable is correlated with the total number of tweets that a senator posts. Put differently, when they begin running for president, senators become more partisan *and* their social media presence increases. In models where we drop the total tweets covariate, senators running for president increase their partisan intensity by 6.8 percent ($p = 0.01$).

Even as promotion seeking affects partisanship, especially in the House, reelection-seeking concerns dramatically change this behavior throughout Congress. In both chambers, those in the least safe seats are much less partisan than their colleagues in very red or blue districts. This is especially pronounced in the Senate. Moreover, the majority party's size substantially changes members' behavior. As Lee (2016) argues, small majorities incentivize both parties to engage in more messaging in an effort to bolster their collective images and win enough contested seats in the next election to become the majority party. The particularly large effect size in the Senate makes sense, given how acrimony often stems from the majority party trying to overcome minority party obstruction and Gelman's (2019) finding that expectations about who will win the majority in the next election are strongly predictive of the Senate's overall level of partisanship.

More generally, the House and Senate display some differences in what motivates partisan intensity. Promotion seeking more strongly affects representatives' behavior. Reelection factors are more associated with senators' partisanship. Yet, a combination of promotion seeking and reelection-seeking is structuring the partisan environment in both chambers.

Promotion Seeking and Changing Partisan Behavior

So far, we have shown that members increase their partisan intensity when they seek and gain influential roles in Congress. In our analysis above, we compared ambitious officeholders who are running for party and leadership committee positions to those who do not. We found support for our theory that promotion-seeking behavior encourages partisanship. In this section, we consider other comparisons that might further buttress our argument that the goal of becoming politically influential is an important factor motivating legislators' partisan behavior.

To do so, we evaluate three promotion-seeking situations and analyze how lawmakers' partisan intensity changes. First, we compare the partisanship of those who won their leadership races against those who lost. We expect that winners should maintain higher intensities while losers become less partisan. Second, we assess if those choosing to leave leadership display less partisanship than their colleagues who are running to keep their current roles or to win new ones. Our expectation is that members who choose to leave decrease their partisanship compared to those who plan to remain a leader. Third, we assess if those who ran for higher office subsequently decreased their intensity once their campaigns were over. Again, we expect that once someone wins higher office, their partisan intensity decreases relative to their previous behavior. Each of these situations provides additional leverage for assessing how trying to become politically influential affects partisan intensity beyond the pooled regression models we previously presented.

Internal Promotion-Seeking Winners and Losers

When House Republicans met to select their party leaders for the 115th Congress, there was no competition for the top spots. But members jockeyed for the low-ranking positions, the springboards to a future as Speaker of the House, majority leader, or whip. The leadership election's undercard, the race for conference secretary, featured Jason Smith (R-MO) and Jackie Walorski (R-IN). Both joined Congress in 2013 and were ambitious members whose safe districts made it likely they had long legislative careers ahead of them.[17]

Our argument, that members change their partisan intensities when they try to move up the party ranks, should produce a consistent pattern. When candidates are running for positions, we expect that they should not vary too much from one another in their partisanship. They are all trying to be good team players. Put differently, Smith's and Walorski's intensities should be similar. Yet, in the next Congress, when one is in leadership and the other is not, their partisanship should diverge. The winner should remain very partisan or even increase their intensity, as demanded by their new role, while the loser becomes less partisan since they no longer need to impress their colleagues.

Smith's and Walorski's partisan behaviors nicely illustrate this trend. In the 114th Congress, when both were trying to establish their Republican bona fides, their intensities were 0.21 (for Smith) and 0.2 (for Walorski). Late in 2016, Smith won the conference secretary spot that both he and Walorski sought. Walorski remained a backbencher. The 115th Congress, Trump's first two years in office, was remarkably partisan. Like most members whose intensity increased from the end of the Obama years, Walorski's partisanship rose, from 0.2 to 0.25. But as expected, Smith's partisanship drastically increased, from 0.21 to 0.37. His win as conference secretary fundamentally changed his partisan behavior. In the next Congress, he became ranking member of the Budget Committee and became one of the most partisan Republicans in the House. Smith's intensity rose to 0.5. In contrast, Walorski remained out of leadership and her partisan behavior leveled off. It was nearly identical in the 115th and 116th Congresses.

The differing trajectories of Jason Smith and Jackie Walorski highlight the diverging partisan path we expect those who win leadership positions to take from those who lose. To test this idea more systematically, we took all the House rank-and-file members who ran for a leadership position and assessed how their intensities changed based on whether they won or lost their election.[18] We excluded those running who were already in leadership since their current positions are associated with them displaying more partisan behavior. The data include 56 winners and 50 losers. We expect that when members are running, the winners' and losers' partisanship is about the same. That is what we find. The winners' average intensity is 0.28, and the losers' average is 0.29 ($p = 0.57$). Yet in the next Congress, once the winners assume their new roles and the losers remain in the rank and file, we see a divergence in the behavior. The winners' average intensity is 0.35, and the losers' average is 0.29 ($p = 0.02$).[19]

Put differently, the members who are not in leadership but are running for a position display similar amounts of partisan intensity. The winners, once in office, become much more partisan, while the losers who remain outside the leadership do not since they no longer need to show off as unusually good team players.

Leaving Leadership Positions

Although we focus on how members secure leadership positions, they often leave these positions as well. Sometimes this happens when a legislator decides to retire. In other cases, they simply return to the rank and file. No matter the reason, choosing to leave positions that require being a good team player should produce a consistent pattern. Those running for reelection, who hope to keep their leadership role, should maintain high levels of partisan intensity. They need to continue to present themselves as dependable team players. Those leaving their positions do not need to show the same commitment to the party. Sure, it is important they support their side, but since they will not be asking their congressional copartisans to vote for them, they can reduce their partisan behavior. Simply put, those trying to stay in leadership should have higher partisan intensities than those leaving.

We tested this prediction by calculating a one-tailed t-test that compared these two groups' average partisan intensity. The data includes 168 members who sought reelection to a leadership position and 52 who were leaving. For the group that was not seeking a return to leadership, we excluded those who intended to run again but unexpectedly left Congress. This includes members who died in office and lost their primary or general elections. We omit them because they were not expecting to leave their position, so they had no reason to reduce their partisan intensity. As we expect, legislators trying to keep their leadership roles are more intensely partisan (0.39) than those leaving these positions (0.32, $p = 0.002$). This provides more evidence that promotion-seeking behavior, in this case, seeking reelection as a party or House committee leader, pushes members to be stronger partisans than those who hold similar positions but are leaving these jobs.

Winners and Losers in Running for Higher Office

We expect to see a slightly different pattern when legislators run for higher office. As we show above, campaigning for a promotion raises members' partisan intensities as they appeal to party insiders and the extended party network. Yet, win or lose, we expect partisanship to decrease in the next term. To understand why, consider the case of Todd Young (R-IN). Young ran for Senate in 2016. Winning his race required that he show off as a staunch team player in order to beat fellow representative Marlin Stutzman (R-IN) in the primary and former Senator Evan Bayh (D-IN) in the general election. Once in office, Young no longer needed to convince his copartisans that he was the best candidate for the Senate seat. As the incumbent, he gets that benefit of the doubt. Instead, he assumed the role of a Senate backbencher who was not seeking a major leadership role. He did not need to impress his fellow Senate Republicans with partisan displays. That being the case, after he won, Young's intensity plummeted from 0.4, when he was a candidate, to 0.16.

We expect Young's partisan trajectory to be the norm among members running for higher office. Unfortunately, our sample size is fairly limited. In the 114th and 115th Congresses, 31 members ran for higher office, but only 13 remained in Congress the next term. These 13 include the 5 senators who ran failed presidential campaigns in 2016 (Cruz, Graham, Paul, Rubio, and Sanders) and 8 representatives who returned as senators the next term.[20] The other 18 candidates either won state-level races, like governor, or lost and did not return to Congress.[21] Since our claim is that legislators who finish running for higher office, win or lose, should subsequently decrease their partisan intensity, we are left to study variation among these 5 losers and 8 winners.

The results, even with such a small sample size, suggest that electoral promotion seeking likely fosters partisanship. When running for higher office, these 13 lawmakers' average partisan intensity was 0.4. The next term, win or lose, it was 0.3.[22] Only 4 of the 13 had higher values in the subsequent Congress. Bernie Sanders's intensity increased as he prepared to run for president again, as did that of Chris Van Hollen, who left the House but immediately joined the Senate Democrats' leadership team.[23] Only Lindsey Graham (R-SC) and Tammy Duckworth (D-IL) ran for higher office and became more partisan afterward without seeking another promotion. The small sample size combined with Sanders's and Van Hollen's unusual political circumstances means we can be less definitive in this assessment. However, what we can say is that for most members who run for higher office, after doing so, their partisan intensity decreases.

What If More Seats Were Competitive?

In this chapter, we have presented evidence that both reelection and promotion-seeking factors are motivating partisan behavior. Some of these factors and their relationship to partisanship, like who is president or the size of the majority party, are not easily changed. In contrast, state legislatures or redistricting commissions have wide latitude to determine how many safe seats are drawn for their House delegations. Our goal is not to review the extensive literature on competitive congressional districts, representational consequences of seat safety, or the situations that produce more competitive maps. Our point is much narrower. We simply note that more competitive seats can reduce partisanship on Capitol Hill. By no means are they a silver bullet, and to be clear, we are not arguing that partisanship is bad per se. Rather, the extreme partisanship that so many others have identified and argued is problematic can be partially mitigated by drawing more competitive districts.

Take, for instance, the top quartile of safe seats.[24] These districts favor one party by at least 17 points, and members holding them display a partisan intensity that is, on average, 8 percent higher than other members. What if these districts were more competitive? How would the lawmakers' partisanship change? To answer this question, we estimated the predicted partisan intensity from model 1 in table 5.6 (see the chapter's appendix). Next, we calculated the same values but at different levels of seat safety. We subtracted the simulated partisan intensity from the predicted value from our analysis. This number is how much a legislator's partisanship would change, all else being equal, if their district was more competitive.[25] In table 5.5, we report the average decrease in a lawmaker's partisanship if their seat, which is currently in the top 25 percent of the safest ones, had an average partisan lean, a 5-point partisan advantage, or had partisan parity.

TABLE 5.5. Predicted Change in Partisan Intensity When the Least Competitive House Seats Become More Competitive

	Avg. Seat Safety *(Seat Safety = 10.6)*	5-Pt. Partisan Advantage *(Seat Safety = 5)*	Partisan Parity *(Seat Safety = 0)*
Change in partisan intensity	−2.3%	−3.3%	−4.2%

Note: Values are calculated for the House seats in the top quartile of the Seat Safety variable.

If the least competitive House seats were redrawn to reduce their partisan advantage to a still comfortable 10.6 points, lawmakers would reduce their partisan intensity by a predicted 2.3 percent. More competitive seats produce even larger decreases. Again, a 3 percent decrease will not end the hyper-partisanship on Capitol Hill. But it would produce, on average, 29 fewer partisan tweets from these members. Over the three Congresses we study, these legislators, if they were still in seats with a 10-point partisan advantage, would in total have posted 11,000 fewer partisan posts. A 4.2 percent decrease is equivalent to 40 fewer partisan messages per member holding a very safe seat each Congress and, in total, over 15,000 fewer partisan tweets. To the extent Congress could benefit from fewer hyper-partisans in it ranks, making the safest seats even a little more competitive would help.[26]

Conclusion

Earlier in the book, we argued that individual-level partisanship is motivated by reelection and promotion-seeking goals. Through a series of statistical tests in this chapter, we find evidence that supports our theory. Factors we identified as affecting legislators' personal or party brand are consistently and predictably associated with changes in partisan behavior. The promotion-seeking variables, which we studied from a number of perspectives, produced similar patterns.

Additionally, by testing common claims about what is creating congressional partisanship, we identified the factors that most strongly related to this behavior. Who is sitting in the White House and the majority party's size play important roles in dictating how much overall partisanship members of a party caucus will display. But factors specific to each individual, like their seat safety, the roles they hold in Congress, and their political ambitions, are also important. As a consequence, legislators in similar political situations might show very different partisan intensities depending on their role or who they want to be in Washington, DC. Other explanations that have been previously proposed are not as important as the reelection and promotion-seeking factors. Like others, we find a partisan asymmetry, but it explains a much smaller slice of partisan intensity. We find little evidence for the cohort hypothesis, perhaps because many of these new members flipped marginal seats in the previous election, and show that longer-serving members, not new firebrands, are more partisan.

More broadly, our results revise the common story that political scientists tell about partisanship. Yes, it is partially a home style that lawmakers use to burnish their and their party's images. But it is also a hill style they adopt to make themselves attractive candidates for leadership positions. For many lawmakers, becoming more politically influential is the main reason they act as dependable partisans. Indeed, two electoral connections are motivating this behavior: the one between members and their voters back home and the one between members and their copartisans in their chamber who elect them to lead the party.

Appendix

(*following page*)

TABLE 5.6. Determinants of Partisan Intensity, by Chamber

	House Models		Senate Models	
	(1)	(2)	(3)	(4)
	Ratio	Count	Ratio	Count
Seat Safety	0.002***	0.008***	0.003**	0.010*
	(0.001)	(0.002)	(0.001)	(0.006)
Majority Party	0.059***	0.288***	0.054	0.403**
	(0.018)	(0.070)	(0.034)	(0.163)
Majority Party Size	−2.971***	−12.030***	−3.342***	−13.809***
	(0.285)	(1.053)	(0.369)	(1.620)
President's Party	−0.064***	−0.224***	−0.077***	−0.348***
	(0.006)	(0.024)	(0.012)	(0.057)
High-Ranking Party Leader	0.094**	0.263**	0.151**	0.468**
	(0.044)	(0.109)	(0.073)	(0.193)
Low-Ranking Party Leader	0.045**	0.161***	0.038	0.151
	(0.021)	(0.060)	(0.027)	(0.117)
Committee Leader	0.067***	0.203***	−0.016	−0.041
	(0.015)	(0.045)	(0.020)	(0.079)
Running for Leadership Position	0.033***	0.115***	−0.033	−0.142
	(0.010)	(0.036)	(0.025)	(0.098)
Running for Higher Office	0.089***	0.399***	0.043	0.222**
	(0.028)	(0.091)	(0.026)	(0.090)
Terms Served	0.001	0.002	0.006**	0.020**
	(0.001)	(0.004)	(0.002)	(0.009)
Republican	0.019*	0.030	0.000	0.000
	(0.010)	(0.039)	(.)	(.)
Ideological Extremity	0.276***	1.109***	0.192***	1.017***
	(0.038)	(0.143)	(0.062)	(0.283)
Democrats 2006	0.033	0.120	0.019	0.091
	(0.026)	(0.084)	(0.024)	(0.093)
Democrats 2008	0.037	0.147	0.023	0.059
	(0.032)	(0.111)	(0.022)	(0.068)
Democrats 2018	−0.057***	−0.210***	−0.102**	−0.404
	(0.016)	(0.067)	(0.050)	(0.319)
Republicans 1994	−0.025	−0.191	0.019	0.001
	(0.029)	(0.122)	(0.021)	(0.086)
Republicans 2010	0.024	0.104*	−0.040*	−0.210*
	(0.016)	(0.063)	(0.023)	(0.116)
Total Tweets	0.020***		0.033***	
	(0.005)		(0.010)	
Constant	1.603***	4.616***	1.648***	5.277***
	(0.174)	(0.600)	(0.225)	(0.873)
N	1,263	1,263	303	303
R^2	0.38	0.03	0.47	0.03
α		0.18**		0.18**

Note: Models 1 and 3 include our proportional measure of partisan intensity and are OLS regressions with robust standard errors clustered by member. Models 2 and 4's DV is a count of partisan tweets and is a negative binomial regression with total tweets as the exposure term and the same cluster robust errors as models 1 and 3. Models 1 and 2 are subset on House members. Models 3 and 4 are subset on senators.

*$p < 0.05$, **$p < 0.01$.

The Negligible Connection Between Legislating and Partisan Intensity

The New York congressional Democrats are a pretty partisan group. The senators represent a reliably blue state, and most of the House members hold safe seats. In the 2018 midterms, the median incumbent from the delegation won 87 percent of the general election vote. Their uncompetitive districts allow them to spend years in Congress moving up the party and committee ranks. In the 116th Congress (2019–20), a New York Democrat served as the Senate minority leader, served as the chair of the House Democratic Caucus, and chaired four House committees. The junior senator, Kirsten Gillibrand, ran for president, and a freshman, Alexandria Ocasio-Cortez, received more public attention and scrutiny than nearly every other member. Given what we have shown is associated with increased partisanship—including seat safety and power seeking in Washington, DC—it is not surprising that so many New York Democrats display high partisan intensities.

What is surprising is that during the 116th Congress, the third most partisan New York Democrat was Paul Tonko, a rank-and-file member who represents Albany and the surrounding area. A liberal rising through the ranks of the Energy and Commerce Committee, Tonko spent the 116th Congress attacking the Trump administration and supporting Joe Biden once he became the Democratic nominee for president. Only Chuck Schumer, the Senate minority leader, and Hakeem Jeffries, the House Democratic Caucus chair, two members with highly visible messaging roles, were more partisan than him.

Why Tonko developed a partisan demeanor is interesting, but so are the potential consequences, or lack thereof, it had on his legislative behavior. A common argument is that partisanship is bad for legislating. The main evidence for this claim is that bipartisanship is associated with lawmaking. However, that finding does not provide a direct answer to this concern. How political scientists measure bipartisanship, which we show later in this chapter, is a mixture of partisan and ideological factors. Because of this, a largely unaddressed question is how partisan behavior seeps into the legislative process and whether it affects cooperation on Capitol Hill, voting patterns, and overall legislative effectiveness.

For Paul Tonko, his extreme partisan intensity in the 116th Congress seems to have had little effect on his relationship with Republicans or his legislative prowess. During those two years, he introduced 32 bills. Even as a strong partisan, he did not focus on writing messaging legislation that tries to make a political point. His bills tended toward the small and mundane. His most high-profile piece of legislation—a bill to require seat belts in limousines— garnered the most attention from his colleagues and attracted 98 cosponsors from across the ideological spectrum. Early in the legislative process, his ideas usually received some bipartisan support, and Tonko avidly signed onto bills sponsored by Republicans. On the floor, he was a loyal partisan. He voted with his party 99 percent of the time on important votes, as measured by *Congressional Quarterly*, and rarely supported Donald Trump's position.

In the end, Tonko's partisan intensity, and voting for that matter, did not have much of an effect on his legislative success. His energy and science policy ideas, which his main committee assignment has jurisdiction over, were positively received in committee, and one of his bills was enacted. His legislative effectiveness score was above average, even after taking into account his majority party status and subcommittee chairmanship. For Tonko, his underlying partisanship seemed to play a role in some of his legislative behaviors. His hyper-partisan voting record reflects his willingness to support his team. However, in other ways, it seemed to have little effect. He supported Republican-sponsored ideas—Tonko is not an ideologue but a partisan team player—and his proposals were not shunned by the other party. In the end, Paul Tonko was able to successfully navigate the legislative process even as one of the most partisan Democrats in one of the most partisan state delegations.

Tonko's legislative experience in the 116th Congress, and the open question of whether his extreme partisan intensity had any effect on his lawmaking behavior, highlights a gap in understanding the link between partisanship and legislating. Research on political behavior suggests an indirect route—that strong partisans can reduce Congress's productivity by politicizing an issue to the point that other legislators no longer feel they can compromise. Perhaps this is what critics mean when they argue that partisanship is bad for lawmaking, and to be fair, in chapter 1 we document evidence that this occurs. However, we are interested in more direct partisanship effects, namely, whether more partisan intensity is associated with being a less successful lawmaker.

In this chapter, we assess these more direct consequences in three ways. First, we examine if partisanship is related to cosponsorship patterns. Are strong partisans less likely to cosponsor bills introduced by the opposition, and are their ideas less likely to receive support from other party lawmakers? Second, we consider how partisanship affects voting patterns, namely, whether it is related to support for the party's or the president's position. Finally, we consider whether partisan intensity is associated with how successful a member is at getting their ideas enacted into law and their broader legislative effectiveness.

In chapter 2, we argue that partisanship comes with few consequences. Our results show that although partisan behavior affects cosponsorship patterns and roll call voting, it does not negatively affect members' legislative productivity. Stronger partisans collaborate less and receive less support from across the aisle when bills are proposed. They are also more loyal to the party and the president, when he is from their party, when voting. However, partisan intensity is not associated with less legislative success or effectiveness. Members are not being penalized for being good team players, at least when Congress is deciding which ideas become law.

Does Partisan Intensity Affect Early Game Cooperation?

One early moment in the legislative process when we might observe partisanship affecting lawmaking is in bill cosponsorship patterns. Political scientists have extensively studied why members cosponsor one another's legislation and have produced a nuanced explanation of this behavior. Broadly speaking, cosponsorship serves several purposes. It signals agenda setters about the measure's level of support (Kirkland 2011; Koger 2003), is a commitment mechanism for future floor votes on the bill (Bernhard and Sulkin 2013), and creates a valuable position-taking opportunity (Rocca and Gordon 2010). For many members, building a bipartisan cosponsorship coalition is an essential step in having their measure seriously considered by committee and party leaders (Wiseman, Volden, and Hill 2020).

Even though legislators cosponsor bills for many reasons, the common denominator is some mutual interest in the policy idea. Most commonly, this includes ideological similarity between the sponsor and cosponsor as well as other reasons, like a shared identity trait or geographic proximity (Bratton and Rouse 2011; Craig et al. 2015). These studies rarely consider a member's partisan behavior and instead conceptualize partisanship as a dummy variable for party or whether the sponsor and cosponsor are in the same party.

Yet, as we discuss in chapter 2, partisan intensity likely affects the cosponsors whom lawmakers' bills attract. When they introduce bills, strong partisans are more likely to propose ideas that politically help their party and damage the opposition. As good team players, they want to create position-taking opportunities that distinguish the parties and make their side look better to voters. Generally, political scientists argue legislation of this sort is ideologically extreme, which in an era of polarization creates partisan cosponsorship coalitions (Lee 2016; Egar 2016). In this scenario, ideologues, not partisans, should attract fewer cosponsors from across the aisle. However, as we have discussed throughout the book, a substantial amount of the bickering between Democrats and Republicans either is not ideological or is a combination of ideological and partisan (Lee 2009). These sorts of issues are ripe for intensely partisan members to offer bills that only attract copartisans and repel the opposition.

To assess whether partisan intensity is associated with the cosponsorship coalitions a member's bills attract, we created a *Cosponsor Coalition's Partisanship* measure. For every House and Senate bill introduced during the time period we analyze, we calculated the cosponsorship coalition's partisan balance, which we operationalize as

$$\frac{\text{\# of Copartisan Cosponsors } - \text{ \# of Opposition Cosponsors}}{\text{Total Cosponsors}}$$

A value of 0 indicates perfect partisan balance as the same number of Democrats and Republicans sponsored the bill. Increasingly positive values indicate that a greater proportion of copartisans are supporting the measure while smaller negative values indicate that more members from the other party have signed onto the bill.[1] We calculate this in two different ways: first, by including all cosponsors, and second, by limiting the calculation to only *original* cosponsors of the bill. This allows us to assess both how partisan the final bill was and how partisan the initial cosponsorship coalition was prior to any bandwagon effects that attract more legislators to sign onto the measure.[2]

Our main independent variables are our measures of partisan intensity.[3] Recall that in chapter 3 we measure partisan intensity in two ways: as a ratio calculated as the number of partisan tweets divided by a member's total tweets and as the number of partisan posts. For both ways we capture this concept, we expect a positive relationship between these factors, which would indicate that as members become more partisan so do their bills' cosponsorship coalitions. We control for a number of factors commonly associated with legislators' bill cosponsorship decisions. First and foremost, we use DW-NOMINATE scores to calculate sponsors' *Ideological Extremity* as the absolute ideological distance from the chamber median. Ideologues propose more extreme bills, which on average are less likely to attract members from the other party. We expect this variable to produce a positive coefficient. Constituent demand may also affect what sorts of bills legislators sponsor. Those representing safe districts may seek more divisive position-taking opportunities relative to those in marginal seats. As such, we include our *Seat Safety* measure, which we describe in chapter 3, and expect it to have a positive coefficient as well.

Additionally, lawmakers often seek out cosponsorship opportunities for bills they think will pass. This allows them to credit claim that they were an early supporter of a new law. That being the case, we include five factors commonly associated with eventual legislative success, namely, serving in the *Majority Party*, as a *Committee Chair*, or as a *Subcommittee Chair*, a member's lagged legislative effectiveness score (*Legislative Effectiveness$_{t-1}$*), and their number of *Terms Served* (Volden and Wiseman 2014). We expect all five to have a negative coefficient, indicating that bills sponsored by these members have less partisan cosponsorship coalitions.[4] Finally, we control for potential differences between House and Senate cosponsorship coalitions with a *Senate* dummy variable,[5] for party differences with a *Republican* dummy variable, and for shifting political environments with Congress fixed effects.

We estimate four models (see table 6.1). Models 1 and 2 include all cosponsored bills. The only difference between them is they include our different measures of partisan intensity (ratio or count). Models 3 and 4 analyze original cosponsors, which only include the members who supported the bill when it was introduced, and, again, the only difference is how we operationalize partisan intensity.

The results suggest that a member's partisan behavior affects who is willing to support their legislation. In analyses that use our ratio measure of partisan intensity, stronger partisans' bills attract fewer supporters from across the aisle and more from their own party. The coefficient when using our count-based

TABLE 6.1. Association Between Partisan Intensity and Cosponsor Partisan Balance

	All Cosponsors		Original Cosponsors	
	(1) Ratio	(2) Count	(3) Ratio	(4) Count
Partisan Intensity	0.20**	0.02	0.28**	0.02
	(0.06)	(0.01)	(0.07)	(0.01)
Ideological Extremity	0.24**	0.28**	0.38**	0.43**
	(0.06)	(0.06)	(0.08)	(0.08)
Seat Safety	0.01*	0.00*	0.01	0.01
	(0.00)	(0.00)	(0.00)	(0.00)
Majority Party	0.07*	0.08*	0.14**	0.15**
	(0.03)	(0.03)	(0.04)	(0.04)
Committee Chair	0.03	0.03	0.06*	0.07*
	(0.02)	(0.02)	(0.03)	(0.03)
Subcommittee Chair	0.01	0.01	−0.01	−0.01
	(0.02)	(0.02)	(0.02)	(0.02)
Terms Served	−0.01	0.00	−0.01	−0.01
	(0.01)	(0.00)	(0.01)	(0.01)
Legislative Effectiveness$_{t-1}$	−0.02*	−0.02*	−0.02*	−0.02*
	(0.01)	(0.01)	(0.01)	(0.01)
Senate	0.04**	0.03*	0.08**	0.07**
	(0.01)	(0.01)	(0.02)	(0.02)
Republican	−0.04*	−0.03	0.15**	0.15**
	(0.02)	(0.02)	(0.02)	(0.02)
Constant	0.45**	0.38**	0.13**	0.06
	(0.04)	(0.06)	(0.05)	(0.07)
N	881	881	881	881
R^2	0.175	0.167	0.178	0.165

Note: Models are OLS regressions with robust standard errors clustered by member and include Congress fixed effects. The dependent variable measures the partisan balance of a cosponsorship coalition with larger numbers representing a more partisan coalition. Ratio models include our ratio measure of partisan intensity. Count models include our logged count measure of partisan intensity.
*$p < 0.05$, **$p < 0.01$.

measure is positive but falls just short of statistical significance. To conceptualize the magnitude of these effects, we plot the predicted partisan balance of a cosponsor coalition in figure 6.1.

The average partisan, whose intensity is 0.28, attracts cosponsorship coalitions that lean heavily toward their party (0.66). Compared to this average, members with the lowest partisan intensity build cosponsorship coalitions that are only three percentage points less partisan. The strongest partisans, with the highest scores in our data, attract cosponsorship groups that are six percentage points more partisan than the average. When recruiting legislators to sign onto a bill as an original cosponsor, the sponsor's partisan intensity

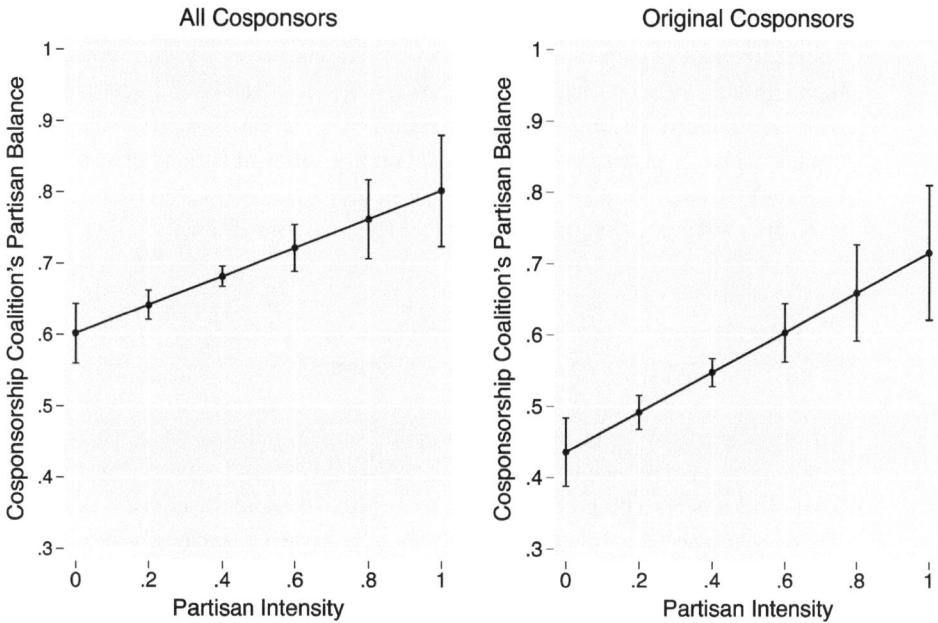

Fig. 6.1. Partisan Balance of Cosponsorship Coalitions

matters more. The cosponsorship balance still leans heavily toward copartisans (0.51). However, the weakest partisans' coalitions are four percentage points more balanced than average, and the most partisan members' coalitions are tilted nine percentage points more partisan. Put simply, as legislators display more partisan intensity, fewer opposition party members cosponsor their bills.

However, a sponsor's partisanship is not the only factor related to who cosponsors a measure. The sponsor's ideological extremity also plays a role. Proposals sponsored by lawmakers with more extreme policy views are also associated with more partisan cosponsorship coalitions. This is not particularly surprising, as ideologues offer fewer ideas that appeal to members from the opposite end of the ideological spectrum.

In this case, even though a bill sponsor's partisanship and ideology affect who supports their measure, the ideological extremity effect is larger. A shift from the least to the most extreme sponsors changes a cosponsorship coalition's partisan balance a predicted 24 percentage points. When subset on original cosponsors, the effect is even larger—a predicted 38 percentage point shift. In contrast, as partisan intensity changes from its minimum to its maximum, the cosponsor's partisan balance only moves at most a predicted 10 percentage points. Even so, a sponsor's partisan intensity is associated with who supports their legislation after taking into account ideological extremity. This contrasts with the standard reasons members cosponsor legislation. They are assessing not just which measures to support based on the policy included but also the sponsor's partisan demeanor. At least early in the legislative process, members pay a price in opposition party support for their partisan intensity.

Are Strong Partisans Less Willing to Support Bills Sponsored by Opposition Members?

Partisanship might affect legislative cooperation another way. More partisan members may be less inclined to cosponsor bills offered by colleagues in the other party. This reflects a common concern on Capitol Hill, and through a series of analyses, we assess whether partisan talk affects behaviors or can be dismissed as mere rhetoric. As we outline in chapter 2, we expect to observe that strong partisans are less bipartisan in their cosponsorship patterns. After all, part of their brand is their unwillingness to work with or compromise with the other side.

However, this reluctance to support measures sponsored by the other party's members is not absolute. Sometimes lawmakers, even very partisan ones, support the ideas being proposed by those in the other party. Perhaps the measure is politically popular or not yet politicized, aligns with their ideological views, or is targeted toward helping their constituents. Whatever the reason, members' partisanship is likely one factor of many that predict their willingness to engage in a bipartisan cosponsorship.

To evaluate if partisan intensity affects which legislation members cosponsor, we used the Lugar Center's Bipartisanship Index scores, which use bill cosponsorships to create a measure of bipartisanship. These scores are our dependent variable. Our models use the same independent variables from table 6.1. Previous studies suggest that the *Ideological Extremity* coefficient will be negative, as ideological extremists are less likely to work across the aisle in developing legislation (Bernhard and Sulkin 2013; Harward and Moffett 2010). However, we expect that our *Partisan Intensity* covariate will also have a negative effect, even after controlling for the ideologues. In figure 6.2 we plot the predicted probabilities from our statistical models to assess if partisan intensity is associated with a member's bipartisanship cosponsorship decisions.

As we expect, members with higher partisan intensities are less likely to support measures sponsored by those in the other party. The predicted bipar-

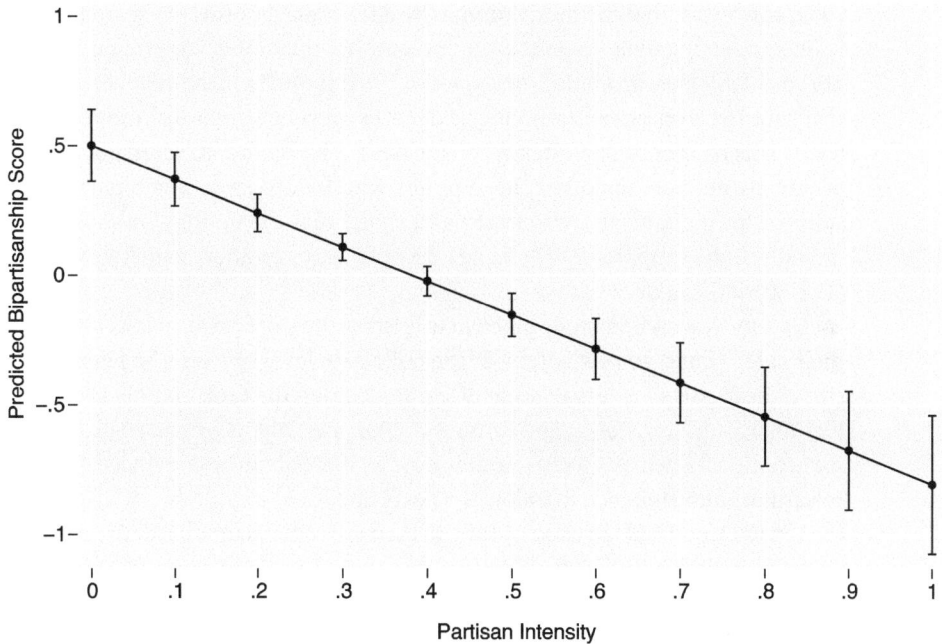

Fig. 6.2. Predicted Bipartisanship Score as Partisan Intensity Changes
Note: Predicted values from model 1 in table 6.2 (see chapter appendix).

tisanship score for the strongest partisans is in the 25th percentile, while the least partisan members' bipartisanship rates near the 75th percentile. Interestingly, both ideology and partisanship affect this behavior, but in this case, ideology's effect is stronger. The most ideologically extreme lawmaker's bipartisanship score rates near the 1st percentile, while the chamber median's is at about the 90th. Although ideology has the stronger effect, it is worth emphasizing that partisanship still matters in how willing a member is to support an idea put forth by someone in the other party. Even after controlling for ideology, a legislator's partisan demeanor substantially affects their willingness to act in a bipartisan way and provides initial evidence that their online partisan personas are related to their legislative activities.

Does Partisan Intensity Affect How Members Vote?

In addition to affecting cooperation early in the legislative process, partisanship may affect the legislative process on the floor when members vote. The basic concern is that the motivation to be a team player prevents lawmakers from supporting ideas from the other team that they otherwise might support on ideological grounds. Consequently, even though a measure is voted on that could pass on its merits, political concerns prevent legislators from voting for it. This happens most often when parties stick together to score political points, by denying the other side a policy win, by not providing bipartisan support for an issue as a way to try and signal that the opposition's idea is extreme, or by supporting (opposing) the president's position no matter what (Lee 2016; Gilmour 1995).

Usually, researchers study partisan teamsmanship, which is used to burnish their side's brand among voters, at the collective level or from the perspective of how party leaders enforce discipline among the rank and file (Krehbiel 2000; McCarty, Poole, and Rosenthal 2001; Lee 2009; Gelman 2020a). As such, political scientists often examine how legislators can be convinced, with rewards or punishments, to follow the party line.

Yet, we argue that lawmakers differ in their willingness to support the party or the president and that their partisan intensity is an important factor that affects this. Stronger partisans want their side to win and want to maintain their reputations as good team players. They do not need cajoling to support their party's position on the floor. Weaker partisans are more willing to break with their side. They have invested less effort in building a partisan persona and instead emphasize other qualities like being a compromiser or an issue expert. Although our analysis is of individual members, the aggregate consequences of a more partisan Congress are clear. Having more legislators with higher partisan intensities means having a smaller pool of those willing to defy the majority of their copartisans and cross party lines on key votes.

We assess whether partisan intensity is associated with roll call voting by analyzing lawmakers' party unity and presidential support scores, both of which we collected from *Congressional Quarterly*. A party unity vote occurs when the majority of Democrats oppose a majority of Republicans on the floor. This measure is widely used in studies of Congress and, in fact, is often how researchers measure partisanship. However, as we discuss in chapter 3, these scores are a weak proxy for the concept as they mix together a member's underlying partisan intensity, ideology, and pressure from leadership to support the party. Presidential support scores reflect how often a member voted with the president when the president took a position on the issue at hand.

Although we contend that partisan intensity should affect party unity voting and presidential support, other factors, such as ideology, likely affect these voting choices. As a first step in assessing these relationships, we plot

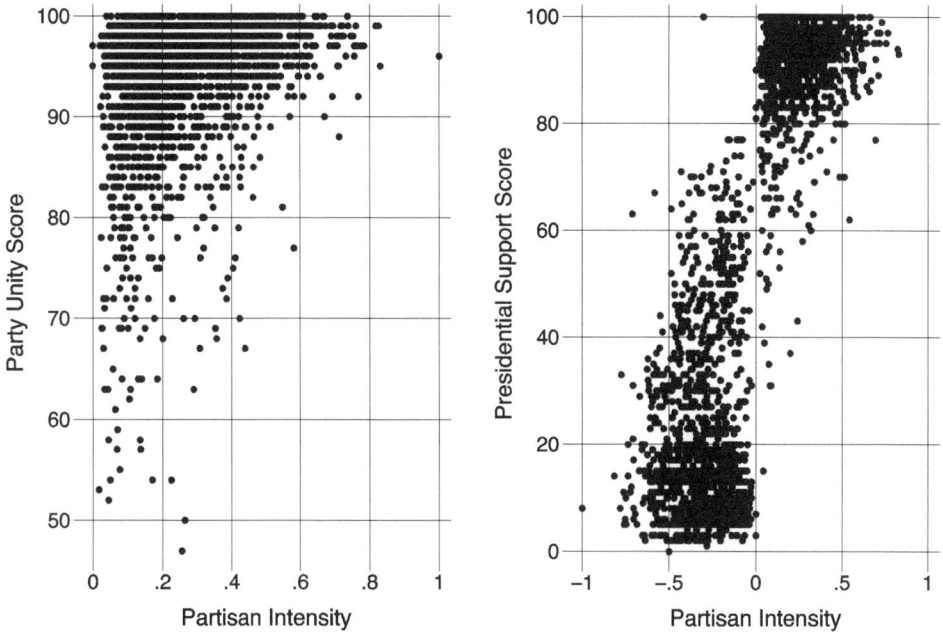

Fig. 6.3. Party Unity and Presidential Support Scores, 2015–20

members' partisan intensity against their party unity and presidential support scores. Notably, in the presidential support plot, we multiply legislators in the party opposite the president by −1 to reflect that those with higher intensities (more negative scores) should vote with the president less often.

As the scatter plots in figure 6.3 show, legislators with low partisan intensities act as we would expect. Their party unity scores are lower, and their presidential support scores cluster toward the middle of the graph. Similarly, stronger partisans vote in lockstep with their party and are more or less inclined to take the president's position, depending on if they are in the same party as him. That said, partisan intensity does not fully explain lawmakers' voting behaviors. This is most apparent in the party unity scatter plot, which shows that a wide range of members vote in near lockstep with their party. Other factors, such as ideology or the partisan composition of a legislator's district, may also affect these voting patterns. As such, we examine to what extent partisan intensity is associated with these legislative behaviors, given other political pressures and a member's ideological orientation.

Next, we examine if partisan intensity predicts lawmakers' party unity voting within a regression framework, using the latter as the dependent variable.[6]

Our main independent variable of interest is our measure of partisan intensity, which we expect to produce a positive effect. Previous research shows that ideological moderates and extremists vote less often with their party (Kirkland and Slapin 2017; Minozzi and Volden 2013). As such, we use first-dimension DW-NOMINATE scores to calculate a member's *Absolute Ideological Distance from the Party Median* and expect this variable to be negative. We also control for a legislator's *District Partisanship*, which is the two-party vote share that the presidential candidate from the legislator's party received in the previous election (Carson et al. 2010; Canes-Wrone, Brady, and Cogan 2002), and we expect it will have a positive coefficient. Additionally, we include control variables for *Party Leaders*, for *Committee Leaders*, for those in the *Republican Party*, for those in the *Senate*, and for *Terms Served* in Congress and account for shifting political environments by including Congress fixed effects.

Our results, included in tables 6.7 and 6.8 in this chapter's appendix, show that both partisan intensity and ideology affect a member's party unity score. As figure 6.4 shows, the most partisan legislators vote, on average, with their party almost always, while the least partisan only do so about 93 percent of the time. This 6 percent difference, while statistically significant, is smaller than ideology's effect. Compared to an ideologically average party member, the most moderate or extreme lawmakers vote with the party 12 percent less often. Put differently, while partisanship increases how often a member votes with the party, their ideological placement in the party is doubly important.

Next, we assess whether partisanship affects voting with or against the president. Figure 6.3 shows a clear and unsurprising partisan divide in presidential support. Recall that we unfold our intensity measure so those in the president's party have positive values and those in the party opposite the president have negative values. As we would expect in contemporary US politics, lawmakers in the president's party almost always support him more than those on the opposing side. However, what happens after we control for party? What else affects presidential support? Is it partisan intensity, ideology, or another factor? In chapter 2, we argue that partisan considerations matter a great deal in determining how much a member supports the president. As the predominate political figure in Washington, DC, he provides a near constant, and fairly easy, target for political point scoring.

To answer these questions, we specify a statistical model where a member's presidential support score is the dependent variable. Our unfolded partisan intensity measure, where those in the party opposite the president have their score multiplied by -1, is our main independent variable. We expect it to be positively associated with presidential support. We followed a similar proce-

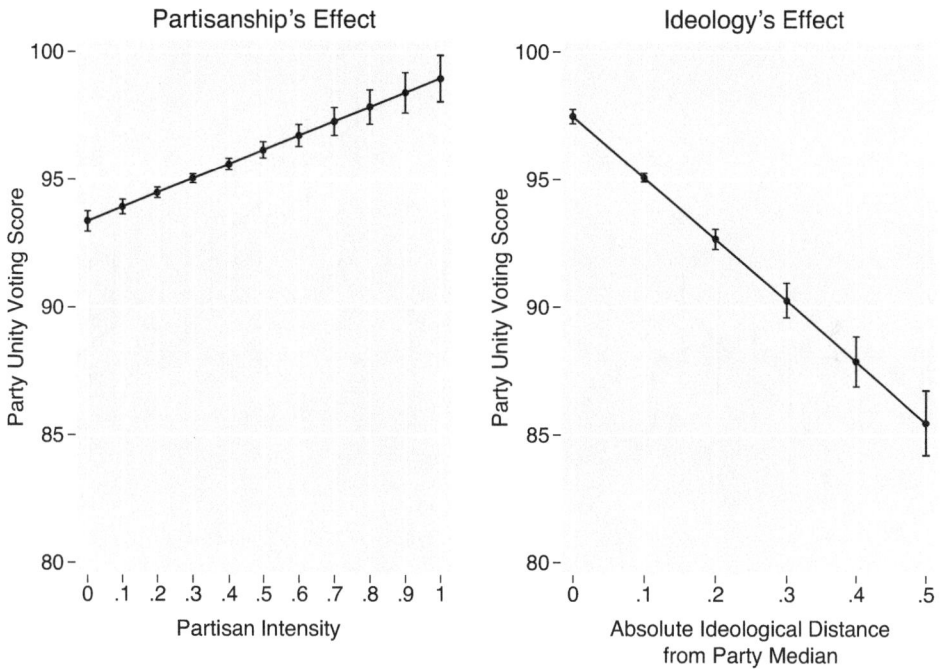

Fig. 6.4. Predicted Party Unity Voting as Partisan Intensity and Ideology Change

dure in transforming our *District Partisanship* variable. Members holding the safest seats in the president's party have the highest scores, and vice versa for those in the opposition. Using Bonica's (2014) CFscores, we control for the *Ideological Distance from the President.*[7] We include the same control variables as above with some modifications. We split the leadership variables in two and control for party and committee leadership in the president's and the opposition's parties. Additionally, we include a *President's Party* dummy instead of the Republican and majority party variables. Finally, we include Senate, terms served, and congressional term controls.[8] We estimate the model using an OLS regression with robust standard errors.

The results produce two notable results. First, and in line with what we see in figure 6.3, being in the president's party is associated with, on average, a 52-percentage-point increase in presidential support. Second, our ratio measure of partisan intensity, which assesses the effect of how much social media rhetoric a legislator devotes to partisanship, is strongly associated with their presidential support score. The partisanship measure that uses the log number of partisan tweets is not. Yet, as figure 6.5 shows, the most intense partisans in

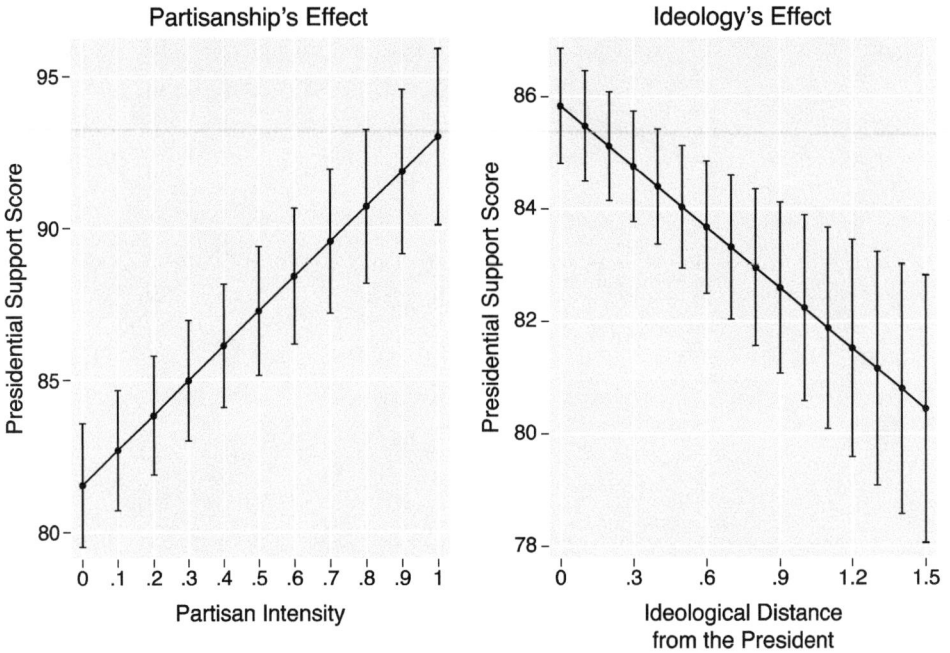

Fig. 6.5. Predicted Presidential Support as Partisan Intensity and Ideology Change
Note: Predicted values from model 1 in table 6.8 (see chapter appendix).

the president's party, measured with our ratio variable, support him about 11 percent more often than the least partisan legislators in the president's party. In contrast, those whose ideology is identical to that of the president vote with him about 4 percent more often than those in his party whose views are most different. In other words, we have some evidence that partisan intensity, after controlling for a legislator's party, is associated with change in presidential support that is three times larger than ideology's effect.

Are Strong Partisans Less Effective Lawmakers?

To this point, we have shown that partisan intensity is associated with legislators' cosponsorship behavior and their voting. The bigger question is whether it affects their legislative effectiveness. In chapter 2, we proposed two possible reasons for how partisanship may affect lawmaking success. First, it may change which sorts of bills a member proposes. Strong partisans, who are motivated by supporting their party and embarrassing the other side, may offer measures whose purpose is to score political points, not make new policy. These messaging bills are fairly common and often include explicitly partisan issues (Gelman 2020a; Lee 2009, 2016). If more partisan members are more likely to introduce ideas that are not intended to become law, then they should be less legislatively effective.

A second possibility is reputational. Members from the opposite party may be less inclined to support ideas proposed by the partisans who regularly bicker with them. While this sort of shunning is interesting to think about, as we discuss in chapter 2, there is little to no evidence it happens. In fact, lawmakers suggest the opposite occurs (Wiseman, Volden, and Hill 2020; Wiseman and Neguse 2021), where they actively seek partners from across the aisle looking for common ground with whomever they can collaborate.

Rather than searching for reasons why strong partisans might be less effective at legislating, we argue that partisanship has no effect on a member's lawmaking prowess. Recall that our argument is twofold. First, many of the same promotion-seeking factors associated with partisanship are also related to being a successful lawmaker. Institutional power, which requires being a good team player, is strongly related to legislative effectiveness (Lewallen 2020; Volden and Wiseman 2014). Yet, even when we disentangle partisanship from other promotion-seeking consequences, like leading a committee, we do not expect these factors to be related. Lawmaking is about building a coalition around shared interests, which usually includes working across the aisle. Even though it is easy to focus on members' hyper-partisan demeanors, in reality, it only makes up part of their behavior. Rather, they spend significant effort developing policy ideas they hope will not be politicized and can be enacted. These range from big, headline-grabbing proposals to small, local issues (Russell 2021b; Grimmer 2013). Regardless of the topic, they regularly search for reliable partners in the other party that can lend bipartisan credibility to their ideas (Wiseman, Volden, and Hill 2020). Thus, even as members try to politicize some issues, score political points, and become more politically influential, they also work to achieve their other goal of passing good public policy. Our contention is that these different goal-seeking behaviors, promotion through partisanship and enacting policy ideas, are largely compartmentalized and do not affect one another.

The first test of our claim that partisanship does not affect lawmaking uses Volden and Wiseman's (2014) legislative effectiveness scores. Their approach measures how successful members are at moving their proposals through the legislative process. Members get credit not just for getting an idea enacted but also for improving its prospects in the future by moving it through Congress.

Statistically, our argument that partisan intensity is not associated with lawmaking prowess means we expect to find null results. Yet, such a finding might arise for a number of reasons, including the variables in our statistical models and other mediating factors. That being the case, we begin by estimating baseline models, and from there, we explore different specifications to evaluate our results' robustness.

We begin by replicating Volden and Wiseman's (2014) main analysis that assesses what factors are correlated with their legislative effectiveness scores. Their original model includes variables unique to the House and excludes senators. We specify a second model that removes the House-specific factors and includes a control for serving in the Senate. For each model, the replication and the one that includes senators, we estimate them using both our ratio and count measures of partisan intensity, resulting in four sets of results. The models in table 6.2 are OLS regressions and are calculated with robust standard errors clustered by member.

We do not find support for partisan intensity being negatively associated with legislative effectiveness. This is best seen in figure 6.6, where we plot the predicted legislative effectiveness scores as a member's partisan intensity changes produced by the models in table 6.2. If partisanship should diminish a lawmaker's legislative prowess, the lines should be negatively sloped. However, as the figure shows, this is not the case. Instead, all four graphs have positive slopes, although only the effects in models 2 and 4 are statistically significant. In other words, we find evidence that partisan intensity has no effect on legislative effectiveness, as we expect, or that more partisan members are actually more legislatively effective!

Of course, these results might be driven by other factors. One possibility is that partisan intensity's effect is being mediated by other variables in the model. As we show earlier in the book, party and committee leaders display more partisanship for promotion-seeking reasons. Volden and Wiseman (2014) show that these positions are also related to legislative effectiveness. There is a similar issue with including measures of seat safety. As a result, having variables that predict both partisan intensity and legislative effectiveness in the model may mediate any association between those variables.

We address this issue in two ways. First, we estimate models that exclude the potential mediators, namely, the leadership and vote share variables. Second, we subset our data to only include legislators in similar political situations. We evaluate the effect of partisan intensity on freshmen and sophomore

TABLE 6.2. Association Between Partisan Intensity and Legislative Effectiveness Scores

	V&W Replication		Both Chambers	
	(1) Ratio	(2) Count	(3) Ratio	(4) Count
Partisan Intensity	0.26	0.07**	0.42	0.09**
	(0.25)	(0.03)	(0.23)	(0.02)
Ideological Extremity	−0.71**	−0.73**	−0.49*	−0.49*
	(0.24)	(0.22)	(0.21)	(0.20)
Legislative Effectiveness$_{t-1}$	0.39**	0.39**	0.46**	0.47**
	(0.05)	(0.05)	(0.04)	(0.04)
State Legislative Experience	−0.06	−0.06	−0.05	−0.04
	(0.09)	(0.09)	(0.08)	(0.08)
State Legislative Exp. × Legislative Prof.	0.21	0.18	0.18	0.19
	(0.27)	(0.27)	(0.24)	(0.23)
Majority Party	0.36*	0.36**	0.60**	0.61**
	(0.14)	(0.14)	(0.13)	(0.13)
Speaker	−1.18**	−1.23**		
	(0.23)	(0.23)		
Majority Leader	0.08	0.03	−0.27	−0.30
	(0.20)	(0.21)	(0.34)	(0.33)
Minority Leader	−0.07	−0.08	−0.40**	−0.43**
	(0.13)	(0.14)	(0.12)	(0.11)
Committee Chair	1.44**	1.43**	0.03	0.02
	(0.27)	(0.27)	(0.10)	(0.09)
Subcommittee Chair	0.14	0.13	−0.11	−0.11
	(0.11)	(0.11)	(0.09)	(0.09)
Terms Served	0.03**	0.03**	0.03**	0.03**
	(0.01)	(0.01)	(0.01)	(0.01)
Vote Share	−0.02	−0.03	−0.03	−0.03
	(0.02)	(0.02)	(0.02)	(0.02)
Vote Share^2	0.00	0.00	0.00	0.00
	(0.00)	(0.00)	(0.00)	(0.00)
Female	0.23**	0.19*	0.22**	0.18*
	(0.09)	(0.09)	(0.08)	(0.08)
African American	0.15	0.15	0.15	0.14
	(0.09)	(0.09)	(0.09)	(0.09)
Latino	−0.02	−0.04	0.03	0.01
	(0.09)	(0.09)	(0.11)	(0.10)
Delegation Size	−0.00	−0.00		
	(0.00)	(0.00)		
Power Committee	−0.27**	−0.26**		
	(0.07)	(0.07)		
Senate			0.01	−0.06
			(0.08)	(0.08)
Constant	1.40	1.26	1.27	0.96
	(0.93)	(0.92)	(0.73)	(0.73)
N	697	697	887	887
R^2	0.485	0.490	0.357	0.364

Note: Models are OLS regressions with robust standard errors clustered by member. The DV is Volden and Wiseman's legislative effectiveness scores. Ratio models include our ratio measure of partisan intensity. Count models include our logged count measure of partisan intensity.

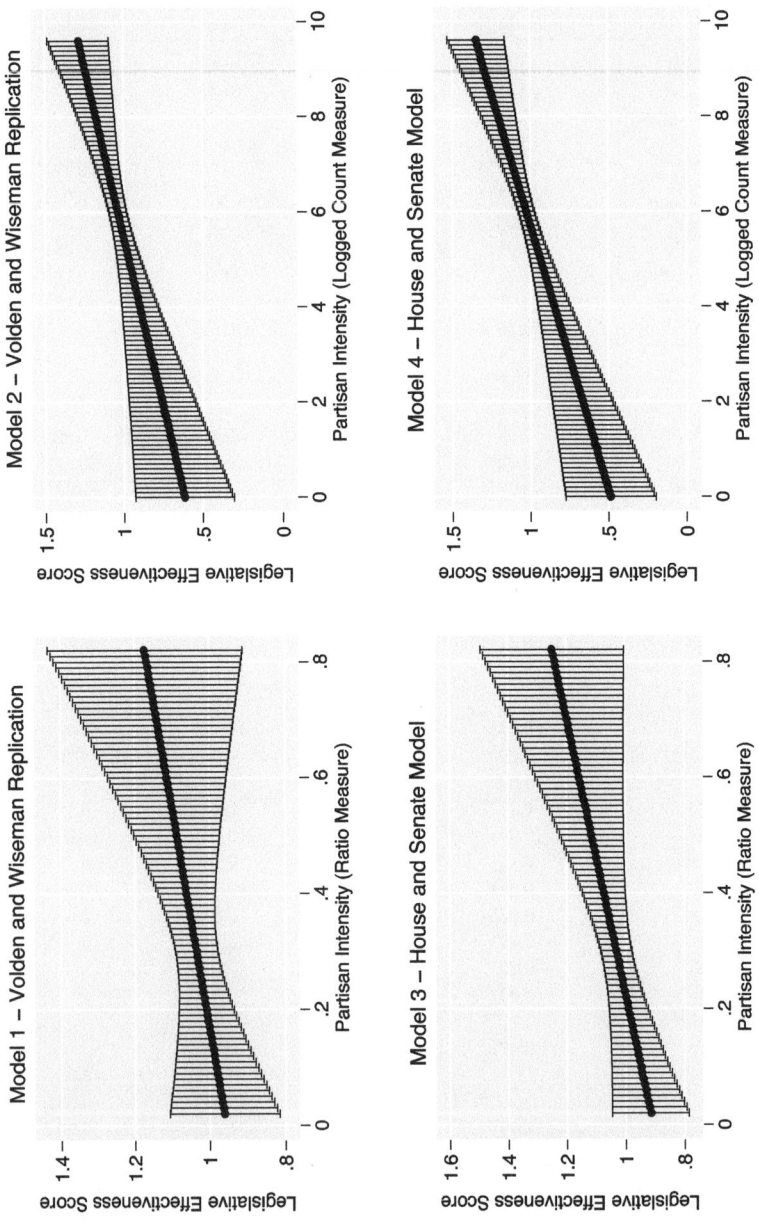

Fig. 6.6. Partisan Intensity's Predicted Effect on Legislative Effectiveness

legislators separately. Freshmen are unique in that they very rarely hold party or committee leadership positions, so those factors are not mediating the relationship between partisanship and effectiveness. Having never won reelection, they may be especially focused on winning their next race and not legislating. Similarly, sophomores rarely hold leadership roles, but we can also control for their partisan reputation from the previous term to assess if members are being punished by the opposition for their previous partisan behavior. We might observe that sophomores, whose reputations for legislative effectiveness and partisanship we control for, see a reduction in their lawmaking abilities based on their current or previous partisan intensity.

Additionally, in another model, we subset the data on committee chairs. Instead of looking for situations where members do not hold institutional power, we study those with similar amounts of power. This way, we can assess if differences in partisan intensity among members who have been successfully promoted to power roles, and who share similar advantages that go with it, affect their effectiveness.

We also consider other situations where partisan intensity might matter. In particular, it is possible majority parties might be more inclined to reward the strong partisans in their party while punishing those in the opposition. We are skeptical this happens, but if it does, we should see partisanship reducing effectiveness in models that only include minority party lawmakers and increasing it in models subset on the majority party.[9]

In table 6.3, we present the coefficients and p-values for our partisan intensity measures from these different specifications. Negative values indicate that members are less effective lawmakers as their partisan intensity increases. Positive values indicate that stronger partisans are, on average, more effective at lawmaking.

In line with our expectations, in most models, partisan intensity is not associated with a member's legislative effectiveness score. The only exception is when we exclude the leadership and vote share mediators. After doing so, our results suggest that stronger partisans are better at legislating, not penalized for their behavior. The common theme across all of these statistical models is that members' lawmaking prowess is not negatively affected by their partisan behavior. Although we have some evidence that partisanship might increase it, our most consistent finding is that these factors are not strongly correlated.

As a final robustness check, we consider whether including certain variables are driving these null results. In fact, in a bivariate regression model, partisan intensity is negative and statistically significant. This raises the question of how sensitive our results are to specific modeling approaches. Fortunately,

TABLE 6.3. Effect of Partisan Intensity on Legislative Effectiveness in Different Specifications

Model	Partisan Intensity (Ratio)		Partisan Intensity (Count)	
	Coefficient	p-value	Coefficient	p-value
No mediators	0.41	0.08	0.08	0.01
Only freshmen	0.01	0.98	0.04	0.53
Only sophomores	0.19	0.79	0.15	0.29
Only committee chairs	0.37	0.69	0.64	0.53
Only minority party	0.21	0.37	0.04	0.26
Only majority party	−0.16	0.40	0.04	0.04

the answer is simple. Once we include a measure of ideological extremity, the absolute ideological distance from the party median, the partisanship effect disappears or becomes positive.

Throughout the book, we have expressed skepticism that measures of ideology, based on scores like DW-NOMINATE, are only capturing members' views on the issues. Others have shown that these variables include some aspect of partisan team play (Aldrich, Montgomery, and Sparks 2014; Lee 2009). Even so, as we show in chapter 3 and earlier in this chapter, partisan intensity and ideological extremity are weakly correlated and, to different degrees, are associated with different legislative behaviors. For instance, as we show above, voting with the president is a predominately partisan exercise, while voting with the party is a mix of partisan and ideological considerations. In this case, and in line with other recent studies (Volden and Wiseman 2014; Casas, Denny, and Wilkerson 2020), ideological extremism reduces legislative effectiveness. We find partisan intensity has no negative relationship with lawmaking prowess.

Are Strong Partisans Less Effective at Getting Their Policy Ideas Enacted?

Legislative effectiveness scores measure how successful members are at moving their ideas through the legislative process. While this is a useful measurement, it is important to consider an even simpler question: Are strong partisans worse at getting their policy ideas enacted? This question means measuring legislative success independent of other aspects captured in the legislative effectiveness scores, like a bill receiving committee consideration.

Assessing this question is not so simple. Researchers have shown that in the contemporary Congress, bills are fungible units that are split, recombined, and usually omnibused into previously unrecognizable forms (Casas, Denny, and Wilkerson 2020). As such, we cannot simply measure if a bill is enacted. Doing so would include significant measurement error. Instead, we assess if a member's policy idea becomes law. This more nuanced dichotomous measure, which is coded as 1 if a legislative section introduced by a member is enacted in any subsequent bill during that congressional term and as 0 otherwise. In analyzing sections, not bills, we follow recent work that tracks policy ideas, not combinations of them bundled into legislation (Wilkerson, Smith, and Stramp 2015). This allows us to more carefully track which measures, proposed by which members, are enacted in the more opaque, unorthodox process that defines the contemporary legislative process (Sinclair 2016).

We provide technical details in the appendix to this chapter, but to do this, we use a decision tree algorithm and training data created by Gelman (2024) for determining if a section was enacted. The basic process is as follows. We split each introduced bill into its separate sections and, for each section, followed a standard procedure in cleaning the text. This includes removing stop words (e.g., "the" or "whereas") and non-legislative text such as the table of contents, tokenizing the text, and removing boilerplate sections that are included as standard practice in numerous bills (e.g., effective date sections). Next, we calculate a number of measures that compare how similar two sections are. These include the percentage of five-word phrases (5-grams) that are in section A and are also in section B (and vice versa), the percentage of two-word phrases (2-grams) that are in the first 100 characters of section A that are also in section B (and vice versa),[10] and finding the longest block of identical text in both sections and measuring what percentage of each section it makes up. We use Gelman's nearly 5,000 hand-coded training set of section dyads and his decision tree algorithm to identify whether two policy ideas are the same or not.

The decision tree predicts if an introduced section was enacted or not in that congressional term by comparing the text of introduced and enacted sections. Once the decision tree matches an enacted section to introduced sections with the same policy idea, we identify the earliest introduced version to determine which member first proposed the idea. Thus, for each section introduced in a bill, we track the sponsor and whether it was enacted in any legislation during that term. This dichotomous measure, 1 if a section is enacted or 0 if not, is our dependent variable.

We specify two statistical models to evaluate if partisan intensity is associated with members getting their policy ideas enacted. First, we use the same

TABLE 6.4. Independent Variables Included in Enacted Policy Idea Models

	Independent Variables
Specification 1 (V&W)	*Partisan Intensity, Lagged Legislative Effectiveness, Ideological Distance from Chamber Median, Seniority, State Legislative Experience, State Legislative Experience × Legislative Professionalism, Majority Party, Majority Party Leadership, Minority Party Leadership, Committee Chair, Subcommittee Chair, Female, African American, Latino, Vote Share, Vote Share², ln(Section Length), 115th Congress, 116th Congress*
Specification 2 (G&W)	*Partisan Intensity, Ideological Distance from Chamber Median, Seat Safety, Majority Party, Party Leader, Committee Chair, Committee Ranking Member, Subcommittee Chair, Terms Served, Republican, Senate, ln(Section Length), 115th Congress, 116th Congress*

independent variables from model 2 outlined in table 6.2, which adopts Volden and Wiseman's (V&W) approach to analyzing legislative effectiveness. However, since their modeling decisions are based on evaluating how bills move through Congress, we use a second model that uses the covariates we have used throughout our analysis to assess how institutional roles, ideology, and partisanship affect whether a section is enacted or not (Gelman & Wilson's [G&W] approach). We summarize the different specifications in table 6.4.

These models include a few noteworthy features. First, we control for a section's complexity by including the natural log of its length.[11] Second, we include congressional dummy variables to account for changing political environments, like divided government, that affect the likelihood a policy idea becomes law. Third, even as aggregated units of policy ideas, bills have different baseline probabilities for enactment. To address this, we include random bill effects for specifications in both models 1 and 2.

Again, our main independent variables are our partisan intensity measures. If partisanship reduces a member's legislative success, this covariate should have a negative coefficient. For reasons we have previously discussed, we are skeptical of such a penalty. Rather, we expect other factors related to lawmaking ability to matter more, like holding positions of institutional power or being an ideological centrist. We test these possibilities with a linear probability model and report the full results in tables 6.10 and 6.11 in the chapter's appendix.

Figure 6.7 plots the predicted probability a section is enacted as a legislator's partisan intensity changes. Partisan intensity in models 2 and 4, which use our logged count measure, has negative coefficients and is significant in model 2 (but not model 4). Substantively, those results predict that the least parti-

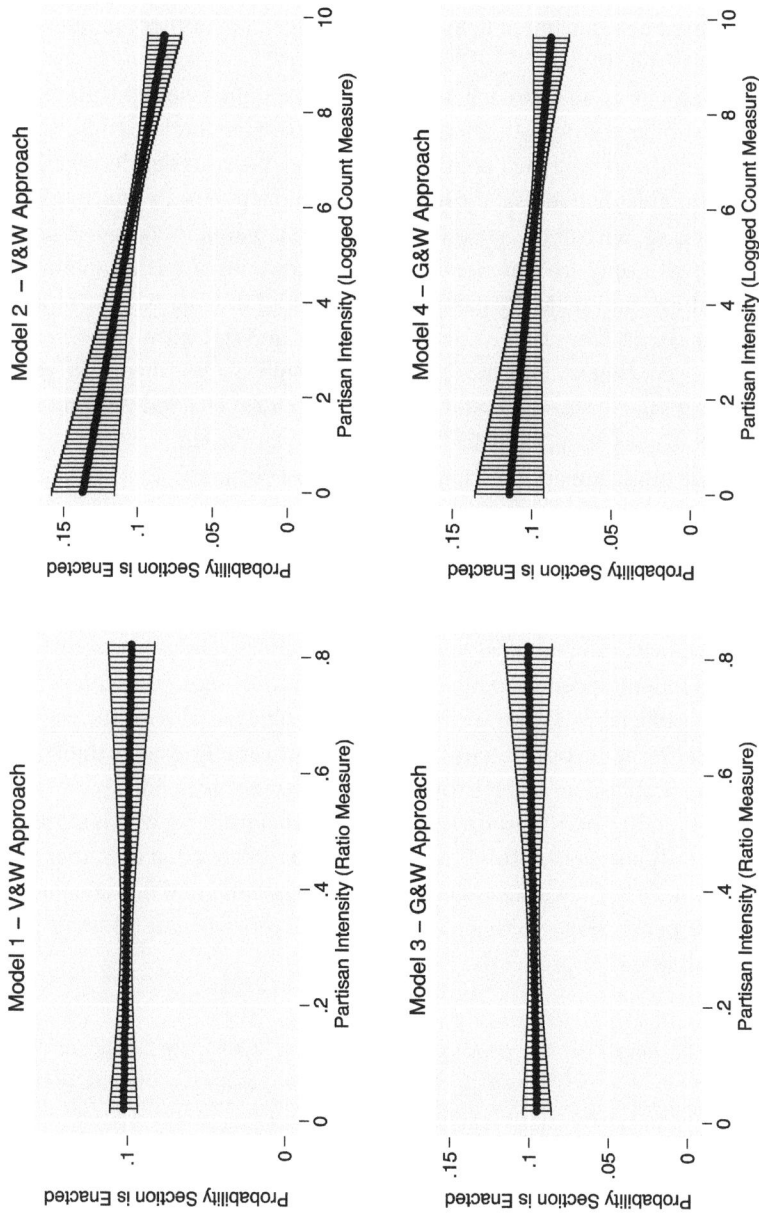

Fig. 6.7. Partisan Intensity's Predicted Effect on a Legislative Section Becoming Law

san legislators have their policy ideas enacted, on average, 5.5 percent more often than the strongest partisans. This provides some evidence that partisan behavior might be a detriment to legislating; however, our other models suggest there is no penalty.

Following our same approach as before, we examine whether legislators who are in similar political situations but whose partisan intensity differs are more successful at getting their policy ideas enacted. We also consider whether mediating variables like seat safety or holding leadership roles are affecting our results. To do so, we run the same wide range of statistical models—without mediators, with only freshmen, sophomores, committee chairs, minority party members, and majority party members—and in table 6.5, we report whether the partisan intensity variable is negative and statistically significant ($p < 0.05$). A checkmark indicates it is, which would suggest that those who act more partisan are less successful in having their ideas enacted. An X means we do not find a negative, statistically significant relationship.

Only one modeling approach, using the V&W covariates and our count version of partisan intensity, produces results that suggest a lawmaking penalty. The bulk of the evidence indicates that members are just as likely to have their policy ideas enacted regardless of their partisan behavior. We also considered whether these null results are because of the specific set of variables we included. Just like in our analysis of legislative effectiveness, specifications that exclude ideological extremity variables produce negative, statistically significant coefficients. When we control for ideology, and with the exception of model 2, the partisan intensity covariate consistently loses its statistical significance. In this case, and mirroring our legislative effectiveness findings, ideology rather than partisanship predominates in determining who is more or less legislatively successful. This is consistent with research that examines the important role of lawmakers' policy views when legislating and that concludes they are not penalized for acting as good team players when developing and advancing their policy proposals.

TABLE 6.5. Tracking If Partisan Intensity Is Negative and Statistically Significant

	Model 1	Model 2	Model 3	Model 4
No mediators	X	✓	X	X
Only freshmen	X	X	X	X
Only sophomores	X	X	X	X
Only committee chairs	X	✓	X	X
Only minority party	X	✓	X	X
Only majority party	X	X	X	X

Conclusion

In this chapter, we test a key claim of our argument: that members do not incur a legislative penalty for their partisan intensity. Our results indicate that the worst outcome for a strong partisan is that their legislation attracts fewer cosponsors from the other party. We find no consistent evidence that it affects their ability to legislate. Although other researchers note that bipartisan collaboration can help members get their ideas enacted, we do not find that partisan intensity affects their legislative effectiveness or ability to get their policy proposals passed into law. We are quick to note that our empirical approach is quite direct in this chapter and that the relationship between cosponsorship, partisanship, and lawmaking may be more complex (Harbridge 2015; Harbridge-Yong, Volden, and Wiseman 2023). What is not as nuanced is where partisanship has its strongest effect: on the floor. It is closely associated with voting with or against the president and the party's position.

To be clear, we are not claiming that partisanship does not matter in the legislative process. In fact, recent research by Curry and Roberts (forthcoming) shows that extreme partisan moments can reduce a member's legislative effectiveness. Moreover, when the president or a party politicizes an issue, it matters a great deal. In the case of presidential position taking, if they are copartisans with the president, strong partisans will almost always support the White House's position even if they disagree with the ideological content. The opposite is true when members are in the other party. Normatively, this is a very troubling finding, as it suggests that those with high partisan intensities in the president's party, who gained their roles by being reliable team players, will rarely, if ever, hold the administration accountable. Similarly, those in the opposite party are very unlikely to work with the president, even when doing so advances the legislators' policy goals or responds to an emergency. To a lesser degree, we see a similar pattern when members must decide to toe the party line or not. Partisanship, independent of ideology, affects this decision-making and, for many legislators, pushes them toward their side and away from compromise.

Indeed, the consequences of a more partisan Congress are not that members become less effective at legislating. It is that it is more difficult to get enough people to vote yes on the House and Senate floor when issues become politicized. Recognizing this, Congress, in reworking the legislative process to emphasize large, omnibus bills that are difficult to politicize, provides a rational response to an institution filled with hyper-partisan members who also happen to be the most influential legislators. By forcing many policy ideas into a single measure, it allows otherwise strong partisans opportunities to legislate *and* prevents them from scoring political points by torpedoing individual components.

More broadly, these results show one reason why partisanship proliferates. The institution, instead of responding by punishing those who politicize issues, adapts how it enacts policy in ways that allow strong partisans to go about their business without consequence. This allows members to pursue their promotion-seeking and policymaking goals without any trade-off between the two.

Appendix

(*following page*)

TABLE 6.6. Likelihood Partisans Engage in Bipartisan Cosponsorships

	(1) Ratio	(2) Count
Partisan Intensity	−1.31**	−0.06*
	(0.20)	(0.02)
Ideological Extremity	−2.37**	−2.68**
	(0.28)	(0.28)
Seat Safety	−0.02**	−0.02**
	(0.00)	(0.00)
Majority Party	−0.98**	−1.05**
	(0.14)	(0.15)
Committee Chair	−0.19*	−0.25**
	(0.09)	(0.09)
Subcommittee Chair	0.09	0.09
	(0.06)	(0.06)
Terms Served	−0.00	−0.01
	(0.01)	(0.01)
Legislative Effectiveness$_{t-1}$	0.21**	0.20**
	(0.03)	(0.03)
Senate	0.14	0.18*
	(0.08)	(0.08)
Republican	0.02	0.05
	(0.06)	(0.07)
Constant	1.82**	1.99**
	(0.19)	(0.23)
N	875	875
R^2	0.490	0.464

Note: Models are OLS regressions with robust standard errors clustered by member and include Congress fixed effects. The dependent variable is the Lugar Center's measure of bipartisanship, which is based on how often a member cosponsors a bill offered by a member from the other party.
*$p < 0.05$, **$p < 0.01$.

TABLE 6.7. Partisanship's Effect on Party Unity Voting

	(1) Ratio	(2) Count
Partisan Intensity	5.51**	0.42**
	(0.62)	(0.09)
Absolute Ideological Distance from the Party Median	−24.40**	−24.71**
	(1.52)	(1.54)
Seat Safety	0.25**	0.26**
	(0.01)	(0.01)
Party Leader	0.57	1.05
	(0.58)	(0.58)
Committee Leader	0.79**	0.99**
	(0.30)	(0.30)
Republican	0.10	0.19
	(0.21)	(0.23)
Terms Served	−0.15**	−0.13**
	(0.02)	(0.02)
Senate	−0.99**	−1.31**
	(0.31)	(0.31)
115th Congress	−0.19	−0.01
	(0.22)	(0.22)
116th Congress	0.75**	0.82**
	(0.24)	(0.25)
Constant	93.70**	92.74**
	(0.29)	(0.50)
N	3,524	3,520
R^2	0.312	0.305

Note: Dependent variable is *CQ*'s annually calculated party unity score. Models are OLS regressions with robust standard errors.

TABLE 6.8. Partisanship's Effect on Presidential Support

	(1) Ratio	(2) Count
Partisan Intensity	12.12**	−0.38*
	(1.34)	(0.17)
Ideological Distance from the President	−3.17**	−4.70**
	(0.86)	(0.88)
District Partisanship	0.35**	0.42**
	(0.02)	(0.02)
President's Party	51.81**	57.77**
	(2.03)	(2.45)
Party Leader—President's Party	−3.83*	0.00
	(1.49)	(1.43)
Party Leader—Opposition Party	5.03	2.60
	(2.76)	(2.81)
Committee Leader—President's Party	−3.44**	−2.71**
	(0.71)	(0.71)
Committee Leader—Opposition Party	4.32**	3.61**
	(0.96)	(0.99)
Terms Served	0.13**	0.08
	(0.05)	(0.05)
Senate	16.14**	15.69**
	(0.60)	(0.60)
115th Congress	7.34**	6.34**
	(0.51)	(0.54)
116th Congress	−1.08*	−1.35**
	(0.43)	(0.45)
Constant	28.27**	27.62**
	(2.03)	(2.10)
N	3,504	3,500
R^2	0.918	0.916

Note: Dependent variable is *CQ*'s annually calculated presidential support score. Models are OLS regressions with robust standard errors.

TABLE 6.9. Effect of Partisan Intensity on Legislative Effectiveness in Different Specifications, Full Models

	No Mediators		Freshmen		Sophomores		Committee Chairs		Minority Party		Majority Party	
	(1) Ratio	(2) Count	(3) Ratio	(4) Count	(5) Ratio	(6) Count	(7) Ratio	(8) Count	(9) Ratio	(10) Count	(11) Ratio	(12) Count
Partisan Intensity	0.41 (0.23)	0.08** (0.02)	0.01 (0.37)	0.04 (0.06)	0.19 (0.72)	0.15 (0.14)	0.37 (0.69)	0.06 (0.10)	0.21 (0.23)	0.04 (0.03)	−0.16 (0.40)	0.04 (0.04)
Ideological Extremity	−1.41** (0.12)	−1.40** (0.11)	−0.87* (0.37)	−0.93** (0.36)	−0.21 (0.71)	−0.53 (0.69)	−0.44 (0.66)	−0.40 (0.69)	−0.05 (0.29)	−0.05 (0.27)	−0.61 (0.38)	−0.70 (0.37)
Legislative Effectiveness$_{t-1}$	0.45** (0.04)	0.46** (0.04)			0.45** (0.14)	0.44** (0.13)	0.41** (0.15)	0.41** (0.14)	0.40** (0.07)	0.40** (0.07)	0.49** (0.07)	0.49** (0.07)
State Legislative Experience	−0.04 (0.08)	−0.05 (0.08)	−0.06 (0.15)	−0.07 (0.15)	0.30 (0.37)	0.27 (0.36)	0.02 (0.22)	0.02 (0.22)	−0.15 (0.09)	−0.16 (0.09)	0.12 (0.15)	0.13 (0.15)
State Legislative Exp. × Legislative Prof.	0.18 (0.23)	0.22 (0.22)	−0.10 (0.45)	−0.06 (0.45)	0.11 (1.19)	−0.13 (1.11)	−0.63 (0.55)	−0.60 (0.56)	0.17 (0.23)	0.17 (0.23)	−0.15 (0.42)	−0.18 (0.41)
Terms Served	0.02* (0.01)	0.02** (0.01)	0.00 (0.00)	0.00 (0.00)	0.00 (.)	0.00 (.)	−0.02 (0.02)	−0.02 (0.02)	0.00 (0.01)	0.00 (0.01)	0.04* (0.02)	0.04* (0.02)
Female	0.20* (0.08)	0.16* (0.08)	−0.20 (0.13)	−0.23 (0.13)	0.28 (0.28)	0.32 (0.28)	0.15 (0.15)	0.14 (0.15)	0.05 (0.07)	0.04 (0.07)	0.24 (0.13)	0.23 (0.14)
African American	0.22* (0.09)	0.22* (0.09)	0.35 (0.26)	0.34 (0.25)	−0.07 (0.25)	−0.20 (0.23)	0.88** (0.32)	0.87* (0.33)	−0.02 (0.09)	−0.02 (0.09)	0.01 (0.14)	0.03 (0.14)
Latino	0.05 (0.11)	0.03 (0.11)	−0.18 (0.16)	−0.19 (0.17)	−0.29 (0.23)	−0.38 (0.24)	−0.23 (0.35)	−0.25 (0.33)	−0.05 (0.09)	−0.05 (0.09)	−0.19 (0.16)	−0.19 (0.16)
Majority Party			0.33 (0.18)	0.32 (0.18)	0.60 (0.38)	0.47 (0.37)						
Vote Share			−0.02 (0.04)	−0.02 (0.04)	−0.11 (0.06)	−0.14* (0.06)	−0.17** (0.06)	−0.16** (0.06)	−0.04 (0.02)	−0.04 (0.02)	−0.05 (0.05)	−0.05 (0.05)
Vote Share^2			0.00 (0.00)	0.00 (0.00)	0.00 (0.00)	0.00* (0.00)	0.00** (0.00)	0.00** (0.00)	0.00 (0.00)	0.00 (0.00)	0.00 (0.00)	0.00 (0.00)
Delegation Size			0.01 (0.00)	0.01 (0.00)	0.01 (0.01)	0.00 (0.01)			−0.00* (0.00)	−0.00 (0.00)	0.00 (0.00)	0.00 (0.00)

	(1)	(2)	(3)	(4)	(5)	(6)	(7)	(8)	(9)	(10)	(11)	(12)
Partisan Intensity$_{t-1}$												
Republican					−2.63* (1.15)	−0.27 (0.19)			−0.36** (0.08)	−0.35** (0.08)	−0.38** (0.11)	−0.33** (0.13)
Subcommittee Chair					−0.20 (0.22)	−0.26 (0.25)					0.10 (0.12)	0.09 (0.12)
Senate							0.26 (0.17)	0.19 (0.21)				
Speaker											−1.21** (0.30)	−1.28** (0.29)
Majority Leader											0.09 (0.21)	0.03 (0.21)
Minority Leader									−0.07 (0.10)	−0.07 (0.10)		
Committee Chair											1.34** (0.27)	1.33** (0.27)
Power Committee									−0.11 (0.06)	−0.11 (0.06)	−0.37** (0.11)	−0.37** (0.11)
Constant	0.86** (0.10)	0.50** (0.16)	1.58 (1.35)	1.43 (1.35)	4.87* (2.32)	6.31** (2.27)	6.34** (2.07)	5.98** (1.93)	1.88* (0.78)	1.71* (0.72)	2.89 (1.77)	2.93 (1.78)
N	888	888	224	224	102	102	76	76	325	325	372	372
R^2	0.332	0.337	0.250	0.252	0.531	0.523	0.439	0.440	0.366	0.367	0.433	0.434

TABLE 6.10. Partisanship's Effect on Probability Bill Section Is Enacted
(Volden & Wiseman Approach)

	(1) Ratio	(2) Count
Partisan Intensity	−0.01	−0.01**
	(0.01)	(0.01)
Ideological Extremity	−0.12**	−0.11**
	(0.01)	(0.01)
Legislative Effectiveness$_{t-1}$	0.01**	0.01**
	(0.01)	(0.01)
State Legislative Experience	0.01	0.01
	(0.01)	(0.01)
State Legislative Exp. × Legislative Prof.	−0.02	−0.02
	(0.02)	(0.02)
Majority Party	−0.03**	−0.03**
	(0.01)	(0.01)
Minority Party Leader	−0.01	0.01
	(0.02)	(0.02)
Majority Party Leader	0.12**	0.12**
	(0.03)	(0.03)
Committee Chair	0.03**	0.03**
	(0.01)	(0.01)
Subcommittee Chair	0.01	0.01
	(0.01)	(0.01)
Terms Served	−0.01**	−0.01**
	(0.01)	(0.01)
Vote Share	−0.01	−0.01
	(0.01)	(0.01)
Vote Share^2	0.01	−0.01
	(0.01)	(0.01)
Female	−0.01	−0.01
	(0.01)	(0.01)
African American	0.01	0.01
	(0.01)	(0.01)
Latino	−0.01	−0.01
	(0.01)	(0.01)
Senate	0.02**	0.03**
	(0.00)	(0.00)
Section Length	−0.01**	−0.01**
	(0.01)	(0.01)
Constant	0.21**	0.22**
	(0.04)	(0.04)
N	84,916	84,916
R^2	0.10	0.10

Note: Models are OLS regressions with bill-level random effects and congressional term dummies. The dependent variable is coded as 1 if a bill section is enacted and 0 otherwise.
*$p < 0.05$, **$p < 0.01$.

TABLE 6.11. Partisanship's Effect on Probability Bill
Section Is Enacted (Gelman & Wilson Approach)

	(1) Ratio	(2) Count
Partisan Intensity	0.01	−0.01
	(0.01)	(0.01)
Ideological Extremity	−0.12**	−0.12**
	(0.01)	(0.01)
Seat Safety	−0.01	−0.01
	(0.01)	(0.01)
Majority Party	−0.02*	−0.02
	(0.01)	(0.01)
Party Leader	0.05**	0.05**
	(0.01)	(0.01)
Committee Leader	0.02**	0.02**
	(0.01)	(0.01)
Subcommittee Chair	−0.01	−0.01
	(0.01)	(0.01)
Terms Served	−0.01	−0.01
	(0.01)	(0.01)
Republican	0.02**	0.02**
	(0.01)	(0.01)
Senate	0.02**	0.02**
	(0.01)	(0.01)
Section Length	−0.01**	−0.01**
	(0.01)	(0.01)
Constant	0.19**	0.21**
	(0.01)	(0.01)
N	85,610	85,610
R^2	0.09	0.09

Note: Models are OLS regressions with bill-level random effects and congressional term dummies. The dependent variable is coded as 1 if a bill section is enacted and 0 otherwise.

$*p < 0.05$, $**p < 0.01$.

TABLE 6.12. Robustness Checks for If Partisan Intensity Is Associated with Section Passage Rates

	No Mediators		Freshmen		Sophomores		Committee Chairs		Minority Party		Majority Party	
	(1) Ratio	(2) Count	(3) Ratio	(4) Count	(5) Ratio	(6) Count	(7) Ratio	(8) Count	(9) Ratio	(10) Count	(11) Ratio	(12) Count
Partisan Intensity	0.01 (0.01)	-0.01** (0.00)	0.01 (0.05)	-0.01 (0.01)	0.08 (0.05)	0.01 (0.01)	-0.02 (0.06)	-0.02** (0.01)	-0.02 (0.02)	-0.01* (0.00)	0.04 (0.02)	-0.01 (0.00)
Ideological Extremity	-0.12** (0.01)	-0.11** (0.01)	-0.10* (0.04)	-0.09* (0.04)	-0.11** (0.04)	-0.09* (0.04)	-0.22** (0.08)	-0.21* (0.08)	-0.08** (0.02)	-0.07** (0.02)	-0.18** (0.02)	-0.17** (0.02)
Legislative Effectiveness$_{t-1}$	0.02** (0.00)	0.02** (0.00)	0.04** (0.01)	0.04** (0.01)	0.02* (0.01)	0.02* (0.01)	0.02** (0.00)	0.02** (0.00)	0.01** (0.00)	0.01** (0.00)	0.02** (0.00)	0.02** (0.00)
State Legislative Experience	0.01 (0.01)	0.00 (0.01)	0.01 (0.02)	0.01 (0.01)	0.05* (0.02)	0.05** (0.02)	-0.07** (0.02)	-0.07** (0.02)	0.02* (0.01)	0.02* (0.01)	-0.01 (0.01)	-0.01 (0.01)
State Leg. Exp. × Leg. Prof.	-0.02 (0.02)	-0.02 (0.02)	-0.06** (0.02)	-0.05* (0.02)	-0.15** (0.06)	-0.15* (0.06)	0.13 (0.07)	0.12 (0.07)	-0.04 (0.02)	-0.04 (0.02)	0.01 (0.02)	0.01 (0.02)
Majority Party	-0.03** (0.01)	-0.02** (0.01)	-0.06** (0.02)	-0.05* (0.02)	-0.01 (0.02)	-0.01 (0.02)						
Terms Served	-0.00 (0.00)	-0.00 (0.00)					-0.01* (0.01)	-0.01 (0.01)	-0.01 (0.01)	-0.01* (0.01)	-0.01** (0.01)	-0.01* (0.01)
Female	-0.01* (0.00)	-0.01 (0.00)	0.00 (0.01)	0.01 (0.01)	-0.00 (0.01)	-0.00 (0.01)	-0.06** (0.02)	-0.06** (0.02)	0.01 (0.01)	0.01 (0.01)	-0.01* (0.01)	-0.02* (0.01)
African American	0.01 (0.01)	0.01 (0.01)	-0.02 (0.02)	-0.02 (0.02)	0.01 (0.02)	0.02 (0.02)	0.07* (0.03)	0.06* (0.03)	-0.00 (0.01)	-0.00 (0.01)	0.03** (0.01)	0.03** (0.01)
Latino	-0.00 (0.01)	-0.00 (0.01)	0.00 (0.02)	0.00 (0.02)	-0.01 (0.02)	-0.01 (0.02)	-0.04 (0.03)	-0.02 (0.03)	-0.00 (0.01)	-0.00 (0.01)	-0.00 (0.01)	-0.00 (0.01)
Senate	0.03** (0.00)	0.03** (0.00)	0.02 (0.02)	0.02 (0.02)	0.02 (0.02)	0.02 (0.02)	0.03 (0.02)	0.04 (0.02)	0.01 (0.01)	0.01* (0.01)	0.05** (0.01)	0.05** (0.01)
Section Length	-0.01** (0.00)	-0.01** (0.00)	-0.01** (0.00)	-0.01** (0.00)	-0.01** (0.00)	-0.01** (0.00)	-0.02** (0.00)	-0.02** (0.00)	-0.01** (0.00)	-0.01** (0.00)	-0.01** (0.00)	-0.01** (0.00)
Minority Leader					0.03 (0.08)	0.04 (0.08)			0.01 (0.02)	0.01 (0.02)		

Majority Leader											0.10**	0.11**
											(0.02)	(0.02)
Committee Chair					-0.03	-0.02	-0.01	-0.01			0.03**	0.03**
					(0.02)	(0.02)	(0.02)	(0.02)			(0.01)	(0.01)
Subcom. Chair			0.02	0.02	-0.01	-0.01	-0.01	-0.01	-0.01	-0.01	-0.01	-0.01
			(0.01)	(0.01)	(0.01)	(0.01)	(0.01)	(0.01)	(0.01)	(0.01)	(0.01)	(0.01)
Vote Share			-0.01	-0.01	0.01	0.01	-0.01	-0.01	0.01	0.01	0.01	0.01
			(0.01)	(0.01)	(0.01)	(0.01)	(0.01)	(0.01)	(0.01)	(0.01)	(0.01)	(0.01)
Vote Share^2			0.01	0.01	0.01	0.01	-0.01	-0.01	0.01	-0.01	-0.01	-0.01
			(0.01)	(0.01)	(0.01)	(0.01)	(0.01)	(0.01)	(0.01)	(0.01)	(0.01)	(0.01)
Constant	0.19**	0.21**	0.33*	0.35*	0.27	0.20	0.14	0.24	0.17**	0.19**	0.15*	0.15*
	(0.01)	(0.01)	(0.16)	(0.17)	(0.15)	(0.14)	(0.14)	(0.15)	(0.06)	(0.06)	(0.06)	(0.06)
N	85,144	85,144	7,346	7,346	7,326	7,326	18,209	18,209	36,815	36,815	48,101	48,101
R^2	0.09	0.09	0.03	0.02	0.02	0.01	0.13	0.10	0.01	0.01	0.11	0.11

Note: Models are linear probability models with bill-level random effects. The unit is the legislative section and the dependent variable is 1 if a section in an introduced bill is enacted in the same congressional term and 0 otherwise. Models include congressional dummies (unreported).

*p < 0.05, **p < 0.01.

TABLE 6.13. Robustness Checks for If Partisan Intensity Is Associated with Section Passage Rates (Gelman & Wilson Approach)

	No Mediators		Freshmen		Sophomores		Committee Chairs		Minority Party		Majority Party	
	(1) Ratio	(2) Count	(3) Ratio	(4) Count	(5) Ratio	(6) Count	(7) Ratio	(8) Count	(9) Ratio	(10) Count	(11) Ratio	(12) Count
Partisan Intensity	0.01	−0.01	0.04	0.01	0.07	0.00	0.06	−0.01	−0.03	−0.01	0.05*	−0.01
	(0.01)	(0.01)	(0.05)	(0.01)	(0.05)	(0.01)	(0.05)	(0.01)	(0.02)	(0.01)	(0.02)	(0.01)
Ideological Extremity	−0.14**	−0.13**	−0.09*	−0.09*	−0.15**	−0.13**	−0.22**	−0.20**	−0.09**	−0.09**	−0.16**	−0.14**
	(0.01)	(0.01)	(0.04)	(0.04)	(0.04)	(0.04)	(0.08)	(0.07)	(0.02)	(0.02)	(0.02)	(0.02)
Majority Party	−0.03**	−0.03**	−0.04	−0.04	−0.02	−0.02	0.31**				0.19**	
	(0.01)	(0.01)	(0.02)	(0.02)	(0.02)	(0.02)	(0.05)				(0.01)	
Terms Served	0.01	0.01					−0.01	−0.01	−0.01	−0.01	−0.01	−0.01
	(0.01)	(0.01)					(0.01)	(0.01)	(0.01)	(0.01)	(0.01)	(0.01)
Republican	0.02**	0.02**	0.01	0.01	0.03*	0.03	−0.01	−0.03	0.03**	0.03**	−0.01	−0.02
	(0.00)	(0.00)	(0.01)	(0.01)	(0.01)	(0.01)	(0.03)	(0.03)	(0.01)	(0.01)	(0.01)	(0.01)
Senate	0.03**	0.03**	0.00	0.00	0.03	0.03	0.00	0.01	0.03**	0.03**	0.04**	0.04**
	(0.01)	(0.01)	(0.01)	(0.01)	(0.01)	(0.01)	(0.02)	(0.02)	(0.01)	(0.01)	(0.01)	(0.01)
Section Length	−0.01**	−0.01**	−0.01**	−0.01**	−0.01**	−0.01**	−0.02**	−0.02**	−0.01**	−0.01**	−0.01**	−0.01**
	(0.01)	(0.01)	(0.01)	(0.01)	(0.01)	(0.01)	(0.01)	(0.01)	(0.01)	(0.01)	(0.01)	(0.01)
Seat Safety	−0.01**	−0.01**	−0.01**	−0.01**	0.01	0.01	−0.01*	−0.01	0.01	0.01	−0.01*	−0.01*
	(0.01)	(0.01)	(0.01)	(0.01)	(0.01)	(0.01)	(0.01)	(0.01)	(0.01)	(0.01)	(0.01)	(0.01)
Party Leader					−0.01	−0.01			−0.01	−0.01	0.12**	0.13**
					(0.07)	(0.07)			(0.02)	(0.02)	(0.02)	(0.02)
Committee Leader					−0.08	−0.06			0.01	0.01	0.04**	0.05**
					(0.11)	(0.11)			(0.01)	(0.01)	(0.01)	(0.01)
Subcom. Chair			0.02	0.02	−0.04*	−0.04*	−0.02	−0.02			−0.00	−0.00
			(0.01)	(0.01)	(0.02)	(0.02)	(0.02)	(0.02)			(0.01)	(0.01)
Constant	0.20**	0.21**	0.20**	0.19**	0.21**	0.21**	0.31**	0.40**	0.16**	0.18**	0.19**	0.21**
	(0.01)	(0.01)	(0.04)	(0.05)	(0.02)	(0.02)	(0.05)	(0.06)	(0.02)	(0.02)	(0.02)	(0.02)
N	85,610	85,610	7,715	7,715	7,378	7,378	18,224	18,224	37,061	37,061	48,549	48,549
R^2	0.09	0.08	0.02	0.02	0.01	0.01	0.10	0.08	0.01	0.01	0.11	0.10

Note: Models are linear probability models with bill-level random effects. The unit is the legislative section and the dependent variable is 1 if a section in an introduced bill is enacted in the same congressional term and 0 otherwise. Models include congressional dummies (unreported).

*$p < 0.05$, **$p < 0.01$.

Decision Tree Information

We use data coded and collected by Gelman (2024), where he tracks whether an introduced legislative section is enacted in a congressional term. This approach allows us to determine whether a policy idea, conceptualized as a section, becomes law even if the original bill it is proposed in is not enacted. This reflects that, as Gelman (2024, 776) notes, the long-standing approach of treating discrete bills as policy ideas is flawed. Bills are best conceived as "fungible amalgamations of numerous policy ideas that are combined, broken up, and reassembled into politically palatable combinations that can be enacted. Usually, this restructuring occurs at the section level, meaning they can be used as a more consistent conceptualization of a policy idea."

He uses a decision tree classification model to match bill sections. Although we use the same training data and classifier that he explains in his article, we briefly outline how this process is implemented. First, Gelman and a research assistant coded 5,000 section pairs to determine whether policy ideas were the same or not. The goal of hand coding the training set was to determine if two sections contained the same policy idea. Except when the text is identical, evaluating this requires some judgment. That being the case, he developed the following coding rules. First, sections were matched as containing the same policy proposal if (1) both proposed making the same policy change and (2) any differences did not change the main policy goal being proposed. For example, a section might contain 80 percent of the same language with the remaining 20 percent difference arising because section A did not include an effective date clause while section B did. In this situation, the policy idea is the same so sections A and B are matched. Differences that did not prevent two sections from being matched as containing the same idea included the following:

1. Minor differences in the text, such as different effective dates or "authorization of appropriations" clauses (see below for an exception). Other instances include reporting requirements, different dates for when a program must begin or end, its duration, or additional requirements to be added in a report (or considerations in producing a report on the same topic)
2. Different agencies or bureaucrats being instructed to implement the program, for example, if section A requires the secretary of defense to create a program but section B requires the secretary of the army to do so.
3. Minor differences in program requirements (e.g., section A has four requirements, and section B has six).

However, some differences in language prevented sections from being matched as containing the same policy ideas. These included the following:

1. Similar language but change different parts of the US Code or accomplish something different. For instance, language that allows for oil drilling in Alaska in section A and oil drilling in the Gulf Coast in section B or requiring a bureaucrat to establish different programs but using similar language.
2. Embedded sections where section A is fully included in section B, which also includes another policy provision.
3. The only policy in the section is authorizing appropriations or specifying a certain percentage of something. Examples include a section that *only* authorizes funds for the armed services but includes different dollar amounts for the army, navy, and air force or a proposed tax rate, one at 15 percent and another at 25 percent.[12]

Using this initial hand-coded sample, Gelman (2024, 777) created a number of similarity statistics that compared shared language in each section. These similarity statistics are as follows:

- Shared 5-grams: The proportion of n-grams that are shared in section A and section B.
- Shared 2-grams in Section Heading: The proportion of n-grams that are shared in the first 100 characters of section A and section B.
- Percentage of Longest Block Length: Identifies the longest block of identical text shared between each section and calculates the percentage of the section that block length makes up (e.g., a 90-gram block of common text in a 100-word section equals 0.9).
- Number of Blocks: A count of the shared 5-grams between each section.

Before running the decision tree model, each section was preprocessed by broadly following the steps outlined by Casas, Denny, and Wilkerson (2020). After scraping each bill text, nonpolicy language is removed that relates from each bill including the table of contents, the procedural head and tail, and a common bill introductory phrase ("Be it enacted by the Senate and House of Representatives of the United States of America in Congress assembled"). After splitting the bill into its respective sections, procedural words as defined

TABLE 6.14. Decision Tree Performance Metrics

		Hand-Coded			
		Same Policy	Different	*Accuracy:*	95.0%
Model Prediction	Same Policy	348	16	*Precision:*	98.3%
	Different	15	865	*Recall:*	98.2%

by Casas, Denny, and Wilkerson (2020) are removed, as are common stop words. Dollar amounts and percentages are retained.

Finally, boilerplate sections that do not create or change a policy, such as sections that specify the policy's effective date, authorize appropriations, define terms, or present Congress's findings, are removed from the dataset. To do so, Gelman created a list of the first 100 characters from each section, which includes the section title, and coded whether it is a boilerplate section that includes common supplemental information that is not directly changing policy.

Matching Sections Using a Decision Tree

These statistics constitute the variables used in a classification decision tree that predicts whether two sections contain the same policy idea. To make these predictions, the decision tree splits each feature (i.e., similarity statistic) by minimizing its Gini index and classifies two sections as containing the same policy idea based on the predictions generated by how a pairwise comparison of sections moves down the tree. The decision tree is useful as a computationally cheap algorithm but can be prone to overfitting or misclassifying data based on specific quirks to the training set. That being the case, the tree's maximum depth and minimum sample for each leaf were set at 5.[13]

To test the decision tree's effectiveness, Gelman randomly selected 25 percent of the hand-coded data and used them as an out-of-sample test. He then trained the algorithm on the other 75 percent of the section comparisons in order to classify them as containing the same policy idea or not, utilizing the decision tree classifier. It performs well, accurately classifying 95 percent of the out-of-sample test tweets, with 98.3 percent precision and 98.2 percent recall.

SEVEN

A Very Affordable Consequence

Estimating Partisanship's Electoral Penalty

To this point, we have shown that members calibrate their partisan intensities to both win reelection and become more politically influential. Their seat safety, concerns over their party's collective brand, and personal ambitions all combine to produce their partisan style. When evaluated with other research, these findings create a contradiction. Political scientists have found that most voters do not reward incumbents, but rather punish them on Election Day, for excessive partisanship (Harbridge and Malhotra 2011; Carson et al. 2010; Koger and Lebo 2017).

In this chapter, we resolve this paradox—that legislators use partisanship to help them win reelection and gain influence but are also electorally punished for it. To do so, we replicate the empirical models that find the electoral penalty. Our results echo and add nuance to these original findings. Yes, incumbents are penalized by voters for their partisanship. However, the decrease in vote share is one that almost all members are comfortable incurring. In most cases, they are free to increase their partisan intensity without fearing they will lose their seat.

Moreover, voters are responding not only to legislators' partisan intensity but also to their tone. As we hypothesized in chapter 2, we find that voters pay attention to tonal differences, but the consequences depend on the type of district the incumbent represents. Voters in safer districts reward more negative partisan rhetoric. In fact, the electoral benefits to negative partisan rhetoric mean that small shifts in how legislators talk allow them to recoup any electoral penalty they incur for their excessive partisanship. Only lawmakers holding the most marginal seats are not rewarded for adopting a caustic partisan tone. In those cases, their tenor does not matter. Notably, cheerleading one's own party is never as politically profitable as bickering with the opposition.

Finally, we move beyond general election consequences and evaluate whether incumbents need to fear attracting a primary challenger for not being partisan enough. We find no evidence that lower partisan intensities attract primary challenges. Rather, our results support other researchers' results that ideological moderates and those in safer districts are more likely to be primaried.

Like we did in chapter 6, we present some normatively challenging conclusions. Most legislators have a relatively free hand to be as partisan as they want. The Election Day penalty they incur is not enough to shift their behavior. Even if they are worried that their partisanship may lose them vote share, they can change how they talk about the parties to offset those losses. Perhaps more troublingly is that negative partisan rhetoric, not a more positive tone or lower levels of partisan intensity, is consistently rewarded. In fact, for nearly every member, disparaging the other party instead of supporting their own side is associated with a higher vote share. Given these results, it is unsurprising that incumbents are not being primaried for lacking party fidelity. In most circumstances, they do not need to balance being a good team player with appealing to general election voters. Instead, they can act in the partisan ways that appeal to primary voters—frequently bickering with the other side—without concern for any substantial Election Day consequences.

Do Partisans Pay a Price on Election Day?

If legislators worry about being reelected, then voters' distaste for partisanship may dampen their partisan intensity. Some evidence suggests this might occur. In a series of analyses, Koger, Lebo, and colleagues argue that members pay a price for their party loyalty. They show that in experiments respondents react negatively toward partisan voting records, not ideologically extreme ones (Carson et al. 2010; Koger and Lebo 2017). Their observational research finds that lawmakers who vote more often with their party receive less support on Election Day. Other survey experiments present a less definitive picture. Harbridge and Malhotra (2011) show that only voters with weak partisan attachments and independents punish partisan behavior, while Flynn and Harbridge (2016) argue that public opinion varies based on the legislative outcome.

Our argument from chapter 2 is that although members may pay a price for partisanship, it is one that most of them can afford. Most legislators come from safe enough districts that allow them to raise their partisan intensity without fear of losing reelection. This follows Fiorina's (1974) argument that members do not try to maximize their vote share. Rather, they are "maintainers" who build enough support to preserve a healthy winning margin, which allows them to pursue other goals. This point is important. Legislators balance their goals, and for most of them, being a good team player, which allows them to become more politically powerful, is worth the cost at the ballot box. Without the opportunity to advance their careers, ambitious members in relatively safe seats face years of puttering around Capitol Hill not being able to fulfill their professional aspirations.

We assess whether members are punished for their partisanship by replicating two influential models that predict incumbent vote share. The first is Canes-Wrone, Brady, and Cogan's (2002) empirical design that tests whether members with more ideologically extreme voting records are punished by voters. We modify their test by adding our measures of partisan intensity to examine if lawmakers are also being punished for their team play.

The second model is Koger and Lebo's (2017). Their version, which uses party unity scores to test if voters punish partisanship, also modifies the Canes-Wrone et al. approach. In Koger and Lebo's view, partisan behavior and electoral success are endogenous, meaning that a member's partisanship influences and is influenced by their vote margin. Additionally, they argue that a lawmaker's ideology does not directly affect their electoral fortunes but instead only affects it through a member's partisanship. Put differently, ideology affects a legislator's willingness to be a good team player, which affects their vote share.

This more complicated model uses a two-stage estimation approach. In the first stage, partisanship is predicted by a member's ideology, their lagged partisanship, their lagged vote share, and the other independent variables included in the Canes-Wrone et al. model. The second stage replicates the Canes-Wrone et al. model plus the predicted partisanship values from the first-stage equation.[1] Our analysis modifies these models in two ways. First, since our data only covers six years, we include Congress fixed effects instead of the variables that vary by congressional term.[2] Second, we include our measures of partisan intensity to evaluate whether legislators are punished for their partisanship. In the Canes-Wrone et al. replication, this means we simply add that term to the regression. In the Koger and Lebo model, we replace party unity scores with our measure.

We recognize that this decision to replace a vote-based measure with a social media–based one is controversial. After all, the premise of both of these studies is that lawmakers are punished for their extreme roll call voting behavior. Yet, as we discuss in chapters 3 and 6, vote-based measures miss a great deal of what goes on in Congress, and party unity scores are an amalgamation of various factors, only two of which are partisanship and ideology. Moreover, as we show below, partisan tone plays an equally important role in how voters evaluate legislators. Our measure captures voter reactions to partisan behavior writ large, not just how often they vote with their party.[3]

To replicate the Canes-Wrone et al. model, we include the following variables. The dependent variable for these analyses is the *Incumbent's Vote Share*.[4] Our main independent variables are our measures of partisan intensity. We also include how they measure a member's *Ideological Extremity* (the absolute value of their DW-NOMINATE score), their *Seat Safety* (average vote share of the incumbent's party from the past two presidential elections), dummy variables for whether they are in the *President's Party*, faced a *Quality Challenger* who previously held elected office, and were a *Freshman* serving their first term in Congress. We also calculated the *Spending Difference* between the incumbent and the challenger by subtracting the natural log of their campaign disbursements. Finally, we include Congress fixed effects and a dummy variable for whether the incumbent served in the Senate.[5]

The second stage of the Koger and Lebo model is identical with two exceptions. First, they remove *Ideological Extremity* from this equation and insert the incumbent's vote share from the previous election. Second, they include a first-stage equation that instruments for partisanship. This additional step includes the *Ideological Extremity* covariate, all of the variables in the second-stage equation, and their lagged partisan intensity.[6] In both models, we expect that the partisan intensity variable will be negative. This would indicate that as members become more partisan, their vote share decreases.

We present the results from four models in table 7.1. Models 1 and 3 include the proportion-based partisan intensity measure, while models 2 and 4 use the natural log of the number of partisan tweets sent by a member. The results present a mixed picture of whether legislators are punished for their partisan behavior. Our argument that most members do not need to worry about the consequences of their partisan behavior on Election Day is supported by the null results in models 1 and 2. However, the premise of models 3 and 4 is that once the endogenous relationships between vote share, partisanship, and ideology are properly accounted for, then we should find that legislators are punished for their partisanship. The negative coefficients on our partisan intensity variables suggest that an electoral penalty exists.[7]

TABLE 7.1. The Electoral Costs of Partisanship

	Canes-Wrone et al. Model		Koger and Lebo Model	
	(1) Ratio	(2) Count	(3) Ratio	(4) Count
Partisan Intensity	1.83	0.16	−13.90**	−2.30**
	(1.29)	(0.16)	(2.79)	(0.47)
Ideological Extremity	−7.33**	−7.07**		
	(1.26)	(1.23)		
Seat Safety	0.74**	0.74**	0.69**	0.68**
	(0.03)	(0.03)	(0.06)	(0.05)
President's Party	−1.48**	−1.49**	−3.50**	−4.49**
	(0.30)	(0.30)	(0.57)	(0.70)
Quality Challenger	−0.88*	−0.93*	−1.41*	−0.75
	(0.41)	(0.41)	(0.58)	(0.61)
Freshman	−0.02	−0.13	0.21	0.71
	(0.38)	(0.38)	(0.80)	(0.88)
Spending Difference	1.50**	1.50**	1.60**	1.60**
	(0.14)	(0.14)	(0.19)	(0.19)
	(0.32)	(0.33)	(0.41)	(0.45)
Senate	−0.86	−0.94	1.12*	2.46**
	(0.54)	(0.57)	(0.56)	(0.74)
Lagged Vote Share			0.11**	0.12**
			(0.04)	(0.04)
Constant	54.39**	53.87**	50.21**	59.86**
	(0.58)	(0.99)	(2.32)	(3.67)
N	1,137	1,137	639	639
R^2	0.744	0.744	0.735	0.720

Note: The dependent variable in all four models is incumbent vote share. Models 1 and 2 are OLS regressions estimated with robust standard errors clustered by members and congressional term fixed effects. Models 3 and 4 are estimated using 2SLS, with Partisan Intensity as the endogenous regressor and Ideological Extremity only included in the first-stage model.

Substantively, however, excessive partisanship is only a concern for a very small group of members, specifically those from marginal districts whose partisan intensity rates as some of the highest in Congress. Take, for example, a member serving in the least safe seat in our data. If they raise their partisan intensity from the 25th percentile of legislators (a score of 0.17) to the 75th percentile (a score 0.36), they will lose a predicted 3 percent of their vote share. Of course, that loss of support probably means they will lose their seat. Yet that only occurs if they more than double their partisan intensity.

More importantly for our argument, most legislators do not run in such dire electoral circumstances. The penalty they incur can be overcome by their already comfortable expected vote share. To better see why this is the case, we plot the electoral loss that members suffer as their partisan intensity increases from the lowest observed value in our data (0.02) to the highest (0.82). In figure 7.1, we include the predicted vote shares from members whose seat safety is in the 1st, 25th, 50th, 75th, and 99th percentiles.

Besides those members in the most vulnerable districts, the electoral penalty from high, even extreme, partisan intensities can reasonably be absorbed by members. The 9 percent drop in vote share from the minimum to the maximum observed values (which never occurs in the data) means that the vote share of a lawmaker in the 25th percentile of seat safety decreases from 63 to 52 percent. In other words, even if they choose to act as the most partisan member of Congress, they would find themselves in a tough race in which they would be favored to win.

Put differently, we find evidence similar to Koger and Lebo that members incur an electoral penalty for being too partisan. Yet, substantively, most can absorb the loss. This nuance helps explain how legislators' partisan behavior affects their home styles and hill styles. Most have the latitude to adopt more partisan personas in an effort to accrue more political influence, even if doing so affects their vote share. As electoral maintainers, not maximizers, they are willing to make this trade as they try to advance their careers in Washington, DC.[8]

Are Legislators Rewarded or Punished for Their Partisan Tones?

Although lawmakers may pay an electoral price for their partisanship, the previous analyses do not speak to how voters may punish or reward different partisan styles. As we show in chapter 4, lawmakers differ not just in how often they act in a partisan way but also in whether they adopt negative or positive tones when they do so.

We argue that voters reward or punish incumbents' partisan tones, but this reaction depends on members' seat safety. In most districts, whose party lean is at least five percentage points toward the incumbent's party, same-party lawmakers are rewarded for emphasizing attacks on the opposition and punished when they focus on cheerleading their own party. This dynamic stems from partisan bickering activating voters' negative partisanship, which increases party loyalty on Election Day. Importantly, this reaction is not limited to strongly partisan voters. Even voters with weak party attachments are motivated by their dislike for the other party (Abramowitz and Webster 2018).

In the most marginal districts, which include more opposition party voters, this reward for negativity disappears. Since bickering with the other party will backfire by activating opposition voters' ire, the best a legislator can do

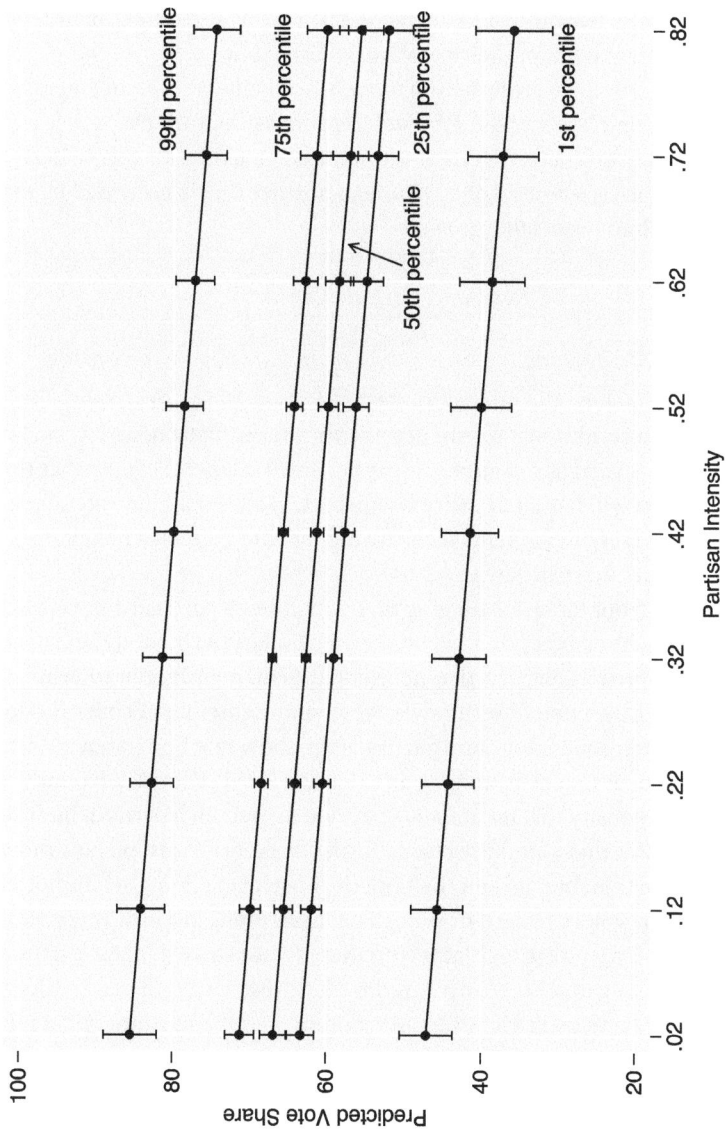

Fig. 7.1. The Effect of Excessive Partisanship on Predicted Vote Share

Note: Predicted values are based on model 3 in table 7.1. All control variables are held at their mean or, for dichotomous ones, at zero.

is to try to sell their party's accomplishments. Doing so may help burnish the party's collective reputation in a hostile district while still allowing the member to portray themselves as a good team player to their copartisans in Congress. As such, we hypothesize (see table 2.5) that as seat safety increases, lawmakers are rewarded for their negative partisan tones.

To test this claim, we replicate the models from table 7.1 but include two new variables. First, we use the *Partisan Tone* measure from chapter 4. It is measured as the summed sentiment of members' partisan tweets, where a negative tweet is −1, a neutral one is 0, and a positive one is 1, divided by the number of partisan tweets they posted:

$$\left(\frac{\Sigma \, Partisan \; Tweets \; Sentiment}{\# \; of Partisan \; Tweets} \right)$$

Second, we include the interaction term *Partisan Tone × Seat Safety*. This accounts for the conditional nature of our hypothesis, that a negative tone is increasingly rewarded as a member's seat becomes safer. We expect that the interaction term will have a negative coefficient.[9] This would indicate that as seat safety increases, incumbents receive a higher vote share when their partisan tone becomes more negative.

The results from table 7.2 suggest that a member's partisan tone affects their vote share, but it is conditional on their seat safety. As before, the Canes-Wrone et al. approach suggests that neither partisan intensity nor tone affect vote share. The Koger and Lebo models, which more carefully account for the relationship between ideology and partisanship, show that both intensity and tone affect an incumbent's vote share and that the tonal effect is independent of the electoral penalty that incumbents pay due to their high partisan intensities. This indicates that voters are evaluating lawmakers not just on how often they act as a partisan but also on the tone they use when doing so. To better understand how voters reward or punish partisan tone, and how it depends on district type, we plot a legislator's predicted vote share as their partisan tone goes from negative to positive in the safest district (99th percentile in seat safety), an average district (50th percentile), and the most marginal one (1st percentile).

For incumbents representing the safest seats, adopting an overly negative partisan tone is associated with a predicted 24-point higher vote share than if they mostly focused on cheerleading. In an average district, the effect is smaller—14 points—but still substantial. Of course, no member shifts their rhetoric in such an extreme way. The average within-member change in par-

TABLE 7.2. The Electoral Consequences of Partisan Tone

	Canes-Wrone et al. Model		Koger and Lebo Model	
	(1) Ratio	(2) Count	(3) Ratio	(4) Count
Partisan Intensity	0.86	0.05	−17.14**	−1.07**
	(1.39)	(0.16)	(3.24)	(0.32)
Partisan Tone	−1.55	−1.66	−6.51**	−2.44
	(1.26)	(1.22)	(2.04)	(1.77)
Seat Safety	0.69**	0.69**	0.59**	0.55**
	(0.04)	(0.04)	(0.07)	(0.06)
Partisan Tone × Seat Safety	−0.10	−0.10	−0.22**	−0.19*
	(0.06)	(0.06)	(0.08)	(0.07)
Ideological Extremity	−6.97**	−6.82**		
	(1.26)	(1.22)		
President's Party	−1.13**	−1.13**	−1.86**	−2.45**
	(0.32)	(0.32)	(0.61)	(0.58)
Quality Challenger	−0.90*	−0.92*	−1.38*	−0.82
	(0.41)	(0.41)	(0.59)	(0.55)
Freshman	−0.01	−0.06	−0.11	0.18
	(0.38)	(0.39)	(0.77)	(0.64)
Spending Difference	1.50**	1.50**	1.63**	1.58**
	(0.14)	(0.14)	(0.19)	(0.18)
Senate	−0.82	−0.84	1.30*	1.32*
	(0.55)	(0.57)	(0.60)	(0.61)
Vote Share$_{t-1}$			0.11**	0.13**
			(0.04)	(0.04)
Constant	54.66**	54.52**	50.52**	52.03**
	(0.61)	(1.01)	(2.30)	(2.31)
N	1,137	1,137	639	639
R^2	0.746	0.746	0.734	0.763

Note: The dependent variable in all four models is incumbent vote share. Models 1 and 2 are OLS regressions estimated with robust standard errors clustered by members and congressional term fixed effects. Models 3 and 4 are estimated using 2SLS, with Partisan Intensity as the endogenous regressor and Ideological Extremity only included in the first-stage model.

tisan tone between Congresses is 0.24, which results in a predicted 2 percent change in vote share.

Only in the least safe districts are members not rewarded or punished for their partisan tones. The difference between the most negatively toned rhetoric to the most positive is only three points of vote share, and that shift is not statistically significant. In these situations, any partisan talk is problematic, positive or negative, as it reminds opposition voters that they are not being represented by one of their own. These results present a harsh truth about how voters perceive partisanship. For most members, attacking the opposition is politically profitable while cheerleading your own party is not.

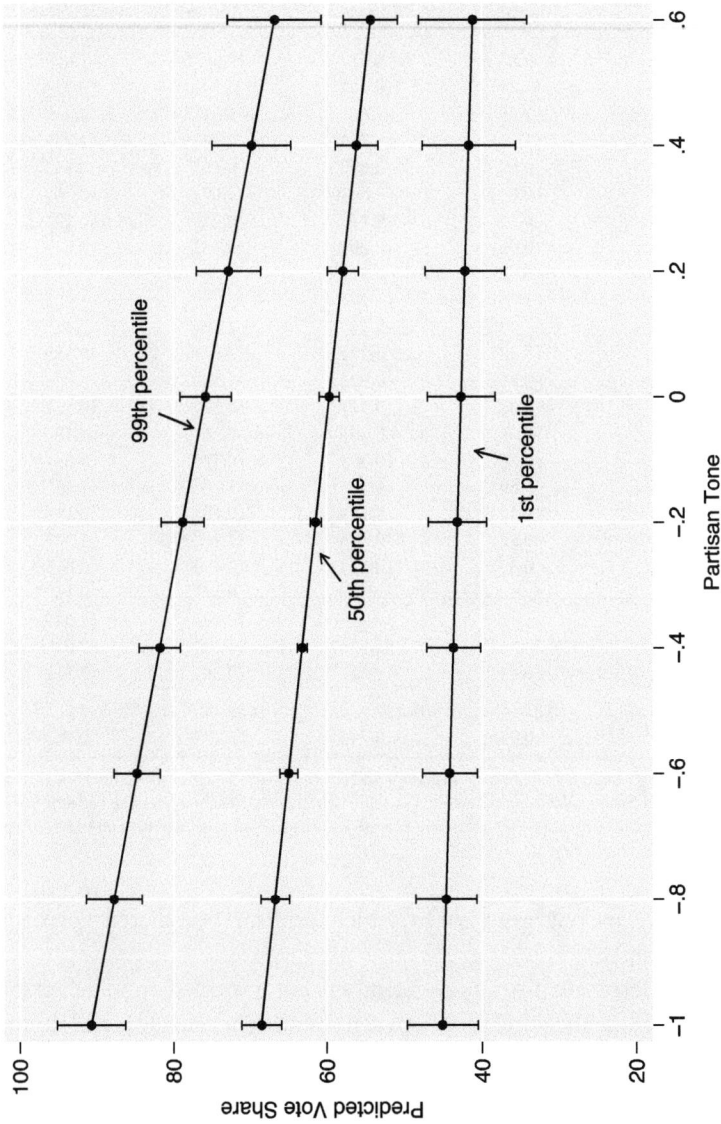

Fig. 7.2. The Effect of Partisan Tone on Predicted Vote Share

Note: Predicted values are based on model 3 in table 7.2. All control variables are held at their mean or, for dichotomous ones, at zero.

Together, these previous analyses show how legislators can strategically use partisan rhetoric to achieve their goals without paying dearly at the ballot box. When they raise their partisan intensity to gain more political influence, they risk an electoral penalty from voters back home. However, they can mitigate these consequences by having built a large enough cushion on Election Day and by making their partisan rhetoric more negative.

This helps resolve what seemed like a contradiction between our theory and the previous research on partisanship. How could this behavior be used to achieve a member's reelection goal, as we argue, if they were penalized for it at the ballot box? The answer is twofold. First, as we show in chapter 5, seat safety and partisan intensity are strongly associated, suggesting that members respond to voter demand for this behavior. Second, even if an electoral penalty exists, lawmakers can compensate by changing the tenor of their rhetoric. For those concerned that their voters will punish them for this behavior, they can simply shift to attacking the other party more frequently. For instance, we estimate that a 10 percent increase in partisan intensity is associated with a 2 percent decrease in predicted vote share. A legislator can maintain that higher partisan intensity and recover those votes by making their partisan tone 12 percent more negative. That change in rhetoric increases vote share by the same 2 percent. Put simply, electoral concerns encourage legislators not to necessarily decrease their partisanship but instead to spend their time bickering with the other party.

Do Weak Partisans Get Primaried?

To date, the link between partisanship and electoral outcomes has focused on general elections. Yet, just as excessive partisan intensity produces a penalty on Election Day, it is possible that not supporting their party enough can generate discontent among party members back home. The threat, then, is that incumbents will attract primary challengers who claim they will be more reliable partisans. Research on political primaries generally does not consider the consequences of legislators' partisanship. Instead, it almost exclusively focuses on ideological challengers trying to unseat incumbents with more liberal or conservative platforms (Boatright 2004; Jewitt and Treul 2019). Yet, as Boatright (2013) shows, most primary challenges are not ideological in nature, and the ones that he does code this way are described as the incumbent being "too moderate or insufficiently partisan" (67). It is possible that one overlooked explanation for why primary challengers join the fray is for partisan, not ideological, reasons.

Indeed, weak partisans might attract primary opponents due to how the parties and politics have changed over the past few decades. Most studies of primaries run through the mid-2010s or earlier. Yet during the time period we study, politics became even more nationalized and party loyalty, particularly during the Trump presidency, took on increasing significance. Republican politicians spoke a great deal about supporting the president while Democrats framed their work in opposition to him. It is possible that partisan, not ideological, primaries became the norm during this time.

Yet, as we discuss in chapter 2, we are skeptical that low levels of partisanship attract primary challengers. Our reasoning is simple. Lawmakers adopt strategies that allow them to claim they are a team player to their voters, even if their actual partisan intensity remains low. Take, for instance, one of the most partisan disputes during the six years we analyze: Brett Kavanaugh's Supreme Court nomination. Every senator, with the exceptions of Joe Manchin (D-WV) and Lisa Murkowski (R-AK), supported their party's position on his nomination. However, as Gelman (2020b) shows, they varied in how vocal they were in their support. Strong partisans talked about Kavanaugh nearly every day for three months. Others did their best to avoid the situation entirely, only mentioning him once or twice. In defending their stances, these weak partisans can point to their support and vote, even if they largely avoided the partisan fray.

Even when members cannot point to a specific vote, as long as they show some support for their party's position they can insulate themselves from intraparty criticism. They can put out lightly read statements of support, say they stand with their party, and only address the topic when directly asked. Put differently, they may be a team player, but not a very active or helpful one.

Moreover, not all situations require legislators to affirm that they support their party. Most issues, even those framed by others as partisan, can be explained in nonpartisan terms (Grose, Malhotra, and Van Houweling 2015). For those unique situations that require members to back the party line, we do not expect to see much deviation that would prompt primary challenges. Party leaders may apply pressure that get their copartisans in line, or lawmakers may understand that the situation requires a unified partisan front to support the collective brand. Those who break from the party in these situations are usually doing so to build a personal reputation that relies on a perception that they are not a typical Democrat or Republican. Their calculation is that being a bad team player is electorally valuable, not a liability.

To evaluate whether weak partisans are more likely to attract primary challengers, we collected data on whether incumbents faced a primary opponent

TABLE 7.3. Determinants of Being Primaried, 2015–20

	Any Primary Challenger		Quality Primary Challenger	
	(1) Ratio	(2) Count	(3) Ratio	(4) Count
Partisan Intensity	0.03	0.03*	−0.04	−0.01
	(0.11)	(0.01)	(0.06)	(0.01)
Ideological Extremity	−0.26**	−0.28**	−0.02	−0.03
	(0.06)	(0.06)	(0.03)	(0.03)
Seat Safety	0.01**	0.01**	0.01*	0.01*
	(0.01)	(0.01)	(0.01)	(0.01)
Terms Served	0.01**	0.01**	−0.01	−0.01
	(0.01)	(0.01)	(0.01)	(0.01)
Age	0.01	0.01	−0.01	−0.01
	(0.01)	(0.01)	(0.01)	(0.01)
Senate	0.15**	0.11	0.05	0.05
	(0.05)	(0.06)	(0.03)	(0.03)
Constant	−1.46	−0.91	2.51	2.49
	(3.05)	(3.05)	(1.65)	(1.66)
N	1,218	1,218	1,218	1,218
R^2	0.062	0.067	0.020	0.020

Note: Models are OLS regressions with state and Congress fixed effects. Models 1 and 3 use the ratio-based partisan intensity measure. Models 2 and 4 use the ln(# partisan tweets) one.

*$p < 0.05$, **$p < 0.01$.

in the three election cycles included in our data (2016–20). Of those members seeking reelection, 46 percent faced at least one challenger. Of course, many primary candidates are amateurs whom legislators, and voters, may not take seriously. Serious challengers, defined as those who have held previous elected office, present a more serious electoral threat, fare much better in these elections, but rarely run (Boatright 2013). We identified 91 primary challengers (7 percent) who held previous office. Based on this data, we created dichotomous measures for whether an incumbent faced any primary challenger or a quality one. These are our dependent variables.

Our main independent variables are our measures of partisan intensity. If being a weak partisan is associated with attracting primary challengers, then they should have negative coefficients. However, we expect these variables will return null results. We also include four variables that Boatright (2013) identifies as being associated with attracting primary opponents. We control for member's *Ideological Extremity* by calculating the absolute distance of their DW-NOMINATE score from the median member from that Congress. If more extreme challengers are primarying more moderate incumbents, then this variable should be negative. Primary challenges are more common in safe dis-

tricts, so we include the same measure of *Seat Safety* we used in tables 7.1 and
7.2. We expect this variable to be positive. Boatright also finds that primary
opponents are motivated to run against longer-serving and older members. As
such, we include the number of congressional terms an incumbent has been in
office (*Terms Served*) and their *Age*. Finally, we include a *Senate* dummy variable, state fixed effects to control for different types of primaries and barriers
to running for office, and Congress fixed effects.

The results in table 7.3 indicate that a member's partisanship, or lack
thereof, is not associated with attracting primary challengers. The partisan
intensity variable is only statistically significant in model 2, but it is in the
wrong direction. Rather, the results seem to confirm Boatright's analysis of
what motivates primary challenges. Ideological moderates are more likely to
attract a primary opponent, as are those in safer seats and those who have
served longer in Congress. We do not find evidence that older lawmakers are
primaried more often. Additionally, like Boatright argues, what motivates
quality primary challengers is more idiosyncratic. None of our variables,
including the partisan intensity or ideology ones, are associated with quality
opponents entering a primary race.

Although the statistical models in table 7.3 are simple, the results are robust
to more complex approaches. We lagged our measures of partisan intensity
and ideological extremity, included lagged vote share, and estimated a two-
step Heckman probit model where the first stage accounted for the probability
a legislator chose to run for reelection. All of these models, which are included
in the chapter's appendix, produced the same result: Partisan intensity is not
associated with a primary challenge.[10]

While our first set of results, for whether incumbents are punished for too
much partisanship, present a more complex picture, these do not. Members
with low levels of partisan intensity do not attract primary challengers, even
less serious amateurs who may be just looking to make a point. Even as lawmakers, especially Republicans, worried about looking like they were in lockstep with their party during these six years, their partisan behavior was not
associated with primary challenges.

Conclusion

In this chapter, we assess whether members' partisanship has any electoral
consequences. Our results largely support our hypotheses and, for those
worried about a hyper-partisan Congress, paint a bleak picture of how vot-

ers evaluate this behavior. Following Koger and Lebo (2017), we considered whether excessive partisanship leads to an electoral penalty at the ballot box. We find mixed evidence for it, and even if incumbents are penalized, for most members the penalty is manageable. As electoral maintainers who have built comfortable Election Day margins, they can increase their partisan intensity without worry.

However, too much partisanship from those in marginal seats can end up hurting their team. A hallmark of the modern Congress is its narrow, insecure majorities. Even if 90 percent of a majority party caucus does not need to worry about acting too partisan, the other 10 percent being ousted for such behavior can swing control of a chamber to the opposition. Take, for instance, the House Democratic Caucus in 2020. Sixteen of its members won by a margin that, if they had increased their partisan intensity by one standard deviation, would have won a predicted vote share below 50 percent. Those narrow electoral wins allowed Democrats to remain in the majority, even as they lost 13 seats. In an alternative world, where those 16 marginal members acted too partisan, the result would have changed Election Day from Democrats incurring manageable losses to Republicans flipping the chamber and preventing two years of unified government. As such, the more precise description of our results is that the vast majority have a free hand to act as partisan as they want. Those in very competitive seats, however, need to be more careful when building their partisan personas. Carelessness not only can cost them their seat but can cost their party a majority.

More troubling, voters only reward negative partisan rhetoric. Incumbents gain no additional support from adopting more positive tones, and the political rewards from bickering with the opposition compensate for any electoral penalty paid for excessive partisanship. In fact, one way that members in most tough districts can improve their electoral prospects is by adopting a more negative partisan tone. Given these results, perhaps unsurprisingly, lawmakers are not primaried for being weak partisans. Between the overwhelmingly negative partisan rhetoric coming out of Congress and incumbents' high partisan intensities, primary voters are likely quite pleased with their representatives' and senators' performances.

Appendix

(*following page*)

TABLE 7.4. Determinants of Being Primaried, with Lagged Partisan Intensity

	Any Primary Challenge		Quality Primary Challenger	
	(1) Ratio	(2) Count	(3) Ratio	(4) Count
Partisan Intensity	−0.22	0.04	−0.15	−0.02*
	(0.19)	(0.02)	(0.08)	(0.01)
Partisan Intensity$_{t-1}$	0.24	−0.01	0.07	0.02
	(0.20)	(0.02)	(0.09)	(0.01)
Ideological Extremity	−0.19*	−0.28**	−0.01	−0.01
	(0.09)	(0.08)	(0.04)	(0.04)
Seat Safety	0.01**	0.01**	0.01	0.01
	(0.01)	(0.01)	(0.01)	(0.01)
Terms Served	0.01	0.01	−0.01	−0.01
	(0.01)	(0.01)	(0.01)	(0.01)
Age	−0.01	−0.01	−0.01	−0.01
	(0.01)	(0.01)	(0.01)	(0.01)
Senate	0.11	0.06	0.09**	0.09**
	(0.07)	(0.07)	(0.03)	(0.03)
Constant	0.81	1.09	2.52	2.49
	(4.32)	(4.32)	(1.93)	(1.93)
N	672	672	672	672
R^2	0.062	0.065	0.029	0.030

Note: Models are OLS regressions with state and Congress fixed effects. Models 1 and 3 use the ratio-based partisan intensity measure. Models 2 and 4 use the ln(# partisan tweets) one.

*$p < 0.05$, **$p < 0.01$.

TABLE 7.5. Determinants of Being Primaried, Robustness Checks

	Any Primary Challenge		Quality Primary Challenger	
	(1) Ratio	(2) Count	(3) Ratio	(4) Count
Partisan Intensity	−0.22	0.04	−0.15	−0.02
	(0.19)	(0.03)	(0.08)	(0.01)
Partisan Intensity$_{t-1}$	0.25	−0.01	0.12	0.02
	(0.21)	(0.02)	(0.09)	(0.01)
Ideological Extremity	−0.18*	−0.26**	0.01	−0.01
	(0.09)	(0.08)	(0.04)	(0.04)
Ideological Extremity$_{t-1}$	0.01	−0.05	−0.07	−0.07
	(0.10)	(0.10)	(0.05)	(0.05)
Vote Share$_{t-1}$	0.01	0.01	−0.01	−0.01
	(0.01)	(0.01)	(0.01)	(0.01)
Seat Safety	0.01**	0.01*	0.01**	0.01*
	(0.01)	(0.01)	(0.01)	(0.01)
Terms Served	0.01	0.01	−0.01	−0.01
	(0.01)	(0.01)	(0.01)	(0.01)
Age	−0.01	−0.01	−0.01	−0.01
	(0.01)	(0.01)	(0.01)	(0.01)
	(0.04)	(0.04)	(0.02)	(0.02)
Senate	0.11	0.06	0.10**	0.10**
	(0.07)	(0.08)	(0.03)	(0.03)
Constant	1.16	1.86	2.97	2.99
	(4.40)	(4.41)	(1.96)	(1.97)
N	669	669	669	669
R^2	0.062	0.066	0.040	0.039

Note: Models are OLS regressions with state and Congress fixed effects. Models 1 and 3 use the ratio-based partisan intensity measure. Models 2 and 4 use the ln(# partisan tweets) one.

*p < 0.05, **p < 0.01.

TABLE 7.6. Determinants of Being Primaried, Two-Stage Model

	Any Primary Challenge		Quality Primary Challenger	
	(1) Ratio	(2) Count	(3) Ratio	(4) Count
Stage 2: Primary Challenge				
Partisan Intensity	−0.10	0.08	−0.53	−0.03
	(0.38)	(0.04)	(0.71)	(0.08)
Ideological Extremity	−0.57**	−0.68**	−0.46	−0.53
	(0.22)	(0.21)	(0.39)	(0.38)
Seat Safety	0.03**	0.02**	0.03*	0.03*
	(0.01)	(0.01)	(0.01)	(0.01)
Terms Served	0.02	0.02	−0.03	−0.03
	(0.02)	(0.02)	(0.03)	(0.03)
Age	−0.01	−0.01	−0.02	−0.02
	(0.01)	(0.01)	(0.01)	(0.01)
Senate	0.33	0.25	0.74**	0.75**
	(0.18)	(0.19)	(0.27)	(0.28)
Constant	8.71	9.13	29.28	29.27
	(11.17)	(11.21)	(20.31)	(20.41)
Stage 1: Run for Reelection				
Terms Served	−0.06**	−0.06**	−0.06**	−0.06**
	(0.02)	(0.02)	(0.02)	(0.02)
Partisan Intensity$_{t-1}$	−0.64	0.07	−0.56	0.06
	(0.49)	(0.05)	(0.49)	(0.05)
Ideological Extremity$_{t-1}$	0.95**	0.78**	1.02**	0.83**
	(0.28)	(0.29)	(0.29)	(0.29)
Vote Share$_{t-1}$	0.01	0.01	0.01	0.01
	(0.01)	(0.01)	(0.01)	(0.01)
Running for Higher Office	−2.49**	−2.54**	−2.48**	−2.53**
	(0.33)	(0.33)	(0.33)	(0.33)
Age	0.01	0.01	0.01	0.01
	(0.01)	(0.01)	(0.01)	(0.01)
Constant	−6.52	−3.72	−6.07	−3.78
	(14.90)	(14.88)	(14.78)	(14.82)
N	757	757	757	757
$Pr > x^2$	0.22	0.24	0.34	0.49

Note: Models are Heckman selection probit models with Congress fixed effects in the first stage. Models 1 and 3 use the ratio-based partisan intensity measure. Models 2 and 4 use the ln(# partisan tweets) one.

*p < 0.05, **p < 0.01.

EIGHT

Conclusion

"Putting party before country."
"Picking a fight to score points."
"Creating gridlock instead of compromising."

These common critiques reflect a core problem people attribute to congressional partisanship: The political theatrics of Congress limit its ability to make good policy. Our evidence suggests that some of these concerns have merit but others are overblown.

As we document, Congress is rife with partisanship. However, it varies dramatically among members, and the consequences from displaying substantial partisan intensity are not what congressional observers and commentators claim. Moreover, being careful about how this concept is measured and defined helps bring into focus different types of conflict that affect Congress and its legislative outcomes in different ways.

Some lawmakers regularly place a partisan frame on how they discuss politics. These include party leaders like Mitch McConnell (R-KY) and Hakeem Jeffries (D-NY), as well as lesser-known legislators. Others see conflict more ideologically by consistently supporting conservative or liberal positions but rarely represent conflict in partisan terms. They are better described as ideologues. As figure 8.1 shows and reinforces from our analysis in chapter 3, these categories are not mutually exclusive and members fall all along both of these partisan and ideological spectrums.

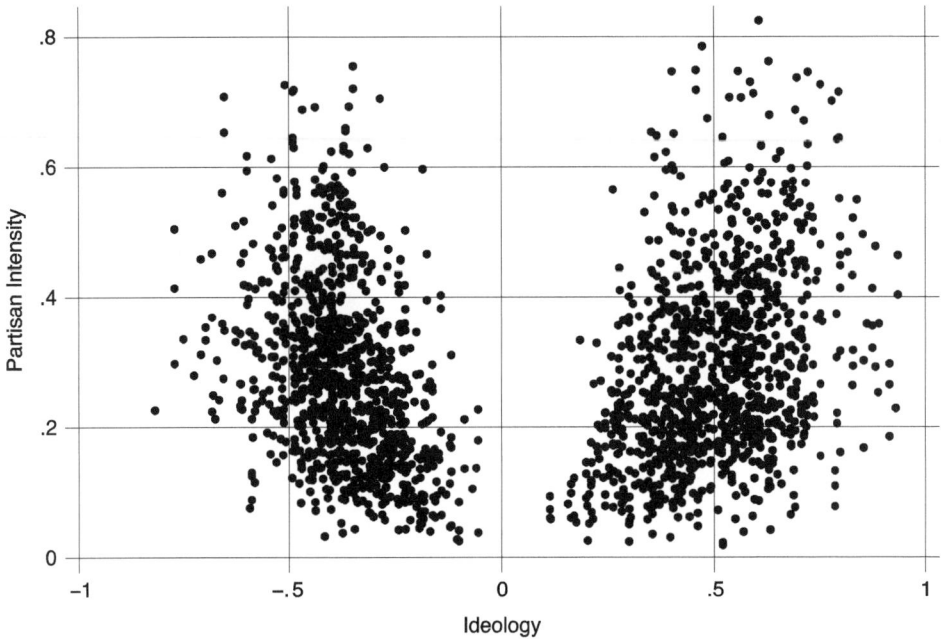

Fig. 8.1. Scatterplot of Partisan Intensity and Ideology Scores, 2015–22
Note: Ideology is measured as first-dimension DW-NOMINATE scores.

Partisanship differs from how political scientists understand ideology in other important ways. Most notably, it is much more malleable and changes with a legislator's political circumstances. This means that reforms that raise or lower the incentives for members to engage in this behavior can meaningfully change the partisan temperature on Capitol Hill. Although it certainly feels like we live in a hyper-partisan time and even though this trend has not changed in recent years, the US Congress is not circumscribed to this sort of politics. It reflects the internal and external political incentives members face. As such, it is worth briefly revisiting why lawmakers choose (or not) to adopt intensely partisan personas and the consequences they face for this behavior. We conclude by documenting that the hyper-partisan atmosphere persisted beyond the first Trump presidency and by proposing reforms that can reduce its prevalence in Congress.

Why Do Lawmakers Adopt Partisan Personas?

One our most striking findings is the wide range of partisan intensities present on Capitol Hill. For some lawmakers, supporting their team consumes their public personas. For others, joining the partisan fray is something they assiduously avoid. Why such stark differences?

We argue and show that partisanship is motivated by both external electoral pressures and internal party politics. One reason lawmakers increase their partisan intensities is to improve their party brand among voters. In an era of nationalized elections with a shrinking incumbency advantage, many voters evaluate members based on their party's performance. As a group, congressional parties are better off on Election Day with strong brands that appeal to voters. Yet, those who build these brands pay a price with some voters who do not like these partisan displays. Like others, we document an Election Day penalty for more partisan members (Carson et al. 2010). As such, strong partisans are more likely to come from safe districts. They can join the partisan fights that tarnish the opposition and burnish their side while easily affording any Election Day penalty.

The second factor that is motivating this behavior is members seeking promotions. Those climbing the party ladder in the House and Senate or running for higher office increase their partisan intensities to display their team play bona fides. Running for higher office or a leadership position, serving as a party leader, and serving as a committee leader in the House are all strongly related to members increasing their partisan intensities. Moreover, once they leave their leadership roles, win higher office, or lose their races, they reduce this type of behavior.

Other factors play a role. Institutional reasons, like serving in the majority party, the size of a chamber's majority, and the president being from the other party, increase partisan behavior across the board. As the parties gain or lose power in Washington, DC, lawmakers adapt. Not only do they change their partisan intensities, but they also change their rhetorical tones. In chapter 4, we show that the change in presidency from Obama to Trump shifted the strongest Democratic partisans from being cheerleaders and opportunists to bickerers. The strongest Republican partisans' tones moved in the opposite direction, with many becoming cheerleaders. Two years later, when Democrats won the House majority and ended Republican unified government, many of the same intensely partisan Republicans continued cheering the Trump administration while criticizing the House Democrats. Many bickerers became opportunists.

Indeed, an important finding worth highlighting is that the shifting control of governing institutions—the presidency, House, and Senate—changes not only who acts as a partisan but also how they act. No matter who is in power at a given moment, ambitious members need to build their partisan résumés. If they are part of the unified government, that means more cheerleading than bickering.

If they are on the other side and out of power, it means constant criticism. Even divided government fosters its own differences, as tone is strongly correlated with whether the member and president are in the same party. Consequently, lawmakers are calibrating their partisan personas in response to their personal circumstances as well as institutional factors outside of their immediate control. This creates an ebb and flow of volume and tone that might seem erratic but when properly contextualized has a predictability to it.

Is Partisanship Hobbling the Lawmaking Process?

A damning critique of partisanship is that it comes at the expense of legislating. Political scientists consistently show that bipartisan initiatives are much more likely to become law than ones only supported by members of one party (Curry and Lee 2020; Harbridge-Yong, Volden, and Wiseman 2023). If that is the case, a reasonable conclusion is that stronger partisans are less successful at lawmaking because they are less cooperative with the opposition.

Our results show that legislators with higher partisan intensities collaborate less with the other party early in the legislative process. They cosponsor fewer bills that are introduced by colleagues from across the aisle. Their measures are cosponsored less often by the opposition as well. However, any effect from this early-stage combativeness dissipates later on. Partisan intensity is not associated with members being less effective at lawmaking or having their ideas enacted. These results are robust even after we take into account that strong partisans tend to also have institutional power as committee and party leaders.

Partisanship's main consequence is not creating a group of ineffective legislators but hardening a member's loyalty to the party when voting on the floor. Intense partisans rarely break from the party line and reliably support or oppose the president's position. As a result, fewer members are likely to emerge as "profiles in courage" who break from their side to create bipartisan coalitions that are sometimes needed to pass important legislation or investigate the executive branch.

To deal with intractable members at the floor stage, over the past few decades, congressional procedure has evolved in ways to keep at least some legislative processes on track.[1] Omnibus procedures insulate measures that would surely be politicized if debated individually and provide a less traceable way for legislators of all sorts, including bickerers, to have their ideas added to laws (Reynolds and Hanson 2023). In the Senate, ending the 60-vote threshold on nominations allows the majority party to circumvent obstructionists and eliminates the need for any minority party support.

On balance, partisanship is not directly hobbling the lawmaking process. It affects, at the margin, legislation's early momentum once introduced. It shapes voting patterns on the floor. It is not making some members less productive than others, and it has forced Congress to adopt new procedures to remain somewhat productive. One effect partisan intensity may have, which is outside the scope of our research, is that it leads to more politicized issues before they arise on the agenda. This sort of influence at the agenda-setting stage, by making an issue too politically toxic to move forward, is another way this behavior might affect lawmaking. We hope political scientists take up this ripe research area in the future.

What Are the Electoral Consequences of This Behavior?

Although partisanship generates complaints, one reason extreme versions of it persist is that voters only lightly punish it at the ballot box. Some voters, especially primary voters, might even prefer it (Anderson, Butler, and Harbridge-Yong 2020). On balance, more partisan incumbents receive lower vote shares than others, after controlling for a myriad of other factors. This reflects other research in this area (Carson et al. 2010; Koger and Lebo 2017). However, we contend that for most legislators, the penalty is easily weathered. If a member increases their partisan intensity 25 percent, they can expect to incur, on average, a two-percentage-point penalty on Election Day. That may seem like a large vote share, but most lawmakers are in districts with at least a ten-point partisan advantage. The choice to win by a little less in order to become a committee or party leader is, for many, an easy decision.

In fact, this small penalty for those in safe seats understates the different political realities partisanship creates between them and others in marginal districts. As we show in chapter 7, the partisan tone legislators adopt also matters but varies by their electoral circumstances. For those in safe seats, a negative, caustic tone mitigates any loss in vote share from their excessive team play. In safe seats, tone matters less as voters punish incumbents for extreme partisanship, regardless of whether it is bickering or cheerleading. Consequently, most members who already hold safe seats have a nearly free hand to act as partisan as they want. The electoral penalty will not endanger their incumbency, and if they become concerned, they can always shift toward a more combative tone. Again, this electoral situation describes most members and helps explain why they feel emboldened to engage in such extreme partisan displays.

The Biden Years

The data we analyze in the previous chapters cover Barack Obama's final two years in office and the entirety of Donald Trump's first term. Academic book publishing's long timelines allowed us to collect and calculate data on legislators' partisan intensity from the 117th Congress, the first two years of Joe Biden's presidency. The results closely follow and support our argument. During the Trump years, Democrats tended to be the most intensely partisan. This dynamic flipped once Biden took office. Nineteen of the 20 most partisan members were Republicans, and their partisan intensity was, on average, 19 points higher than Democrats.

Additionally, as our theory predicts, most of these team players were ambitious members holding or seeking positions of power. The most partisan Republicans were the two House party leaders (Kevin McCarthy and Steve Scalise), two committee ranking members (Virginia Foxx and Jason Smith), and two seemingly ambitious backbenchers holding safe seats (Andrew Clyde and Lance Gooden).

On the Democratic side, the entire House leadership team announced they would step down at the end of the term. Their replacements, Hakeem Jeffries (5th), Katherine Clark (25th), Pete Aguilar (17th), and Ted Lieu (13th), ranked as some of the most partisan Democrats during those two years as they auditioned for their new roles. The least partisan members from each party were not surprises. On the Democratic side, Senator Kyrsten Sinema, who eventually left the party to become an independent, displayed a very low partisan intensity. Similarly, the least partisan Republican was Senator Susan Collins. Although principally viewed as an ideological moderate, Collins rarely engaged in team play.

The 117th Congress also showed that the partisan behavior during those Trump years was not an aberration and is likely to persist. The plot on the left in figure 8.2 displays members' partisan intensity by congressional term. It shows that the uptick during Trump's first presidency persisted during Biden's first two years in office. The plot on the right only includes the freshmen for each of the four congressional terms. During the final Obama years and the Trump ones, new members adopted less intense partisan personas than their more experienced colleagues. Since they generally are not promotion seeking

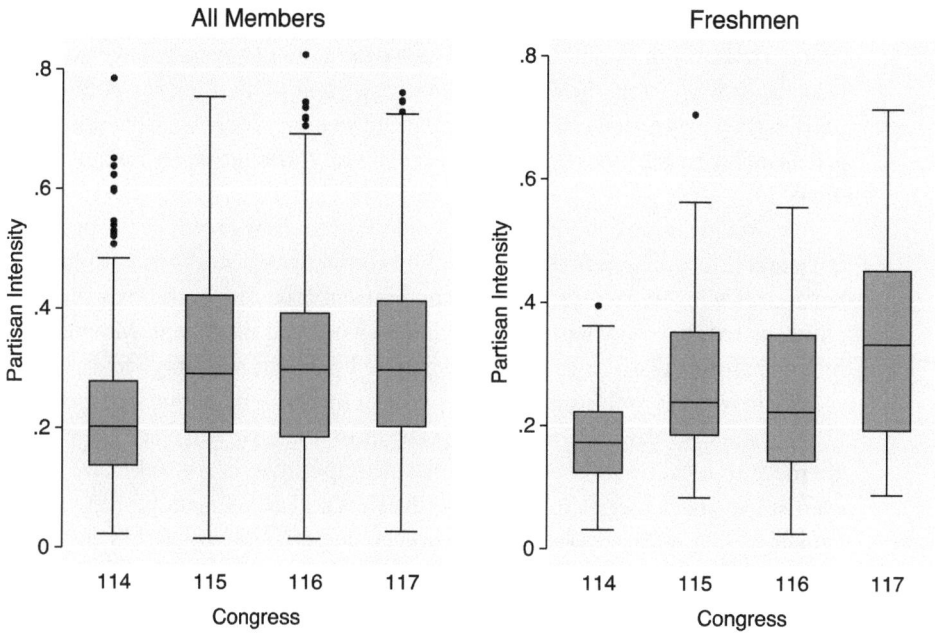

Fig. 8.2. Partisan Intensity by Congress for All Members and Freshmen

so early in their careers, even the strongest freshman partisans' behavior paled to the team play displayed by leadership and those running for higher office.

The freshman class in the 117th Congress is different. Their partisan intensity is, on average, higher than the other members and includes some of the most partisan legislators during those two years. Although this change may have arisen for a number of reasons, our interest is in what it means for Congress moving forward. This shift in new member behavior suggests that that partisanship was not just an Obama- or Trump-era phenomenon but a feature of the contemporary US Congress. Even new legislators, still finding their feet in Washington, DC, rely on framing issues as pitting Democrats versus Republicans.

Turning Down the Partisan Heat

To the extent that partisanship is an omnipresent feature in Congress, a natural question is, What can be done about it? Before providing recommendations on reducing partisan intensity, we are quick to note that eliminating congressional partisanship is neither possible nor desirable. Lawmakers have good reasons for supporting their side, and even if we bellyache about the political parties, they play a vital role in organizing and shaping Congress. That said, it is reasonable to ask how the partisan excesses in Washington, DC, might be reined in.

We provide three concrete recommendations for how to reduce the partisan temperature on Capitol Hill. First, more competitive districts will produce lawmakers who are reluctant to join the partisan fray. Although not a silver bullet, as we show in chapter 5, this change would be significant. Moving a member from a district with an average-sized partisan advantage to a very competitive one would reduce their partisan intensity by about 2 percent. Shifting the safest lawmakers, who have the most incentive and electoral wiggle room to bicker with the opposition, to competitive seats would have an even larger effect. Legislators in tough districts still act as team players and benefit from a strong party brand. However, any electoral price they might pay from excessive partisanship can make them pause and consider whether a fight between the parties is worth joining.

Second, providing lawmakers more pathways to political influence that do not rely on support from the party caucus/conference will also lower the partisan temperature. In the House, becoming a committee leader requires being a good team player because fellow party members select who leads these panels. As we show in chapter 5, this increases the chair's and the ranking member's partisan intensity. Adopting other selection mechanisms that emphasize fidelity to the committee itself, and not to fellow party members, will reduce the incentive for ambitious representatives to adopt these intense partisan personas. For instance, having committee members vote for their leadership makes them the chair's and ranking member's constituents, not the party caucus at large. One likely and positive consequence from this change is that committee leaders will further emphasize building their committee's power rather than using their agenda-setting powers to pick fights with the opposing party.

Third, dampening promotion-seeking behavior will reduce the number of members acting as extreme partisans. To be clear, we are not claiming you can stop politicians from seeking more power and prestige in Washington, DC. For some, their goal is to become president or senator or to lead their party or committee. For others, retaining their seat and having some influence are enough. As power has centralized to party leadership, avenues for backbenchers to gather some power have dissipated. The emergence of important caucuses provides one outlet for the rank and file to accumulate influence without seeking a promotion in the party or to higher office. Providing subcommittees more power is the obvious reform, especially in the House, that may incentivize more legislators to remain in their current seats rather than pining for their next opportunity in the leadership ranks or Senate.

Looking Backward

In chapter 1, we spent a few pages discussing the scope and external validity of a book that only analyzes six years of congressional politics. Now that we have made our argument in full, regression tables and all, we wish to briefly return to this topic. Any reader, with a PhD in political science or not, should naturally ask the question of whether the ideas here extend beyond our timeframe of study. It is a fair and reasonable point of skepticism. Indeed, tracing partisan intensity in the past is challenging. Venues where voters, copartisan legislators, and researchers can all observe the same behavior are rare, and this is one reason social media data is so valuable. However, moments from the past can provide some sense that the ideas in this book did not begin with our data from 2015.

Take, for instance, one of the most partisan situations in Congress: a presidential impeachment. To prosecute its case before the Senate, the House majority party appoints impeachment managers from its membership. Although they are selected for various reasons, agreeing to serve means taking on a high-profile partisan role.[2] Per our argument, one of the main reasons someone might agree to do this is that they hold an important position they wish to keep or have political ambitions beyond their current position.

Although the congressional careers of the Democratic impeachment managers from 2019 and 2020 are still unfolding, the careers of the 13 Republican managers from Bill Clinton's 1998 impeachment have mostly reached their endpoint. Almost all of them either have achieved what is likely their final political office or are no longer in politics (or, in a few cases, no longer alive). One of our key arguments is that those who take on such high-profile partisan roles do so in part because they are ambitious ladder climbers. If that is the case, then their career paths are more likely to include seeking leadership positions or higher office in the future. Did this happen? What were their career trajectories like after serving as impeachment managers? Was it different than other Republicans at the time?

Of the 13 managers, only 4 never became a committee chair in the House or sought a higher office. The other 9, or 69 percent of the group, had varied paths but showed the ambition we expect of highly partisan members. Four (Henry Hyde, Jim Sensenbrenner, Steve Buyer, and Steve Chabot) all held House committee chairmanships. Hyde was the Judiciary Committee chair at the time, so being an impeachment manager may have stemmed from slightly different motivations. Three (Bill McCollum, Lindsey Graham, and Ed Bryant) ran for higher office. Two were appointed to high-level positions in the Bush administration. Asa Hutchinson left his House seat for his position. James Rogan took his position after losing his reelection race to future Democratic impeachment manager and eventual US Senator Adam Schiff.

Is 69 percent (or 62 percent if we exclude Rogan's more idiosyncratic situation) a high or low percentage of members holding or pursuing leadership positions or higher offices? One possibility is that most House members eventually become a committee chair, run for higher office, or are appointed as a high-ranking administration official. In reality, that is not the case. As a comparison group, consider the 1994 House Republican freshmen class that brought about the Republican revolution. Even with a more expansive understanding of political ambition (e.g., being appointed as a federal judge), only 44 percent held a chairmanship or sought a higher office.

Finding historical moments where we can observe variation in partisan intensity is challenging. However, the places where we can plausibly assess how and why some members shoulder the party's work provide additional context for the arguments we present. Social media makes studying this topic easier. It does not mean it created the concepts we study here.

Looking Forward: Twitter and Measuring Partisan Intensity

In that vein, a central argument of this book is that partisan intensity, the relative level of team play that members engage in, is important as it helps explain congressional politics in ways that other concepts cannot. We operationalize it using posts from the social media microblogging site Twitter. At the time, Twitter was the predominate place where legislators regularly communicated with their constituents. To be fair, it was not the only way. They also used newsletters, press releases, and other social media sites to disseminate their messages. But the sheer number of posts, the near ubiquitous use, and its high-profile nature due to Donald Trump's omnipresence on the platform made Twitter the best, most comprehensive source to document this concept.

Social media sites lead short lives, and even as we write, it seems Twitter, now branded X, is at the beginning of its end as a centralized hub for politicians' communications to their constituents. That does not mean the idea of partisan intensity dies with it. Rather, we contend that it has always existed in Congress, likely ebbing and flowing with the times. Indeed, if we were starting this project right now, in 2025, we would likely collect data from multiple social media websites, as the places lawmakers post has balkanized. For the six years we analyze, Twitter as it existed then, members' widespread use of the platform, and advances in computational social science simply made it possible for us to operationalize and examine partisan intensity. Even though tweets may not be the way legislators display their partisan personas in the coming years, this behavior will persist on other social media websites. By facilitating constant messaging opportunities, platforms like Twitter, Facebook, and whatever comes next allow lawmakers to broadcast their participation in the partisan bickering, and perhaps even to incentivize more of it, that was much less visible in the past. As such, we hope political scientists will continue to consider and measure partisan intensity's importance, even if it involves data that is different than what we present here.

Final Thoughts

Congress scholars have spilled a great deal of ink thinking about when, and even if, partisanship matters. In many cases, partisanship has been conceptualized as if a legislator votes with their party on the floor. That certainly is a type of partisan behavior, and one that is easily measured. In our view, it is only a conceptual snippet and includes a fair amount of measurement error. Team play on Capitol Hill happens during floor votes but more often occurs off the record in the daily bickering and cheerleading that permeates the institution. Our focus on this day-to-day partisanship captures dynamics that votes and formal speeches do not and even predicts that behavior.

Congressional partisanship is like oxygen. It is essential and omnipresent, but its concentration varies. Sometimes it is intense, defining conflict and pulling in lawmakers inclined to support their side. In other cases, it exists in the background, taking a back seat to ideology or local, parochial concerns. Understanding when and why partisanship matters, and its consequences, has been our goal in this book.

People worry a lot about partisanship. They are right to be alarmed, but not always for the reasons that are commonly cited. Partisanship is not breaking the legislative process or hobbling the institution. Congress has adapted to a hyper-partisan environment and continues to pass significant amounts of policy and to spend increasingly large sums of money. What we view as problematic is that to become powerful, a legislator generally needs to be a good team player. More pathways to power in Washington, DC—besides via the parties, and through avenues that emphasize legislating and developing expertise—will improve the institution. The old systems that decentralized power in the mid-20th century were problematic and not the way forward. But as Congress evolves, new avenues to influence, whether it be through caucuses, committees, or something else, can provide a counterweight to partisanship when it runs amok.

Notes

1. Twitter, now called X, is a social network that allows users to post short, public messages.

2. Throughout the book, we present tweets as they were written, including spelling and grammar errors. Additionally, we refer to these posts as tweets, which is what they were called when written.

3. As of writing, we do not know who sent those posts.

4. The analysis of aggregate media statistics comes from searching the *ProQuest Central* database for news articles related to the SCIF incident.

5. Per the *ProQuest Central* database, only 10 or so media pieces, on TV, in newspapers or magazines, mentioned the event in the days after October 24. Although it was discussed rarely through the first week of November, by early November, Republicans began using the SCIF to try to discredit the impeachment on transparency grounds while ignoring the October 23 stunt.

6. The extent of, reasoning for, and durability of these differences are explored in a wide range of settings. More optimistic accounts suggest that factual disagreements are about partisan cheerleading and that over time partisans' views eventually converge to the truth (Bullock et al. 2013; Hill 2017; Stimson and Wager 2020).

7. Others have documented how partisanship has changed lawmaking at the collective level, especially during the agenda-setting and negotiation phases of lawmaking. As we discuss throughout the book, at the individual level, a member's partisan intensity is not strongly correlated with their ability to attract cosponsors for their bills or their overall legislative effectiveness. However, we note here and later that Republicans who voted against certifying the 2020 election, a textbook definition of partisan behavior, subsequently suffered a significant decrease in these areas (Curry and Roberts, forthcoming).

8. Other types of congressional communications do not share these features. Constituents must subscribe to newsletters. Press releases are sent much less frequently than social media posts and do not allow for the same types of interactions between users.

9. In February 2023, Musk also ended free use of the Twitter/X application programming interface, which forced us to conclude our data collection. We use data from the 117th Congress in the final chapter.

10. For an accessible review on the early formation of congressional political parties, see chapter 3 in Aldrich (1995).

11. Increasingly this is true of Senate chairs as well, as we note in chapter 2.

CHAPTER 2

1. He also suggests that the first presidents' skepticism of parties was hypocritical. When winning their terms in office, presidents like Madison had no problem encouraging party unity but returned "to their denunciations of it after every defeat" (Van Buren 1867, 5).

2. Gaining political influence has both individual components (e.g., becoming a committee leader) and collective ones (e.g., serving as a committee chair, which is more valuable than being the ranking member). As we detail below, both factors, moving up in Washington, DC, and serving in the majority party, are related to changes in a member's partisan intensity.

3. It is worth noting that even at its height in usage, most Americans did not use Twitter (Dinesh and Odabas 2023). Our argument does not depend on how many voters saw a tweet when it was posted. Rather, the public nature of social media is the essential component.

4. Even members in marginal seats must satisfy primary electorates made up of strong partisans. This likely creates a floor of partisan fidelity, which provides a rationale for why this behavior is ubiquitous.

5. The correlation between a member's party unity voting score and their seat safety is 0.4. The correlation between seat safety and our measure of partisan intensity is 0.32. These are calculated using the partisan intensity and seat safety measures that we outline in chapters 3 and 5.

6. Moran consistently rated around the 10th percentile in his partisanship, while Roberts hovered around the 75th.

7. Writing at the same time, Mayhew (1974) has similar insight. Like Fiorina, he argues that members are not vote maximizers, but seek to "win comfortably" (47). They do this by adopting a minimax strategy, where they adopt public behaviors that minimize the chance they lose on Election Day. Yet unlike Fiorina, Mayhew does not think about how those with comfortable margins act in Congress after achieving them. His focus is on how they maintain such margins in the face of future uncertainty. However, implicitly, he seems to agree with Fiorina. Members winning by comfortable margins are unlikely to place much effort in gaining more votes but instead maintain their comfortable margin. He does not expand on what they do instead, but it is reasonable to interpret that they engage in other activities, like pursuing powerful positions or writing public policy.

8. This measure, which is calculated for the districts in our sample, is based on the vote share the presidential candidate from the incumbent's party received in the past two elections (Canes-Wrone, Brady, and Cogan 2002).

9. The chamber's flipping control is not necessarily correlated with narrow majorities, but as Lee (2016) convincingly shows, members' behaviors change as majority size decreases.

10. Other less-trodden avenues exist, such as leading influential caucuses or building a support base among a certain segment of the party. These strategies may rely on displaying different behaviors like ideological extremity or even stoking within-party disagreement.

11. We acknowledge two other paths to influence. First, members spend years cultivating their power in committees by leading subcommittees and developing issue expertise. Besides moving up the committee system, another option is members can lead important caucuses or legislative service organizations. These positions certainly matter and can be influential; however, the logic for being promoted into leading them is more idiosyncratic and varies based on their membership and goals.

12. Following others, when we discuss leaders through this chapter, we mean those in the party leadership structure as well as the party's top-ranking member on a committee (Cox and McCubbins 2005). Recognizing that incentives for partisan team play may differ between these two groups, we analyze them separately in the empirical section.

13. Committees vary in their bipartisan reputations. Appropriations and Armed Services in both chambers, for example, are often seen as bastions of relative comity. Yet in recent years, and during the time we examine, many of these formerly collegial committees have become venues for intense ideological and partisan disputes (e.g., Price 2013). Nevertheless, we acknowledge these differences but argue that the selection process, not the committee's jurisdiction, is what increases leaders' partisan intensity.

14. Recent leadership selection to the Senate Judiciary Committee suggests partisanship may play a role for both parties. Lindsey Graham was selected to lead the Republicans after his fierce defense of Brett Kavanaugh's confirmation. Dianne Feinstein (D-CA) stepped down as the lead Democrat on the Senate Judiciary Committee after being widely criticized for not more stridently opposing Amy Coney Barrett's late-term Supreme Court confirmation ("Sen. Feinstein Announces She Will Not Seek Judiciary Chair" 2020). Of course, the Senate Judiciary Committee is such a unique panel that we are not willing to generalize beyond these recent cases.

15. The cohort argument is usually made about specific cohorts. However, wave cohorts may differ in how they came to office, like whether they mostly replace former members in their own party, flip marginal districts, or emerge due to a broader realignment. We do not seek to adjudicate the partisan behavior of specific cohorts, and in the subsequent chapters, we test these related arguments in a number of ways. Additionally, these cohort hypotheses often conflate partisanship with polarization, although as Theriault (2013) argues, it is often impossible to distinguish between the two.

16. Congressional Democrats' reaction to Republicans who voted against certifying Joe Biden's 2020 presidential election win are a good example of this. Prior to these votes, Democrats would seek bipartisan partners, no matter their partisan inten-

sity. But, after the January 6 insurrection, many Democrats refused to cooperate with the Republicans who voted against certifying the election. Democrats' explanations emphasize that before January 6, they would work with anyone and cite various partnerships with partisan and ideological extreme Republicans (Caldwell 2021).

17. See Costa (2020) for an alternative view on whether primary voters are motivated by partisan animosity. Others have studied this balancing act between reelection and primary constituencies by examining legislator ideology, not partisanship (Brady, Han, and Pope 2011).

18. See Gelman (2020b) for an in-depth treatment of partisanship during Kavanaugh's confirmation.

CHAPTER 3

1. His lack of success may owe to his career as a federal judge ending after being impeached and removed from the bench by Congress for bribery and perjury.

2. From this perspective, partisanship is zero-sum. However, situations can arise in which partisan behavior can benefit the opposition party. One example might be presidential election endorsements producing counter-mobilizing behavior. Thus, an even more precise definition is behavior *intended* to support your party and harm the other party, even if doing so sometimes produces unintended consequences.

3. Most Republicans rarely spoke in opposition to the president, and if they did, it was in some extraordinary situations. A few notable exceptions, such as Justin Amash (who eventually left the party), Mitt Romney, Liz Cheney, and Adam Kinzinger (both late in Trump's term), stand out as exceptions.

4. In our initial coding of congressional tweets, we tracked cross-partisan posts. They accounted for 0.4 percent of the data (82 out of 20,000).

5. A good example is the literature on party voting. Party cohesiveness is studied from a partisan perspective in which leadership induces the rank and file to act as a voting bloc on the floor, often overriding reluctant members' ideological preferences (Lawrence, Maltzman, and Smith 2006). It is also studied from an ideological one in which scholars track partisan differences in DW-NOMINATE scores over time. Roberts and Smith (2003) nicely capture how these terms are used as synonyms. They note that "no feature of congressional politics during the past three decades has received more notice than the increase in partisanship" (305), which in their conceptualization is partisan polarization.

6. The Republicans who voted to impeach or convict Trump and the Democrats who voted against impeachment acted in a bipartisan way.

7. See the final passage vote on 116-HJRes-107.

8. Democrats' nuking of the filibuster for lower court and executive branch nominees was an equally partisan move.

9. See his floor speech on March 26, 2019.

10. An important strand in this literature considers how disciplined parties are in their floor voting. In these studies, the unit is measured at the party level and assesses the caucus's strength, cohesion, or discipline (McCarty, Poole, and Rosenthal 2001; Krehbiel 2000).

11. An implicit assumption in these studies is that bipartisanship is the antithesis to partisanship.

12. Russell's (2018, 2020) research analyzes Twitter posts and, as we discuss below, does not have the measurement challenges as these other approaches.

13. Partisan agenda control presents a problem for using amendments to measure partisanship. Reynolds (2017) recognizes this problem and uses data on Senate vote-a-ramas to study partisan amending activity.

14. See 116-HRes-755 and roll call votes 695 and 696.

15. Another concern might be that older legislators, especially during the period we are studying, knew very little about social media or were less likely to use it. However, the data does not bear this out. The correlation between the total number of tweets a legislator posted during a congressional term and their age is 0.12.

16. Even if some tweets are deleted, what remains is the partisan intensity a legislator wishes to publicly display. In addition, as we have largely collected data in real time over the period in question, our data includes tweets that may have been deleted after the fact.

17. Our data excludes 19 legislators who removed their accounts before we could collect their tweets. We also exclude members who sent fewer than 50 tweets during a congressional term. While Twitter use is nearly ubiquitous, these low-usage legislators may not use the platform as a consistent means of communication. All of our results are substantively similar if we include these low-usage members. See the supplementary materials in Gelman and Wilson (2022) for lists of members not included in the analyses.

18. The House and Senate have established rules for how members can use their official accounts. Generally speaking, legislators can only use their official Twitter account for business related to their position and not for campaigning (Straus and Glassman 2016). We include all accounts, as it presents the most comprehensive record of a member's partisan brand and legislators vary in which account type they most frequently use.

19. Besides explicitly partisan language and events, we also classify certain campaign rhetoric as partisan. We argue tweets that ask followers to vote for a candidate, ask them to volunteer for their campaign, or announce an endorsement are inherently partisan. Such campaign rhetoric constitutes 4 percent of partisan tweets.

20. We coded a random sample of 1,000 partisan tweets by category. Mentions of the president, his administration, or prominent officials were the most common type of partisan post (48 percent). The explicit use of partisan labels (21 percent) was the second most common type.

21. Information on intercoder reliability is presented in the supplementary material in Gelman and Wilson (2022).

22. As we note in our earlier work on this topic, "the settings described are very typical for these applications, and the results are robust to adding more layers or tweaking the particular parameterizations. For parsimony, we use the simplest settings for the results" (Gelman and Wilson 2022, 251).

23. The overall results of our findings are robust to not using this technique; however, through iterative testing it improves the out-of-sample accuracy of the neural nets.

24. In our hand-coded sample, the most common link is to a picture of a constituent meeting.

25. One concern is that this approach might introduce more false positives. We examined this by taking a random sample of 1,500 links. Less than 1 percent were coded as false positives. The rest accurately captured an otherwise miscoded partisan tweet and reclassified it as such.

26. We also trained independent neural nets on each Congress to evaluate whether it would be better to treat each Congress independently for classification purposes. Overall, the single unified neural net performed marginally better across the board, and so we opted for its usage.

27. Second-dimension DW-NOMINATE scores are even more weakly correlated (-0.07) than first-dimension ones.

CHAPTER 4

1. We explicitly avoid using the term "negative partisanship," which has a very different meaning in political behavior research.

2. Legislators certainly think it does, because as exhaustively documented by political scientists, they strategically and predictably vary their tones and emotional appeals (e.g., Gelman, Wilson, and Petrarca 2021; Macdonald, Russell, and Hua 2023; Russell 2021).

3. This literature is large, with active debates about whether affective polarization's origins are social or policy based, what causes these views, and how it can be reduced. See Iyengar et al. (2019) for a recent review.

4. In this case, we use the term "nonpartisan" to mean any tweet not classified as partisan. These tweets could have no partisan content, bipartisan, or cross-partisan.

5. The differences between all these values are statistically significant at the $p < 0.0001$ level.

6. See Mechkova and Wilson (2019) for the details of the tweets from the American public, from which we borrowed the random samples.

7. Or, hypothetically, it means a member is entirely neutral in their partisan tone, which is never the case.

8. One possibility is that members who are more extreme in tone and/or intensity are just "more online." The chapter's appendix includes a bubble chart, where each data point corresponds to the number of tweets a legislator posts in a congressional term. That plot shows little relationship between social media activity and partisan tone or intensity.

9. We explored creating these measures based on party (e.g., the most partisan Democrats or Republicans) but sought to avoid false equivalencies that might arise where a bickerer in one party is much less negative or partisan than a bickerer in the other party. These sorts of asymmetries are worth exploring more, not papering over with party-specific groupings.

10. We created these categories based on whether members were one standard deviation above the mean in intensity and above or below the mean in partisan tone. The correlation between a standard deviation approach and the one we define in the text is as follows: Warriors—0.70, Opportunists—0.53, Cheerleaders—0.82.

11. Trump subsequently appointed him director of the Office of Management and Budget.

12. Figure 4.3 is from a standardized regression model, where the mean of each variable is set at 0 and the standard deviation at 1.

13. Any results we find might stem from how we defined our categories, and in particular, we might misclassify opportunists just on the cutoff with bickerers and cheerleaders. To test this possibility, in table 4.6 we include an analysis where we shrink the definition of opportunists to those in middle 40th percentile in tone and expand the bickerer and cheerleader categories to include members who were close to our original cutoffs. Both models are estimated with robust standard errors clustered by member. We do not include Congress fixed effects, as doing so prevented the models from converging.

14. Table 4.4 is based on the percentage change in the odds of a legislator being a partisan type and is calculated using a Z-test.

15. The p-value for seat safety distinguishing between opportunists and cheerleaders is 0.1.

CHAPTER 5

1. For instance, on December 19, 2019, he tweeted, "Whether you agree with impeachment or not, Trump Derangement Syndrome has reached a new level. House Democrats refusing to send the Articles of Impeachment to the Senate because they don't like the way we may do the trial—that is just scary."

2. As Caldera (2020) notes, Graham maintains he did nothing wrong.

3. Graham and Chuck Grassley (R-IA) traded the chairmanship over three Congresses as they cycled between leading the Judiciary and Finance Committees. Moreover, Senate chairs are not selected by rank-and-file copartisans, but Graham's selection as Judiciary Committee chair by his fellow Republican committee members was based on his partisan goals of confirming judges and investigating the Clinton and Biden campaigns (Levine 2019; Zwirz 2019).

4. In chapter 2, we discuss how Senate committee leaders may not be selected by rank-and-file copartisans. We use this institutional variation to test our claims about power seeking later in this chapter.

5. See our discussion in chapter 2 for a review of these arguments. An additional argument is that those who fear a primary challenge adopt more partisan personas. We address this possibility in chapter 7. Additionally, a recent primary challenge could change an incumbent's behavior. We don't think this is likely, as the conventional wisdom is that members fear a future primary challenge, not a past one. However, we examined whether a quality primary challenger affected partisan intensity in the 115th and 116th terms. The coefficient was negative, not positive, signed, meaning a quality challenger in the last election reduces subsequent partisan intensity. Moreover, the coefficient was not statistically significant ($p = 0.27$).

6. We do not include senators continuing as committee leaders, because as we previously discuss, Senate committee leaders are not selected by the caucuses and conferences.

7. The articles we reviewed suggest this sometimes happens. For instance, very

early in this process, candidates' names may be floated, probably by their own offices, but they never run for the leadership position.

8. The only case in which a House member ran for a state-level office other than governor was Keith Ellison (D-MN), who ran for Minnesota's attorney general (Xavier Becerra was appointed California's attorney general).

9. The count model does not include the total tweets covariate since it is included as the exposure term. Our results are robust to a regression model that uses the natural log of partisan tweets as the dependent variable. In addition, a zero-inflation specification is unnecessary in the count model because the nearly universal usage of Twitter by members of Congress means there is no zero inflation in the data.

10. Measuring the low-ranking party leader variable by chamber, by creating an interaction term between the Senate and low-ranking party leader variables, does not change the results. The effect in the House is stronger but is still not statistically significant.

11. A one standard deviation change in terms served has less than a 1 percent effect on partisan intensity. The effect in table 5.3 can be interpreted as the difference between freshmen and the longest serving members.

12. A one standard deviation increase in seat safety increases partisan intensity by about 2 percent.

13. Top House leadership was fairly stable, especially on the Democratic side. However, top positions were contested, like Tim Ryan (D-OH) challenging Nancy Pelosi (D-CA) for minority leader in 2016, Diana DeGette (D-CO) running against Jim Clyburn for House whip, and Jim Jordan (R-OH) challenging Kevin McCarthy for the minority leader position in 2018. For lower-level positions, House races were hotly contested, often with multiple candidates.

14. Patty Murray's (D-WA) elevation to assistant minority leader when Dick Durbin (D-IL) became whip is the most prominent example.

15. It is possible that partisanship driven by reelection considerations works differently in the Senate than in the House. Since only one-third of the Senate runs in an election year, those facing their voters may change their partisan intensity differently than senators not on the ballot. We examined this possibility by interacting a dummy variable for those running for reelection with our reelection covariates. We found no evidence that being the Senate class facing voters had an effect on partisan intensity.

16. These models include some collinearity among the majority party, president's party, Republican, and Congress fixed effects variables, which requires us to estimate more restricted models. By dropping the Republican and Congress fixed effects, we are able to retain our main reelection and promotion-seeking variables of interest in the models.

17. Walorski tragically passed away in 2022 in a car crash, so we cannot further track how her and Smith's careers may have diverged.

18. We exclude the Senate, since during these six years, we did not document any losers for party or committee leadership positions and committee leadership positions are not selected by the party caucus/conference.

19. When we include the Senate winners, there is no difference between winners and losers when they are both running (0.28 and 0.27, respectively). Winners' intensity is 0.31, while losers' intensity is 0.29 ($p = 0.27$).

20. All won their elections except Martha McSally, who ran and lost but was then appointed to the Senate by Arizona's governor to fill a vacant seat. The seven winners were Van Hollen, Young, Duckworth, Cramer, Blackburn, Sinema, and Rosen.

21. The data for the losers was collected from OpenSecrets' "casualty lists" for the 114th and 115th Congresses.

22. A one-tailed t-test produces a p-value of 0.053.

23. Given the extremely small sample size, removing Sanders and/or Van Hollen from the sample produces much smaller p-values.

24. Since Senate seats cannot be redrawn, we only analyze House members in this section.

25. Of course, a second reason partisanship might decrease if seats were more competitive is that more partisan members would lose reelection more often!

26. Our data does not include a redistricting cycle, so we cannot do an in-depth analysis with exogenous changes in district competition. However, the 2022 midterm elections, taking place under new maps, will be the first case where partisan intensity data measured using social media posts can be used to determine if the changing district competitiveness affects incumbents' partisan intensity.

CHAPTER 6

1. We only include bills that are cosponsored. For ones without cosponsors, setting those values to zero would misrepresent the number of perfectly balanced cosponsorship coalitions in the data.

2. We explored other measures to account for the size of the cosponsorship coalition. For instance, one that multiplies the number of total sponsors and the measure we describe above suggests that higher partisan intensity may be associated with larger, more partisan cosponsorship coalitions. However, all of these alternative measures have their own measurement and interpretation issues, so we focus on the more straightforward one we present in the text.

3. Since partisan intensity and bill introductions/cosponsorships are co-occurring, using a member's lagged partisan intensity might help identify the variable's effect. In specifications with the lagged term, we find substantively similar results.

4. These variables are based on Volden and Wiseman (2014) and Stewart and Woon (2022a, 2022b) data. Including the lagged legislative effectiveness drops the entire 114th Congress. When we omit this variable, which allows us to include one-third of our data, we find substantively similar results.

5. Our main results are the same in models subset on representatives or senators.

6. *Congressional Quarterly* calculates party unity scores annually, so we estimated annual partisanship scores for these models.

7. Presidential DW-NOMINATE scores are based on the votes they take public positions on. As such, they are constructed from the same votes used to calculate presidential support scores. This creates the exact endogeneity problem that Jackson and Kingdon (1992) caution about. CFscores are derived from campaign contributions and are highly correlated with DW-NOMINATE scores (Bonica 2014).

8. Our results are robust to models that include year dummies.

9. In fact, conventional wisdom in Congress is that the opposite happens. Majority

parties are more likely to withhold credit-claiming opportunities from minority party members in marginal districts. This would show up in table 6.3 as stronger partisans being more effective legislators. However, we do not find evidence for this either.

10. Section headings are not consistently formatted in bills. Yet, similarly or identically titled sections are much more likely to include the same policy topic. Subsetting on the first 100 characters addresses this lack of formatting and captures common 2-grams in the title and, in some cases, the first few lines of the section. Although this measure is not perfectly capturing section title similarity, it substantially improves the decision tree's classification of sections containing the same policy ideas.

11. This measure is based on the cleaned sections, which has stop words removed and is a count of the section's characters.

12. To account for these differences, the cleaned corpus included dollar amounts and percentages.

13. Lower values for depth may lead to underfitting, which will produce a more conservative match for whether two ideas are the same.

CHAPTER 7

1. Because of the lagged measures, we drop one-third of our data (the entire 114th Congress) in these analyses.

2. This includes variables that measure the change in personal income, presidential popularity, and whether the upcoming election is a midterm race.

3. We also estimate both models with party unity scores and find similar results.

4. Following both of these previous studies, we exclude members who received over 99 percent of the vote.

5. The Canes-Wrone et al. and the Koger and Lebo models focus on House members. Our House-specific models produce very similar results.

6. The second-stage equation is as follows:

$IncumbentVote_{it}$

$$= \tau_{2t} + \gamma_1 Unity_{it} + \beta_0 + \beta_1 District_{it} + \beta_2 Challenger_{it}$$
$$+ \beta_3 SpendGap_{it} + \beta_4 Freshman_{it} + \beta_5 President'sParty_{it}$$
$$+ B_6 IncumbentVoteShare_{it-1} + B_7 114thCongress$$
$$+ B_8 115thCongress + v_{it}$$

The first-stage equation is as follows:

$$Unity_{it} = \tau_{it} + \delta_1 District_{it} + \delta_2 Challenger_{it} + \delta_3 SpendGap_{it} + \delta_4 Freshman_{it}$$
$$+ \delta_5 President'sParty_{it} + \delta_6 IncumbentVoteShare_{it-1}$$
$$+ \delta_7 114thCongress + \delta_8 115thCongress + \theta_1 Extermism_{it}$$
$$+ \theta_2 Unity_{it-1}$$

7. A concern with our model is that we omit the actual party unity score, which Koger and Lebo (2017) use as their main measure of partisanship. In other words,

a member's voting, not their partisan intensity, is what creates the penalty. We find the exact opposite. In models where we instrument for party unity score and partisan intensity, including the lagged values for both, only the intensity measure is negative and statistically significant. Moreover, it has a much larger effect than the vote score. This suggests that at least during this time, partisan persona plays a larger role in vote share than aggregate partisan voting records.

8. A second way to assess if members pay an electoral penalty is to see if partisan intensity is correlated with winning a general election. Our argument is that maintainers can safely adopt more partisan behaviors without worrying about losing on Election Day. In fact, that is exactly what we see in the data. The only maintainer who lost was Mike Honda (D-CA) to a fellow Democrat in California's top-two primary system. Reflecting our argument, only maximizers lost and those who won tended to lower their partisan intensities. However, more complex models that try to parse out this difference, like subsetting election results on maintainers to see if they pay the ultimate political penalty for their partisanship, have no observations.

9. We do not have an expectation for the sign on the *Partisan Tone* variable, as we are agnostic about whether negative partisan tone is punished or rewarded in districts with a perfect partisan split.

10. One way partisanship may affect primary challenges that fall outside our large-N statistical approach is when legislators are expected to fall in line during very high-profile events. Those who do not do so risk being primaried. A recent example of this is Republicans who voted to impeach Trump after the events of January 6 attracted primary challenges and in most cases lost. We acknowledge this occurs but note that members know this too, so except in rare cases, they will adopt the party line, although some studies have explored similar situations (e.g., Nyhan et al. 2012).

CHAPTER 8

1. Some may argue that these changes are due to ideological polarization, not partisanship. We remind our readers that these concepts are often intertwined, and as Lee (2009) shows, many of the issues that generate partisan acrimony have no real ideological content.

2. After all, majority parties in modern American politics do not try to impeach presidents from their own party.

References

Abramowitz, Alan I., and Steven W. Webster. 2018. "Negative Partisanship: Why Americans Dislike Parties but Behave Like Rabid Partisans." *Political Psychology* 39 (February): 119–35. https://doi.org/10.1111/POPS.12479

Albertson, Bethany, Lindsay Dun, and Shana Kushner Gadarian. 2020. "The Emotional Aspects of Political Persuasion." In *Oxford Handbook of Electoral Persuasion*, edited by Elizabeth Suhay, Bernard Grofman, and Alexander Treschel, 169–83. New York: Oxford University Press.

Aldrich, John. 1995. *Why Parties? The Origins and Transformation of Political Parties in America*. Chicago: University of Chicago Press.

Aldrich, John, Jacob M. Montgomery, and David B. Sparks. 2014. "Polarization and Ideology: Partisan Sources of Low Dimensionality in Scaled Roll Call Analyses." *Political Analysis* 22:435–56. https://doi.org/10.1093/pan/mpt048

Alduncin, Alexander, David C. W. Parker, and Sean M. Theriault. 2017. "Leaving on a Jet Plane: Polarization, Foreign Travel, and Comity in Congress." *Congress & the Presidency* 44 (2): 179–200. https://doi.org/10.1080/07343469.2016.1270370

American Political Science Association. 1950. "Summary of Conclusions and Proposals." *American Political Science Review*, "Toward a More Responsible Two-Party System," 44 (3): 1–14. https://doi.org/10.2307/1950998

Anderson, Sarah E., Daniel M. Butler, and Laurel Harbridge-Yong. 2020. *Rejecting Compromise: Legislators' Fear of Primary Voters*. New York: Cambridge University Press.

Ansolabehere, Stephen, James M. Snyder Jr., and Charles Stewart III. 2001. "The Effects of Party and Preferences on Congressional Roll-Call Voting." *Legislative Studies Quarterly* 26 (4): 533–72. https://doi.org/10.2307/440269

Arnold, R. Douglas. 1990. *The Logic of Congressional Action*. New Haven: Yale University Press.

Balsamo, Michael, and Mary Clare Jalonick. 2019. "Chaotic Scene as Republicans Disrupt Impeachment Deposition." AP English Language News. October 23. Accessed December 17, 2024.

Banda, Kevin K., and John Cluverius. 2018. "Elite Polarization, Party Extremity, and Affective Polarization." *Electoral Studies* 56 (December): 90–101. https://doi.org/10.1016/J.ELECTSTUD.2018.09.009

Barber, Michael, and Jeremy C. Pope. 2019. "Does Party Trump Ideology? Disentangling Party and Ideology in America." *American Political Science Review* 113 (1): 38–54. https://doi.org/10.1017/S0003055418000795

Barberá, Pablo. 2015. "Birds of the Same Feather Tweet Together: Bayesian Ideal Point Estimation Using Twitter Data." *Political Analysis* 23 (1): 76–91. https://doi.org/10.1093/PAN/MPU011

Barberá, Pablo, Andreu Casas, Jonathan Nagler, Patrick J. Egan, Richard Bonneau, John T. Jost, and Joshua A. Tucker. 2019. "Who Leads? Who Follows? Measuring Issue Attention and Agenda Setting by Legislators and the Mass Public Using Social Media Data." *American Political Science Review* 113 (4): 883–901. https://doi.org/10.1017/S0003055419000352

Barnes, Julian E., Nicholas Fandos, and Adam Goldman. 2019. "Republican Senators Are Cool to Trump's Choice for Top Intelligence Post." *New York Times*, July 29. https://www.nytimes.com/2019/07/29/us/politics/trump-ratcliffe-national-intelligence.html

Baum, Matthew. 2011. "Red State, Blue State, Flu State: Media Self-Selection and Partisan Gaps in Swine Flu Vaccinations." *Journal of Health Politics and Policy* 36 (6): 1021–59. https://doi.org/10.1215/03616878-1460569

Berman, Russell. 2019. "Elijah Cummings, Reluctant Partisan Warrior." *The Atlantic*, October 17. https://www.theatlantic.com/politics/archive/2019/10/elijah-cummings-dead-republicans/600208/

Bernhard, William, and Tracy Sulkin. 2013. "Commitment and Consequences: Reneging on Cosponsorship Pledges in the U.S. House." *Legislative Studies Quarterly* 38 (4): 461–87. https://doi.org/10.1111/LSQ.12024

Bernhard, William, and Tracy Sulkin. 2018. *Legislative Style*. Chicago: University of Chicago Press.

Binder, Sarah, and Frances Lee. 2013. "Making Deals in Congress." In *Negotiating Agreement in Politics*, edited by Jane Mansbridge and Cathie Jo Martin, 54–72. Washington, DC: American Political Science Association.

"Bipartisan Index." 2021. The Lugar Center. https://www.thelugarcenter.org/ourwork-Bipartisan-Index.html

Bisgaard, Martin, and Rune Slothuus. 2018. "Partisan Elites as Culprits? How Party Cues Shape Partisan Perceptual Gaps." *American Journal of Political Science* 62 (2): 456–69. https://doi.org/10.1111/AJPS.12349

Boatright, Robert. 2004. *Expressive Politics: Issue Strategies for Congressional Challengers*. Columbus: Ohio State University Press.

Boatright, Robert. 2013. *Getting Primaried: The Changing Politics of Congressional Primary Challenges*. Ann Arbor: University of Michigan Press.

Bonica, Adam. 2014. "Mapping the Ideological Marketplace." *American Journal of Political Science* 58 (2): 367–86. https://doi.org/10.1111/ajps.12062

Brady, David W., Hahrie Han, and Jeremy C. Pope. 2011. "Primary Elections and Candidate Ideology: Out of Step with the Primary Electorate?" *Legislative Studies Quarterly* 32 (1): 79–105. https://doi.org/10.3162/036298007X201994

Bratton, Kathleen A., and Stella M. Rouse. 2011. "Networks in the Legislative Arena:

How Group Dynamics Affect Cosponsorship." *Legislative Studies Quarterly* 36 (3): 423–60. https://doi.org/10.1111/J.1939-9162.2011.00021.X

Broder, David. 1971. *The Party's Over: The Failure of Politics in America*. New York: Harper & Row.

Buck, Ken, and Bill Blankschaen. 2017. *Drain the Swamp: How Washington Corruption Is Worse Than You Think*. Washington, DC: Regnery.

Bullock, John G., Alan Gerber, Seth J. Hill, and Gregory A. Huber. 2013. "Partisan Bias in Factual Beliefs About Politics." National Bureau of Economic Research. https://doi.org/10.3386/w19080.

Caldera, Camille. 2020. "Fact Check: Claim About Sen. Lindsey Graham's Calls to State Officials Is Misleading." *USA Today*. https://www.usatoday.com/story/news/factcheck/2020/11/20/fact-check-claim-lindsey-graham-calls-georgia-arizona-nevada-misleading/6341301002/

Caldwell, Leigh Ann. 2021. "House Democrats Draw the Line: No Bipartisan Cooperation with Republicans Who Questioned the Election." NBC News. https://www.nbcnews.com/politics/congress/house-democrats-draw-line-no-bipartisan-cooperation-republicans-who-questioned-n1261015

Canes-Wrone, Brandice, David W. Brady, and John F. Cogan. 2002. "Out of Step, Out of Office: Electoral Accountability and House Members' Voting." *American Political Science Review* 96 (1): 127–40. https://doi.org/10.1017/S0003055402004276

Carper, Thomas. 2017. "RT @EPWDems: Senate Democrats call on Republican leaders to postpone final vote on nomination of Scott Pruitt to lead the EPA." February 17. Twitter.

Carson, Jamie L., Gregory Koger, Matthew J. Lebo, and Everett Young. 2010. "The Electoral Costs of Party Loyalty in Congress." *American Journal of Political Science* 54 (3): 598–616. https://doi.org/10.1111/j.1540-5907.2010.00449.x

Casas, Andreu, Matthew J. Denny, and John Wilkerson. 2020. "More Effective Than We Thought: Accounting for Legislative Hitchhikers Reveals a More Inclusive and Productive Lawmaking Process." *American Journal of Political Science* 64 (1): 5–18.

Castor, Kathy. 2018. "Trump/GOP repeal of #NetNeutrality goes into effect today even though most Americans support free, open internet. This will hurt small businesses & consumers! @SpeakerRyan @HouseGOP blocking @USRepMikeDoyle resolution to #SavetheInternet even after Senate voted to do so!" June 11. Twitter.

Clymer, Adam. 2017. "Robert Michel Dies at 93; House G.O.P. Leader Prized Conciliation." *New York Times*, February 17. https://www.nytimes.com/2017/02/17/us/robert-michel-dies.html

Converse, Phillip. 1964. "The Nature of Belief Systems in Mass Publics." In *Ideology and Its Dimensions*, edited by David E. Apter. New York: Free Press of Glencoe.

Cortez-Masto, Catherine. 2018. "Today is the day. @SenateDems are officially filing the petition that allows us to force a vote on the Senate floor to save #NetNeutrality. But we still need #OneMoreVote to get it done. If you want to protect a free, open internet, make your voices heard before it's too late!" May 9. Twitter.

Costa, Mia. 2020. "Ideology, Not Affect: What Americans Want from Political Representation." *American Journal of Political Science* 65 (2): 342–58. https://doi.org/10.1111/ajps.12571

Cox, Gary, and Mathew D. McCubbins. 1991. "On the Decline of Party Voting in Congress." *Legislative Studies Quarterly* 16 (4): 547–70. https://doi.org/10.2307/440017

Cox, Gary, and Mathew McCubbins. 2005. *Setting the Agenda: Responsible Party Government in the U.S. House of Representatives*. New York: Cambridge University Press.

Craig, Alison W. 2021. "It Takes a Coalition: The Community Impacts of Collaboration." *Legislative Studies Quarterly* 46 (1): 11–48. https://doi.org/10.1111/LSQ.12324

Craig, Alison, Skyler J. Cranmer, Bruce A. Desmarais, Christopher J. Clark, and Vincent G. Moscardelli. 2015. "The Role of Race, Ethnicity, and Gender in the Congressional Cosponsorship Network." arXiv, December 18. https://arxiv.org/abs/1512.06141v1

Crespin, Michael H., David W. Rohde, and Ryan J. Vander Wielen. 2011. "Measuring Variations in Party Unity Voting: An Assessment of Agenda Effects." *Party Politics* 19 (3): 432–57. https://doi.org/10.1177/135406881140757

Crosson, Jesse M., Alexander C. Furnas, Timothy Lapira, and Casey Burgat. 2021. "Partisan Competition and the Decline in Legislative Capacity among Congressional Offices." *Legislative Studies Quarterly* 46 (3): 745–89. https://doi.org/10.1111/lsq.12301

Currinder, Marian. 2003. "Leadership PAC Contribution Strategies and House Member Ambitions." *Legislative Studies Quarterly* 28 (4): 551–77. https://doi.org/10.3162/036298003X201006

Currinder, Marian. 2008. *Money in the House: Campaign Funds and Congressional Party Politics*. Boulder: Westview Press.

Curry, James. 2015. *Legislating in the Dark: Information and Power in the House of Representatives*. Chicago: University of Chicago Press.

Curry, James, and Frances E. Lee. 2020. *The Limits of Party: Congress and Lawmaking in a Polarized Era*. Chicago: University of Chicago Press.

Curry, James, and Jason Roberts. Forthcoming. "Interpersonal Relationships, Bipartisanship, and January 6th." *American Political Science Review*, 1–7. https://doi.org/10.1017/S000305542400114X

Dancey, Logan, and Jasmine Masand. 2017. "Race and Representation on Twitter: Members of Congress' Responses to the Deaths of Michael Brown and Eric Garner." *Politics, Groups, and Identities* 7:267–86. https://doi.org/10.1080/21565503.2017.1354037

Dancey, Logan, and Geoffrey Sheagley. 2018. "Partisanship and Perceptions of Party-Line Voting in Congress." *Political Research Quarterly* 71 (1): 32–45.

Deering, Christopher J., and Paul J. Wahlbeck. 2006. "U.S. House Committee Chair Selection: Republicans Play Musical Chairs in the 107th Congress." *American Politics Research* 34 (2): 223–42. https://doi.org/10.1177/1532673X05284410

Dietrich, Bryce J. 2021. "Using Motion Detection to Measure Social Polarization in the U.S. House of Representatives." *Political Analysis* 29:250–59. https://doi.org/10.1017/pan.2020.25

Dinesh, Shradha, and Meltem Odabas. 2023. "8 Facts About Americans and Twitter as It Rebrands to X." Pew Research Center, July 26. https://www.pewresearch.org/short-reads/2023/07/26/8-facts-about-americans-and-twitter-as-it-rebrands-to-x/

Dingell, John. 2014. "When Congress Worked." National Press Club, June 27. https://www.youtube.com/watch?v=LYdC5MEoAz8

Dobbs, Lou, and John Roberts, dirs. 2019. "October 23, 2019." *Lou Dobbs Tonight*. Fox

News. https://www.proquest.com/pq1academic/other-sources/adding-historic
-successes-trump-on-syria-let/docview/2308328450

Dodd, Lawrence C., and Scot Schraufnagel. 2013. "Taking Incivility Seriously." In *Politics to the Extreme: American Political Institutions in the Twenty-First Century*, edited by Scott A. Frisch and Sean Q. Kelly, 71–91. New York: Palgrave MacMillan US.

Doherty, Carroll, and Jocelyn Kiley. 2016. "Key Facts About Partisanship and Political Animosity in America." Pew Research Center, June 22. https://www.pewresearch.org/fact-tank/2016/06/22/key-facts-partisanship/

Doherty, Carroll, Jocelyn Kiley, Nida Asheer, and Talia Price. 2023. "Americans' Dismal Views of the Nation's Politics." Pew Research Center, September 19. https://www.pewresearch.org/politics/2023/09/19/americans-dismal-views-of-the-nations-politics/

Druckman, James N., Erik Peterson, and Rune Slothuus. 2013. "How Elite Partisan Polarization Affects Public Opinion Formation." *American Political Science Review* 107 (1): 58–79. https://doi.org/10.1017/S0003055412000500

Egan, Patrick J. 2013. *Partisan Priorities: How Issue Ownership Drives and Distorts American Politics*. New York: Cambridge University Press.

Egar, William T. 2016. "Tarnishing Opponents, Polarizing Congress: The House Minority Party and the Construction of the Roll-Call Record." *Legislative Studies Quarterly* 41 (4): 935–64. https://doi.org/10.1111/LSQ.12135

Elkind, Elizabeth. 2024. "Democratic Pols Ditch Twitter After Elon Musk Takeover, Report Shows." *Fox News* (blog), December 27. https://www.foxnews.com/politics/democratic-pols-ditch-twitter-after-elon-musk-takeover-report-shows

Everett, Burgess. 2019. "Former Mississippi Sen. Thad Cochran Dies at 81." *Politico*, May 30. https://www.politico.com/story/2019/05/30/thad-cochran-dead-1347664

Everson, Phil, Rick Valelly, Arjun Vishwanath, and Jim Wiseman. 2016. "NOMINATE and American Political Development: A Primer." *Studies in American Political Development* 30:97–115. https://doi.org/10.1017/S0898588X16000067

Fenno, Richard. 1978. *Home Style: House Members in Their Districts*. Glenview, IL: Scott, Foresman.

Fiorina, Morris. 1974. *Representatives, Roll Calls, and Constituencies*. Lexington, MA: Lexington Books.

Flynn, D. J., and Laurel Harbridge. 2016. "How Partisan Conflict in Congress Affects Public Opinion: Strategies, Outcomes, and Issue Differences." *American Politics Research* 44 (5): 875–902. https://doi.org/10.1177/1532673X15610425

Foran, Claire. 2019. "Trump Insults Mitt Romney After Republican Senator's Tough Criticism of President." CNN Politics, October 5. https://www.cnn.com/2019/10/04/politics/romney-trump-china-ukraine-rebuke/index.html

Fowler, James H. 2006. "Connecting the Congress: A Study of Cosponsorship Networks." *Political Analysis* 14 (4): 456–87. https://doi.org/10.1093/pan/mpl002

Franken, Al. 2017. *Al Franken: Giant of the Senate*. New York: Hachette Book Group.

Gadarian, Shana Kushner, Sara Wallace Goodman, and Thomas B. Pepinsky. 2021. "Partisanship, Health Behavior, and Policy Attitudes in the Early Stages of the COVID-19 Pandemic." *PLOS One* 16 (4): e0249596. https://doi.org/10.1371/journal.pone.0249596

Garlick, Alex. 2015. "'The Letter After Your Name': Party Labels on Virginia Ballots."

State Politics & Policy Quarterly 15 (2): 147–70. https://doi.org/10.1177/1532440 015573015

Gelman, Jeremy. 2018. "If Congress Is So Dysfunctional, Why Is Its Staff So Busy? A Congressional Fellow's Perspective." *PS: Political Science & Politics* 51 (2): 494–95. https://doi.org/10.1017/S1049096518000288

Gelman, Jeremy. 2019. "In Pursuit of Power: Competition for Majority Status and Senate Partisanship." *Party Politics* 25 (6): 782–93. https://doi.org/10.1177/1354068 8177497

Gelman, Jeremy. 2020a. *Losing to Win: Why Congressional Majorities Play Politics Instead of Make Laws*. Ann Arbor: University of Michigan Press.

Gelman, Jeremy. 2020b. "Partisan Intensity in Congress: Evidence from Brett Kavanaugh's Supreme Court Nomination." *Political Research Quarterly* 74 (2): 450–63. https://doi.org/10.1177/1065912920911464

Gelman, Jeremy. 2024. "The Deaths of Ideas in Congress." *Political Research Quarterly* 77 (3): 772–886. https://doi.org/10.1177/10659129241246003

Gelman, Jeremy, and Steven Lloyd Wilson. 2022. "Measuring Congressional Partisanship and Its Consequences." *Legislative Studies Quarterly* 47 (1): 225–56. https://doi.org/10.1111/lsq.12331

Gelman, Jeremy, Steven Lloyd Wilson, and Constanza Sanhueza Petrarca. 2021. "Mixing Messages: How Candidates Vary in Their Use of Twitter." *Journal of Information Technology and Politics* 18 (1): 101–15. https://doi.org/10.1080/19331681.2020.18 14929

Gerber, Alan, and Gregory A. Huber. 2010. "Partisanship, Political Control, and Economic Assessments." *American Journal of Political Science* 54 (1): 153–73. https://doi.org/10.1111/j.1540-5907.2009.00424.x

Gervais, Bryan T. 2017. "More Than Mimicry? The Role of Anger in Uncivil Reactions to Elite Political Incivility." *International Journal of Public Opinion Research* 29 (3). https://doi.org/10.1093/ijpor/edw010

Gervais, Bryan T. 2019. "Rousing the Partisan Combatant: Elite Incivility, Anger, and Antideliberative Attitudes." *Political Psychology* 40 (3): 637–55. https://doi.org/10 .1111/pops.12532

Gervais, Bryan T., and Irwin L. Morris. 2018. *Reactionary Republicanism: How the Tea Party Paved the Way for Trump's Victory*. New York: Oxford University Press.

Gervais, Bryan T., and Walter Wilson. 2017. "New Media for the New Electorate? Congressional Outreach to Latinos on Twitter." *Politics, Groups, and Identities* 7:305–23. https://doi.org/10.1080/21565503.2017.1358186

Gilmour, John. 1995. *Strategic Disagreement: Stalemate in American Politics*. Pittsburgh: University of Pittsburgh Press.

Golbeck, Jennifer, Justin Grimes, and Anthony Rogers. 2010. "Twitter Use by the US Congress." *Journal of the American Society for Information Science and Technology* 61 (8): 1612–21. https://doi.org/10.1002/asi.21344

Goldmacher, Shane. 2013. "Dana Rohrabacher: Chairman of the Trolling Caucus." *National Journal*, September 24. https://www.nationaljournal.com/s/69843/da na-rohrabacher-chairman-trolling-caucus

Gosar, Paul. 2019. "I'm Joining @RepMattGaetz and Other Colleagues This Morning Demanding Transparency in This Sham Impeachment Inquiry. What Do Democrats Have to Hide? The American People Deserve the Truth!" October 23. Twitter.

Graham, Lindsey. 2019. "Whether you agree with impeachment or not, Trump Derangement Syndrome has reached a new level. House Democrats refusing to send the Articles of Impeachment to the Senate because they don't like the way we may do the trial—that is just scary." December 19. Twitter.

Green, Matthew N., and Douglas B. Harris. 2019. *Choosing the Leader: Leadership Elections in the U.S. House of Representatives.* New Haven: Yale University Press.

Grimmer, Justin. 2013. *Representational Style in Congress: What Legislators Say and Why It Matters.* New York: Cambridge University Press.

Grimmer, Justin, Solomon Messing, and Sean J. Westwood. 2012. "How Words and Money Cultivate a Personal Vote: The Effect of Legislator Credit Claiming on Constituent Credit Allocation." *American Political Science Review* 106 (4). https://doi.org/10.1017/S0003055412000457

Grose, Christian R., Neil Malhotra, and Robert Van Houweling. 2015. "Explaining Explanations: How Legislators Explain Their Policy Positions and How Citizens React." *American Journal of Political Science* 59 (3): 724–43. https://doi.org/10.1111/AJPS.12164

Grossmann, Matt, and David A. Hopkins. 2015. "Ideological Republicans and Group Interest Democrats: The Asymmetry of American Party Politics." *Perspectives on Politics* 13 (1): 119–39. https://doi.org/10.1017/S1537592714003168

Hall, Richard. 1996. *Participation in Congress.* New Haven: Yale University Press.

Harbridge, Laurel. 2015. *Is Bipartisanship Dead? Policy Agreement and Agenda-Setting in the House of Representatives.* New York: Cambridge University Press.

Harbridge, Laurel, and Neil Malhotra. 2011. "Electoral Incentives and Partisan Conflict in Congress: Evidence from Survey Experiments." *American Journal of Political Science* 55 (3): 494–510. https://doi.org/10.1111/J.1540-5907.2011.00517.X

Harbridge-Yong, Laurel, Craig Volden, and Alan E. Wiseman. 2023. "The Bipartisan Path to Effective Lawmaking." *Journal of Politics* 85 (3): 1048–63. https://doi.org/10.1086/723805

Harward, Brian M., and Kenneth W. Moffett. 2010. "The Calculus of Cosponsorship in the U.S. Senate." *Legislative Studies Quarterly* 35 (1): 117–43. https://doi.org/10.3162/036298010790821950

Hassell, Hans J. G. 2016. "Party Control of Party Primaries: Party Influence in Nominations for the US Senate." *Journal of Politics* 78 (1): 75–87. https://doi.org/10.1086/683072

Heberling, Eric S., and Bruce A. Larson. 2012. *Congressional Parties, Institutional Ambition, and the Financing of Majority Control.* Ann Arbor: University of Michigan Press.

Heitkamp, Heidi. 2018a. "@FCC North Dakota businesses are worried about higher online business costs, & many working families & millennials are anxious about rising internet rates & limited access. Let's #SaveTheInternet & allow North Dakotans to thrive." April 23. Twitter.

Heitkamp, Heidi. 2018b. "In May, the President signed my bipartisan #Relief4MainStreet bill into law which included provisions I fought for to help boost investments in #smallbiz & startups in ND & rural America by eliminating unnecessary red tape. Read more @emergingprairie." October 2. Twitter.

Hibbing, John R. 1986. "Ambition in the House: Behavioral Consequences of Higher Office Goals Among U.S. Representatives." *American Journal of Political Science* 30 (3): 651–65. https://doi.org/10.2307/2111094

Hill, Seth J. 2017. "Learning Together Slowly: Bayesian Learning About Political Facts." *Journal of Politics* 79 (4): 1403–18. https://doi.org/10.1086/692739

Hill, Seth J., and Gregory A. Huber. 2019. "On the Meaning of Survey Reports of Roll-Call 'Votes.'" *American Journal of Political Science* 63 (3): 611–25. https://onlineli brary.wiley.com/doi/full/10.1111/ajps.12430

Hong, James, Jacob Ritchie, Jeremy Barenholtz, Will Crichton, Daniel Fu, Ben Hannel, Xinwei Yao et al. 2021. "Analysis of Faces in a Decade of US Cable TV News." In *Proceedings of the 27th ACM SIGKDD International Conference on Knowledge Discovery & Data Mining.* Association for Computing Machinery.

Hopkins, Daniel J., and Hans Noel. 2022. "Trump and the Shifting Meaning of 'Conservative': Using Activists' Pairwise Comparisons to Measure Politicians' Perceived Ideologies." *American Political Science Review* 116 (3): 1133–40. https://doi.org/10 .1017/S0003055421001416

Huber, Gregory A., and Neil Malhotra. 2017. "Political Homophily in Social Relationships: Evidence from Online Dating Behavior." *Journal of Politics* 79 (1): 269–83. https://doi.org/10.1086/687533

Huddy, Leonie, Lilliana Mason, and Lene Aaroe. 2015. "Expressive Partisanship: Campaign Involvement, Political Emotion, and Partisan Identity." *American Political Science Review* 109 (1): 1–17. https://doi.org/10.1017/S0003055414000604

Iyengar, Shanto, Yphtach Lelkes, Matthew Levendusky, Neil Malhotra, and Sean J. Westwood. 2019. "The Origins and Consequences of Affective Polarization in the United States." *Annual Review of Political Science* 22:129–46. https://doi.org/10.11 46/annurev-polisci-051117-073034

Iyengar, Shanto, Gaurav Sood, and Yphtach Lelkes. 2012. "Affect, Not Ideology: A Social Identity Perspective on Polarization." *Public Opinion Quarterly* 76 (3): 405–31. https://doi.org/10.1093/POQ/NFS038

Jackson, John E., and John W. Kingdon. 1992. "Ideology, Interest Group Scores, and Legislative Votes." *American Journal of Political Science* 36 (3): 805–23. https://doi .org/10.2307/2111592

Jacobson, Gary. 2015. "It's Nothing Personal: The Decline of the Incumbency Advantage in US House Elections." *Journal of Politics* 77 (3): 861–73. https://doi.org/10 .1086/681670

Jacobson, Gary. 2017. "The Electoral Connection, Then and Now." In *Governing in a Polarized Age: Elections, Parties, and Political Representation*, edited by Alan Geber and Eric Schickler, 35–64. New York: Cambridge University Press.

Jacobson, Gary. 2019. "Extreme Referendum: Donald Trump and the 2018 Midterm Elections." *Political Science Quarterly* 134 (1): 9–38. https://doi.org/10.1002/po lq.12866

Jenkins, Jeffrey A., Michael H. Crespin, and Jamie L. Carson. 2005. "Parties as Procedural Coalitions in Congress: An Examination of Differing Career Tracks." *Legislative Studies Quarterly* 30 (3): 365–89. https://doi.org/10.3162/036298005X201590

Jenkins, Jeffery A., and Nathan W. Monroe. 2012. "Buying Negative Agenda Control in the U.S. House." *American Journal of Political Science* 56 (4): 897–912. https://doi .org/10.1111/J.1540-5907.2012.00593.X

Jewitt, Caitlin, and Sarah A. Treul. 2019. "Ideological Primary Competition and Congressional Behavior." *Congress & the Presidency* 46 (3): 471–94. https://doi.org/10 .1080/07343469.2019.1600173

Jungherr, Andreas. 2016. "Twitter Use in Election Campaigns: A Systematic Literature Review." *Journal of Information Technology and Politics* 1:72–91. https://doi.org/10.1080/19331681.2015.1132401

Kanthak, Kristin. 2007. "Crystal Elephants and Committee Chairs: Campaign Contributions and Leadership Races in the U.S. House of Representatives." *American Politics Research* 35 (3): 389–406. https://doi.org/10.1177/1532673X0629807

Kelly, Caroline, and Manu Raju. 2020. "Georgia Secretary of State Says Lindsey Graham Implied He Should Try to Throw Away Ballots." CNN Politics, November 17. https://www.cnn.com/2020/11/16/politics/georgia-secretary-of-state-lindsey-graham-ballots-cnntv/index.html

Kirby, Jen. 2018. "Lindsey Graham Rages in Kavanaugh Hearing: 'This Is the Most Unethical Sham.'" *Vox*, September 27. https://www.vox.com/2018/9/27/17911604/kavanaugh-lindsey-graham-ford-hearings

Kirkland, Justin. 2011. "The Relational Determinants of Legislative Outcomes: Strong and Weak Ties Between Legislators." *Journal of Politics* 73 (3): 887–98. https://doi.org/10.1017/S0022381611000533

Kirkland, Justin, and Jonathan Slapin. 2017. "Ideology and Strategic Party Disloyalty in the US House of Representatives." *Electoral Studies* 49:26–37. https://doi.org/10.1016/j.electstud.2017.07.006

Koger, Gregory. 2003. "Position Taking and Cosponsorship in the U.S. House." *Legislative Studies Quarterly* 28 (2): 225–46. https://doi.org/10.3162/036298003X200872

Koger, Gregory, and Matthew J. Lebo. 2017. *Strategic Party Government: Why Winning Trumps Ideology*. Chicago: University of Chicago Press.

Krehbiel, Keith. 1993. "Where's the Party?" *British Journal of Political Science* 23 (2): 235–66. https://doi.org/10.1017/S0007123400009741

Krehbiel, Keith. 2000. "Party Discipline and Measures of Partisanship." *American Journal of Political Science* 44 (2): 212–27. https://doi.org/10.2307/2669306

Kriner, Douglas, and Liam Schwartz. 2008. "Divided Government and Congressional Investigations." *Legislative Studies Quarterly* 33 (2): 295–321. https://doi.org/10.3162/036298008784310993

Lawless, Jennifer, Sean Theriault, and Samantha Guthrie. 2018. "Nice Girls? Sex, Collegiality, and Bipartisan Cooperation in the US Congress." *Journal of Politics* 80 (4): 1268–82. https://doi.org/10.1086/698884

Lawrence, Eric D., Forrest Maltzman, and Steven S. Smith. 2006. "Who Wins? Party Effects in Legislative Voting." *Legislative Studies Quarterly* 31 (1): 33–69. https://doi.org/10.3162/036298006X201724

Lawrence, John A. 2018. *The Class of '74: Congress After Watergate and the Roots of Partisanship*. Baltimore: Johns Hopkins University Press.

Lee, Frances. 2009. *Beyond Ideology*. Chicago: University of Chicago Press.

Lee, Frances. 2016. *Insecure Majorities: Congress and the Perpetual Campaign*. Chicago: University of Chicago Press.

Levine, Marianne. 2019. "Lindsey Graham Will Give Judiciary Chairmanship Back to Chuck Grassley." *Politico*, October 31. https://www.politico.com/news/2019/10/31/graham-judiciary-chairmanship-grassley-062993

Lewallen, Jonathan. 2020. "Booster Seats: New Committee Chairs and Legislative Effectiveness." *Journal of Legislative Studies* 26 (4): 496–522. https://doi.org/10.1080/13572334.2020.1771890

Macdonald, Maggie, Annelise Russell, and Whitney Hua. 2023. "Negative Sentiment and Congressional Cue-Taking on Social Media." *PS: Political Science & Politics* 56 (2): 201–6. https://doi.org/10.1017/S1049096522001299

Maddow, Rachel, dir. 2019. "The Rachel Maddow Show for October 23, 2019." *The Rachel Maddow Show*. MSNBC, October 23. https://www.proquest.com/pq1ac ademic/other-sources/rachel-maddow-show-october-23-2019-msnbc/docview /2308719085

Madison, James. 1787. "Federalist No. 10." *The Federalist Papers*. Available at Avalon Project, Yale Law School. https://avalon.law.yale.edu/18th_century/fed10.asp

Maltzmann, Forrest, and Lee Sigelman. 1996. "The Politics of Talk: Unconstrained Floor Time in the U.S. House of Representatives." *Journal of Politics* 58:819–30.

Mann, Thomas, and Norman Ornstein. 2012. *It's Even Worse Than It Looks*. New York: Basic Books.

Manning, Christopher D., Mihai Surdeanu, John Bauer, Jenny Finkel, Steven J. Bethard, and David McClosky. 2014. "The Stanford CoreNLP Natural Language Processing Toolkit." In *Proceedings of the 52nd Annual Meeting of the Association for Computational Linguistics: System Demonstrations*, 55–60. Baltimore: Association for Computational Linguistics.

Mason, Lilliana. 2018. *Uncivil Agreement: How Politics Became Our Identity*. Chicago: University of Chicago Press.

Mathes, Michael. 2019. "Republicans Storm Secure Impeachment Deposition, Delay Testimony." AFP International Text Wire, October 23. https://www.proquest.com /pq1academic/wire-feeds/republicans-storm-secure-impeachment-deposition /docview/2307854864

Mayhew, David. 1974. *Congress: The Electoral Connection*. New Haven: Yale University Press.

McCarty, Nolan. 2019. *Polarization: What Everyone Needs to Know*. New York: Oxford University Press.

McCarty, Nolan, Keith T. Poole, and Howard Rosenthal. 2001. "The Hunt for Party Discipline in Congress." *American Political Science Review* 95 (3): 673–87. https:// doi.org/10.1017/S0003055401003069

McCarty, Nolan, Keith T. Poole, and Howard Rosenthal. 2016. *Polarized America: The Dance of Ideology and Unequal Riches*. Cambridge, MA: MIT Press.

McGrath, Robert J. 2013. "Congressional Oversight Hearings and Policy Control." *Legislative Studies Quarterly* 38 (3): 349–76. https://doi.org/10.1111/LSQ.12018

McPherson, Lindsey. 2018. "Here Are All the Republicans Jockeying for Committee Leadership Positions (So Far)." *Roll Call*, August 29. https://rollcall.com/2018/08 /29/here-are-all-the-republicans-jockeying-for-committee-leadership-positions -so-far/

Mechkova, Valeriya, and Steven Wilson. 2021. "Norms and Rage: Gender and Social Media in the 2018 US Midterm Elections." *Electoral Studies* 69:102268. https://doi .org/10.1016/j.electstud.2020.102268

Meinke, Scott. 2009. "Presentation of Partisanship: Constituency Connections and Partisan Congressional Activity." *Social Science Quarterly* 90 (4): 777–1038. https://doi.org/10.1111/j.1540-6237.2009.00666.x

Meyer, Chase B. 2021. "Getting 'Primaried' in the Senate: Primary Challengers and the Roll-Call Voting Behavior of Sitting Senators." *Congress & the Presidency*. https:// doi.org/10.1080/07343469.2021.1922541

Minozzi, William, and Craig Volden. 2013. "Who Heeds the Call of the Party in Congress?" *Journal of Politics* 75 (3): 787–802. https://doi.org/10.1017/S0022381613 000480

Miras, Nicholas S. 2019. "Polls and Elections: Resistance Is Not Futile: Anti-Trump Protest and Senators' Opposition to President Trump in the 115th Congress." *Presidential Studies Quarterly* 49 (4): 932–58. https://doi.org/10.1111/PSQ.12575

"Morning Consult Senator Rankings." 2019. Morning Consult. https://morningconsult.com/senator-rankings/ (accessed June 21, 2021).

Morris, Jonathan S. 2001. "Reexamining the Politics of Talk: Partisan Rhetoric in the 104th House." *Legislative Studies Quarterly* 26 (1): 101–21. https://doi.org/10.23 07/440405

Nocera, Kate. 2014. "House Democrats Try to Shake Down Members for Dues Payments." BuzzFeed News, March 10. https://www.buzzfeednews.com/article/kate nocera/house-democrats-try-to-shake-down-members-for-dues-payments

Nyhan, Brendan. 2014. "The Partisan Divide on Ebola Preparedness." *New York Times*, October 16. https://www.nytimes.com/2014/10/17/upshot/the-partisan-divide -on-ebola-preparedness.html

Nyhan, Brendan, Eric McGhee, John Sides, Seth Masket, and Steven Greene. 2012. "One Vote Out of Step? The Effects of Salient Roll Call Votes in the 2010 Election." *American Politics Research* 40 (5): 844–79. https://doi.org/10.1177/15326 73X11433

Obama, Barack. 2020. *A Promised Land*. New York: Random House.

Parker, David C. W., and Matthew Dull. 2009. "Divided We Quarrel: The Politics of Congressional Investigations, 1947–2004." *Legislative Studies Quarterly* 34 (3): 319–45. https://doi.org/10.3162/036298009788897790

"The Partisan Divide on Political Values Grows Even Wider." 2017. Pew Research Center, October 5. https://www.pewresearch.org/politics/2017/10/05/the-partisan -divide-on-political-values-grows-even-wider/

Patterson, Samuel C., and Gregory A. Caldeira. 1988. "Party Voting in the United States Congress." *British Journal of Political Science* 18 (1): 111–31. https://doi.org/10.10 17/S000712340000497X

Pearson, Kathryn. 2015. *Party Discipline in the U.S. House of Representatives*. Ann Arbor: University of Michigan Press.

Pink, Sophia L., James Chu, James N. Druckman, David G. Rand, and Robb Willer. 2021. "Elite Party Cues Increase Vaccination Intentions Among Republicans." *Proceedings of the National Academy of Sciences* 118 (32): e2106559118. https://doi.org /10.1073/pnas.2106559118

Polsby, Nelson. 2004. *How Congress Evolves*. New York: Oxford University Press.

Price, David. 2013. "The Twilight of Appropriations." *Politico*, September 22. https:// www.politico.com/story/2013/09/budget-twilight-appropriations-david-price-09 7171

Ragusa, Jordan M. 2016. "Partisan Cohorts, Polarization, and the Gingrich Senators." *American Politics Research* 44 (2): 296–325. https://doi.org/10.1177/1532673X15 597746

Reagan, Ronald. 1990. *An American Life*. New York: Simon and Schuster.

Reynolds, Molly. 2017. "Who Fights the Good (Party) Fight? Individual Incentives to Engage in Partisan Messaging in the US Senate." In *NCAPSA American Politics Workshop*, 1–24.

Reynolds, Molly, and Peter Hanson. 2023. "Just How Unorthodox? Assessing Lawmaking on Omnibus Spending Bills." *The Forum* 21 (2): 213–38. https://doi.org/10.15 15/for-2023-2021

Rhodes, Jesse H., and Zachary Albert. 2017. "The Transformation of Partisan Rhetoric in American Presidential Campaigns, 1952–2012." *Party Politics* 23 (5): 566–77. https://doi.org/10.1177/1354068815610968

Rippere, Paulina S. 2016. "Polarization Reconsidered: Bipartisan Cooperation Through Bill Cosponsorship." *Polity* 48 (2): 243–78. https://doi.org/10.1057/pol.2016.4

Roberts, Jason M., and Steven S. Smith. 2003. "Procedural Contexts, Party Strategy, and Conditional Party Voting in the U.S. House of Representatives, 1971–2000." *American Journal of Political Science* 47 (2): 305–17. https://doi.org/10.1111/15 40-5907.00021

Rocca, Michael S., and Stacy B. Gordon. 2010. "The Position-Taking Value of Bill Sponsorship in Congress." *Political Research Quarterly* 63 (2): 387–97. https://doi.org /10.1177/1065912908330347

"Rules for the Democratic Conference." 2022. Senate Democratic Conference, December 21. https://www.democrats.senate.gov/rules-for-the-democratic-conference

Russell, Annelise. 2018. "U.S. Senators on Twitter: Asymmetric Party Rhetoric in 140 Characters." *American Politics Research* 46 (4): 695–723. https://doi.org/10.1177 /1532673X17715619

Russell, Annelise. 2021a. "Minority Opposition and Asymmetric Parties? Senators' Partisan Rhetoric on Twitter." *Political Research Quarterly* 74 (3): 615–27. https:// doi.org/10.1177/1065912920921239

Russell, Annelise. 2021b. *Tweeting Is Leading: How Senators Communicate and Represent in the Age of Twitter*. New York: Oxford University Press.

Sanders, Bernie. 2018. "The repeal of #NetNeutrality hands the internet over to a handful of corporations while people of color, low-income families, disabled communities and rural towns get pushed offline. with @mediajustice." May 16. Twitter.

Scalise, Steve. 2019. "RT @Robert_Aderholt This Impeachment Process Is Literally Being Conducted in the Basement of the Capitol, behind Closed Doors, to Keep You from Seeing What Is Taking Place. It Is a Mockery! #StopTheSchiffShow." October 23. Twitter.

Schaffner, Brian F., and Matthew J. Streb. 2002. "The Partisan Heuristic in Low-Information Elections." *Public Opinion Quarterly* 66 (4): 559–81. https://doi.org /10.1086/343755

Seelye, Katharine Q. 2021. "Alcee Hastings, Longtime Florida Congressman, Dies at 84." *New York Times*, April 6. https://www.nytimes.com/2021/04/06/us/politics /alcee-hastings-dead.html

"Sen. Feinstein Announces She Will Not Seek Judiciary Chair." 2020. KPIX, November 23. https://sanfrancisco.cbslocal.com/2020/11/23/sen-feinstein-announces-she -will-not-seek-judiciary-chair/

Shutt, Jennifer. 2020. "Candidates for Appropriations Gavel Laying Groundwork." Roll Call, February 18. https://rollcall.com/2020/02/18/candidates-for-appropriations -gavel-laying-groundwork/

Sinclair, Barbara. 2006. *Party Wars: Polarization and the Politics of National Policymaking*. Norman: University of Oklahoma Press.

Sinclair, Barbara. 2016. *Unorthodox Lawmaking: New Legislative Processes in the U.S. Congress*. Washington, DC: Congressional Quarterly Press.

Slothuus, Rune. 2010. "When Can Political Parties Lead Public Opinion? Evidence from a Natural Experiment." *Political Communication* 27 (2): 158–77. https://doi.org/10.1080/10584601003709381

Slothuus, Rune, and Claes H. de Vreese. 2010. "Political Parties, Motivated Reasoning, and Issue Framing." *Journal of Politics* 72 (3): 630–45. https://doi.org/10.1017/S0022381610000006X

Smith, Steven. 2014. *The Senate Syndrome*. Norman: University of Oklahoma Press.

Snyder, James M., Jr., and Tim Groseclose. 2000. "Estimating Party Influence in Congressional Roll-Call Voting." *American Journal of Political Science* 44 (2): 193–211. https://doi.org/10.2307/2669305

Socher, Richard, Alex Perelygin, Jean Wu, Jason Chuang, Christopher Manning, Andrew Ng, and Christopher Potts. 2013. "Recursive Deep Models for Semantic Compositionality Over a Sentiment Treebank." In *Proceedings of the 2013 Conference on Empirical Methods in Natural Language Processing*, 1631–42. Seattle: Association for Computational Linguistics.

Stapleton, Carey E., and Ryan Dawkins. 2021. "Catching My Anger: How Political Elites Create Angrier Citizens." *Political Research Quarterly* 75 (3): 754–65. https://doi.org/10.1177/10659129211026972

Stewart, Charles, III, and Jonathan Woon. 2022a. "Congressional Committee Assignments, 103rd–115th Congresses, 1993–2017: House." Available at https://web.mit.edu/17.251/www/data_page.html#2

Stewart, Charles, III, and Jonathan Woon. 2022b. "Congressional Committee Assignments, 103rd–115th Congresses, 1993–2017: Senate." Available at https://web.mit.edu/17.251/www/data_page.html#2

Stimson, James A., and Emily A. Wager. 2020. *Converging on Truth: A Dynamic Perspective on Factual Debates in American Public Opinion*. New York: Cambridge Elements.

Straus, Jacob R., Matthew Eric Glassman, Colleen J. Shogan, and Susan Navarro Smelcer. 2013. "Communicating in 140 Characters or Less: Congressional Adoption of Twitter in the 111th Congress." *PS—Political Science and Politics* 46 (1): 60–66. https://doi.org/10.1017/S1049096512001242

Straus, Jacob, Raymond Williams, Colleen J. Shogan, and Matthew Glassman. 2014. "Social Media as a Communication Tool in Congress: Evaluating Senate Usage of Twitter in the 113th Congress." In *American Political Science Association Annual Meeting*, 1–22. https://papers.ssrn.com/sol3/papers.cfm?abstract_id=2452781

Strong, Jonathan, and Abby Livingston. 2012. "Busy Chris Van Hollen Looking at Leadership?" *Roll Call*, October 24. https://rollcall.com/2012/10/24/busy-chris-van-hollen-looking-at-leadership/

Sykes, Charles. 2019. "The Humiliation of Lindsey Graham." *Politico*, October 7. https://www.politico.com/magazine/story/2019/10/07/trump-lindsey-graham-syria-kurds-turkey-229541/

Tapper, Jake, dir. 2019. "Trump Declares Victory in Handling of Syria Crisis; Republicans Forcibly Crash Impeachment Testimony." *The Lead with Jake Tapper*. CNN, October 23. https://transcripts.cnn.com/show/cg/date/2019-10-23/segment/01

Theriault, Sean. 2008. *Party Polarization in Congress*. New York: Cambridge University Press.

Theriault, Sean. 2013. *The Gingrich Senators: The Roots of Partisan Warfare in Congress*. New York: Oxford University Press.

Theriault, Sean. 2015. "Party Warriors: The Ugly Side of Party Polarization in Congress." In *American Gridlock: The Sources, Character, and Impact of Political Polarization*, edited by James A. Thurber and Antoine Yoshinaka, 152–70. New York: Cambridge University Press.

Treul, Sarah. 2009. "Ambition and Party Loyalty in the U.S. Senate." *American Politics Research* 37 (3): 449–64. https://doi.org/10.1177/1532673X08322260

Uslaner, Eric M. 1993. *The Decline of Comity in Congress*. Ann Arbor: University of Michigan Press.

Valentino, Nicholas, Ted Brader, Eric Groenendyk, Krysha Gregorowicz, and Vincent Hutchings. 2011. "Election Night's Alright for Fighting: The Role of Emotions in Political Participation." *Journal of Politics* 73 (1): 156–70. https://doi.org/10.1017/S0022381610000939

Van Buren, Martin. 1867. *Inquiry into the Origin and Course of Political Parties in the United States*. New York: Hurd and Houghton.

Van Pykeren, Sam. 2021. "All of Lindsey Graham's Flagrantly Self-Serving Flip-Flops on Trump: A 5-Act Play." *Mother Jones*, January 11. https://www.motherjones.com/politics/2021/01/all-of-lindsay-grahams-flagrantly-self-serving-flip-flops-on-trump-a-5-act-play/

Victor, Jennifer Nicholl. 2011. "Legislating Versus Campaigning: The Legislative Behavior of Higher Office-Seekers." *American Politics Research* 39 (1): 3–31. https://doi.org/10.1177/1532673X10382854

Volden, Craig, and Alan E. Wiseman. 2014. *Legislative Effectiveness in the United States Congress*. New York: Cambridge University Press.

Wang, Amy B. 2016. "Sen. Lindsey Graham: 'I Voted Evan McMullin for President.'" *Washington Post*, November 8. https://www.washingtonpost.com/politics/2016/live-updates/general-election/real-time-updates-on-the-2016-election-voting-and-race-results/sen-lindsey-graham-i-voted-evan-mcmullin-for-president/

Wang, Ianne S., and Samara Klar. 2022. "Partisanship and Public Opinion." In *Handbook on Politics and Public Opinion*, edited by Thomas Rudolph, 168–77. Northampton, MA: Elgar.

Washington, George. 1796. "Farewell Address." Available at Avalon Project, Yale Law School. https://avalon.law.yale.edu/18th_century/washing.asp

Westwood, Sean J., Erik Peterson, and Yphtach Lelkes. 2019. "Are There Still Limits on Partisan Prejudice?" *Public Opinion Quarterly* 83 (3): 584–97. https://doi.org/10.1093/poq/nfz034

Wilkerson, John, David Smith, and Nicholas Stramp. 2015. "Tracing the Flow of Policy Ideas in Legislatures: A Text Reuse Approach." *American Journal of Political Science* 59 (4): 943–56. https://doi.org/10.1111/ajps.12175

Wiseman, Alan, and Joe Neguse. 2021. "Discussing Legislative Effectiveness with Representative Joe Neguse." Center for Effective Lawmaking. https://thelawmakers.org/video/discussing-legislative-effectiveness-with-representative-joe-neguse

Wiseman, Alan, Craig Volden, and French Hill. 2020. "Discussing Legislative Effectiveness with Representative French Hill." Center for Effective Lawmaking. https://thelawmakers.org/conversations-with-lawmakers/discussing-legislative-effectiveness-with-representative-french-hill

Wojcik, Stefan, and Adam Hughes. 2019. "Sizing Up Twitter Users." Pew Research Center, April 24. https://www.pewresearch.org/internet/2019/04/24/sizing-up-twitter-users/

Woon, Jonathan, and Jeremy C. Pope. 2008. "Made in Congress? Testing the Electoral Implications of Party Ideological Brand Names." *Journal of Politics* 70 (3): 823–36. https://doi.org/10.1017/S002238160808078X

Wulfsohn, Joseph A. 2018. "How Lindsey Graham Single-Handedly Saved Kavanaugh's Confirmation." *The Federalist*, October 1. https://thefederalist.com/2018/10/01/how-lindsey-graham-single-handedly-saved-kavanaughs-confirmation/

Zapler, Mike. 2012. "Lugar Unloads on Unrelenting Partisanship." *Politico*, May 9. https://www.politico.com/blogs/on-congress/2012/05/lugar-unloads-on-unrelenting-partisanship-122891

Zwirz, Elizabeth. 2019. "Lindsey Graham Elected Senate Judiciary Committee Chairman." Fox News, January 9. https://www.foxnews.com/politics/lindsey-graham-elected-senate-judiciary-committee-chairman

Index

Note: Page references in *italics* indicate tables and figures

Absolute Ideological Distance from the Party Median, 126
ACA. *See* Affordable Care Act
accountability, 57
across-the-aisle vetting, 34
Aderholt, Bob, 1
affective rhetoric, 76
Affordable Care Act (ACA), 4, 73–74
AFP International Text Wire, 2
agenda, 9, 28, 185n7
agenda-setting effects, 59
Aguilar, Pete, 178
Almanac of American Politics, 40
Amash, Justin, 188n3
American Political Science Association (APSA), 18
Appropriations Committee, 187n13
APSA. *See* American Political Science Association
Armed Services Committee, 187n13
Arnold, R. Douglas, 25
Associated Press, 2
Association Between Partisan Intensity and Cosponsor Partisan Balance, *120*
Association Between Partisan Intensity and Legislative Effectiveness Scores, *131*

"authorization of appropriations" clauses, 151–52

backbenchers, 14–15, 29, 107, 180
bad faith, 47, 56
Barrett, Amy Coney, 94, 187n14
Bayh, Evan, 109
Becerra, Xavier, 192n8
Benghazi hearings, 4, 52, 60
BERT. *See* Bidirectional Encoder Representations from Transformers
bickering, 41, 50, 81, 183, 191n13; ACA and, 74; cheerleading compared to, 6, 156; cosponsorship relation to, 36; Democrats and, 82; higher office and, 89; in marginal districts, 160, 162; opinion formation relation to, 75–76; opportunists and, 175; partisan acrimony and, 96; for partisan fidelity, 83; partisan intensity and, 88; partisan tone score and, 16, 79; partisan warriors and, 76–77; of party leadership, 84; politicization and, 86–87; rhetoric of, 74; seat safety and, 6, 75, 87; team players and, 39–40; Trump and, 49
Biden, Joe, 16, 82, 115, 178, 187n16

Bidirectional Encoder Representations from Transformers (BERT), 65
bill development process, 134–35, 136, 151, 193n1; hyper-partisan environment relation to, 9; partisan intensity relation to, 139–40
bipartisan rhetoric, 62
bipartisanship, 29, 48, 187n13; ACA and, 73–74; cosponsorship and, 11, 34–35, 36, 57, 122, *141*; credibility and, 129; credit-claiming opportunities and, 54; ideological extremity relation to, 122, 123; legislative effectiveness relation to, 116, 176; partisan warfare relation to, 76; party warriors relation to, 49; policy ideas relation to, 139; politicization relation to, 37
Bipartisanship Index scores, 122
Boatright, Robert, 40, 165, 167–68
Bonica, Adam, 127
Brady, David W., 157
Broder, David, 18
Brooks, Mo, 55
Burr, Richard, 94

Canes-Wrone, Brandice, 157–58, 162
Capuano, Michael, 40
Carper, Tom, 56
Castor, Kathy, 53–54
centrists, 136
CFScores, 101, 193n7
cheerleading, 49, 51, 76–77, 78, 190n10, 191n13; bickering compared to, 6, 156; higher office and, 89; for Kavanaugh, 41; of Mulvaney, 81, 82; partisan intensity and, 88; partisan tone score and, 16, 79; party brand and, 74; of party leadership, 84; president relation to, 87; public image relation to, 76; team players and, 39–40, 87; of Trump, 49; in unified government, 175–76. *See also* credit-claiming opportunities
Cheney, Liz, 188n3
civil rights issues, 52
Clark, Katherine, 178
Clinton, Bill, 181
Clinton, Hillary, 4, 9, 52, 60
Clyburn, Jim, 192n13

Clyde, Andrew, 178
Cochran, Thad, 45
CODELS. *See* fact-finding congressional delegations
Cogan, John F., 157
cohort hypothesis, 32, 103, 187n15
collective party goals, 19
Collins, Susan, 67, 68, 178
committee leaders, 31, 133, 180, 187n11; in House of Representatives, 29; legislative effectiveness of, 36; promotion-seeking behavior and, 104; in Senate, 30, 98
Common Explanations for Legislators' Partisanship, *103*
compelling behavior argument, 8
competitive districts, 22–23, 169; maximizers in, 24, 25; partisan intensity in, 6–7, 111, 180
Congress. *See specific topics*
congressional communication, 20, 61, 186n8
congressional dummy variables, 136
Congressional Quarterly (publication), 116, 124
conservative judges, 57
Cooper, Laura, 2
copartisans, 48, 62, 83–84; cosponsorship of, 50; party leadership relation to, 97, 166; with president, 139; reelection of, 30–31; tone of, 87
Cornyn, John, 104
Cosponsor Coalition's Partisanship measure, 118
cosponsorship, *58*, 59, 96, 117–19, *121*, 139; of bill development process, 193n1; bipartisanship and, 11, 34–35, 36, 57, 122, *141*; of copartisans, 50; ideology and, 47; partisan intensity relation to, 120, *120*, 121–22, 123, *123*, 128–29, 176, 185n7, 193nn2–3; partisan personas and, 6
counter-mobilizing behavior, 188n2
Cramer, Kevin, 54–55
credibility, bipartisanship and, 129
credit-claiming opportunities, 25, 37; bipartisanship and, 54; cosponsorship and, 119; minority party status and,

193n9; party brand and, 74, 76; rhetoric for, 56; tone and, 49
cross-party rhetoric, 62
Crowley, Joe, 40
Cruz, Ted, 68
Cummings, Elijah, 45
Curry, James, 139

Davis, Rodney, 2
decision tree algorithm, 135, 151–52, 153, *153*
DeGette, Diana, 192n13
DeMint, Jim, 73
Democrats, 2–3, 9, 15, 33, 115; ACA and, 73–74; bickering and, 82; Biden relation to, 178, 187n16; partisan polarization and, 51–52; party leadership of, 192n13; primary challengers to, 40; public opinion of, 17; Republicans compared to, 84, 95, 96, 101; Trump relation to, 166, 175, 188n6; on Twitter/X, 13
Denham, Jeff, 29, 30
Department of Justice, 63
DeSantis, Ron, 46
Determinants of a Legislator's Partisan Tone, *91*
Determinants of Being Primaried: 2015–20, *167*; with Lagged Partisan Intensity, *170*
Determinants of Being Primaried, Robustness Checks, *171*
Determinants of Being Primaried, Two-Stage Model, *172*
Determinants of Congressional Partisanship, *102*
Determinants of Partisan Intensity, by Chamber, *113*
Determinants of Partisanship, by Chamber, *105*
Determinants of Strong Partisans' Tone, *92*
Distribution of Legislators' Partisan Intensity, *69*
Dot Plot of Legislators' Partisan Intensity, *69*
Duckworth, Tammy, 110
Durbin, Dick, 192n14
DW-NOMINATE, 33, 55, 70, 71, 134,

188n5; *Absolute Ideological Distance from the Party Median* and, 126; ideological extremity and, 84, 100, 119, 158, 167; ideology relation to, 96; president and, 193n7

effective date clause, 151
The Effect of Excessive Partisanship on Predicted Vote Share, *161*
Effect of Partisan Intensity on Legislative Effectiveness in Different Specifications, *134*, *144–45*
The Effect of Partisan Tone on Predicted Vote Share, *164*
electioneering, rhetoric and, 68, 70
electioneering committee, 30–31
elections: partisan intensity relation to, 6, 16, 20, 22; for party caucuses, 14; for party leadership, 4–5, 6, 30, 100, 104; for president, 105–6; 2020, 185n7, 187n16. *See also* reelection
The Electoral Consequences of Partisan Tone, *163*
The Electoral Costs of Partisanship, *159*
electoral penalty, 38–39, 155–56, 160, 168–69, 177, 195n8; maintainers relation to, 42; party unity scores and, 40–41; tone relation to, 165. *See also* reelection
Eleventh Commandment, 49
Ellison, Keith, 192n8
Energy and Commerce Committee, 115
Engel, Eliot, 40
Environmental Protection Agency (EPA), 63
Era of Good Feelings, 18
Example Tweets About Donald Trump, *64*
extended party network, 5, 6
external URLs, 65, 66

fact-finding congressional delegations (CODELS), 50, 58
Factors That Affect a Member's Partisan Tone, *86*
Factors That Differentiate Strong Partisans Based on Tone, *88*
false negatives, 65, 66
family separation, 3

fast-moving news stories, 61
"Federalist No. 10" (Madison), 17
Feinstein, Dianne, 187n14
Fenno, Richard, 20–21
Fiorina, Morris, 24, 157, 186n7
five-word phrases (5-grams), 135, 152
floor discipline, 29
floor speeches, 50, 60, 61
floor voting, 21, 50, 188n10
Floyd, George, 46
Flynn, D. J., 156
Fox News, 2, 94
Foxx, Virginia, 178
Freedom Caucus, 55
fundraising, teamsmanship and, 11–12

Gaetz, Matt, 1
Garland, Merrick, 53
Gillibrand, Kirsten, 23, 115
Gingrich, Newt, 8–9
"Gingrich Senators," 32, 33, 94
goals: partisan intensity relation to, 19–21,
    95, 97; of party warriors, 49; rhetoric
    for, 165; team players and, 157
Gooden, Lance, 178
GOP-written tax cuts (2017), 4
Gorsuch, Neil, 53
Gosar, Paul, 1
Gowdy, Trey, 60
Graham, Lindsey, 93–94, 110, 187n14,
    191n3
Grassley, Chuck, 20, 191n3
Graves, Sam, 29
Group of Six, 73–74

Harbridge-Yong, Laurel, 38, 156
hardball tactics, 50
Harris, Mark, 40
Hastings, Alcee, 45–46
healthcare policies, 3
Heitkamp, Heidi, 54
Helsinki conference, 52
higher office, 100, 105; cheerleading and,
    89; electoral penalty and, 38; influence
    of, 31; partisan intensity relation to, 31,
    107; rhetoric for, 87; tone and, 85
High-Ranking Party Leader variable, 98
Hill, French, 35

hill style, 95, 97, 160
home style, 23, 42, 61, 94, 112; maintain-
    ers and, 25–26; partisan behavior rela-
    tion to, 160; partisan personas and, 97;
    reelection relation to, 22, 98; Republi-
    cans and, 33
Honda, Mike, 195n8
Hopkins, Daniel J., 55
House Budget Committee, 107
House committee chairs, 14
House Committee Leader and *Senate Com-
    mittee Leader* measures, 98
House Democratic Caucus, 169
House Intelligence Committee, 1, 68
House Judiciary committee, 59
House of Representatives, 98; committee
    leaders in, 29; impeachment relation
    to, 181–82; party leadership in, 192n13;
    Senate compared to, 104, 105
House Oversight Committee, 45
House Rules Committee, 46
Hutchinson, Asa, 182
hyper-partisan environment, 9–10, 174,
    183–84

Ideological Distance from the President, 127
ideological extremity, 33–34, 70, 103,
    187n10; bipartisanship relation to,
    122, 123; cosponsorship relation to,
    121; DW-NOMINATE and, 84, 100,
    119, 158, 167; electoral penalty for, 38;
    legislative effectiveness relation to, 138;
    partisan intensity and, 101, 134, 168;
    tone and, 80, *80*
ideological polarization, 8, 47, 51–55,
    195n1
ideologues, 173
ideology, 9, 47; DW-NOMINATE relation
    to, 96; partisan intensity relation to,
    71, 173, 174, *174*; primary challengers
    and, 40, 165; rhetoric and, 53; Scatter
    Plot of Partisan Intensity and, *71, 174*;
    teamsmanship and, 55, 157; vote-based
    measures relation to, 59
ill-advised posts, 61
impeachment, 1–3, 57, 59, 181–82
incivility, 10, 47, 55–56, 75–76
incumbency advantage, 175

incumbents, 177; partisan intensity relation to, 155; partisan personas of, 39
Incumbent's Vote Share, 158
Independent Variables Included in Enacted Policy Idea Models, *136*
individual performance rule, 25
influence, 20, 42, 186n2, 187n11; of higher office, 31; partisan intensity relation to, 27–28, 39, 97, 165; of party leadership, 50; promotion-seeking behavior and, 180–81
institutional power, 136
institutional resources, legislative effectiveness and, 36
intensity-based approach, 59
interparty fighting, 70, 96
intraparty fighting, 62
issue experts, 27, 36, 37, 124

Jacobson, Gary, 15, 23
Jeffries, Hakeem, 115, 173, 178
Jewitt, Caitlin, 40
Jordan, Jim, 192n13
judicial confirmations, 58
judicial nominations, 12

Kavanaugh, Brett, 12, 53, 166, 187n14; Graham relation to, 93–94; Republicans relation to, 41
Kinzinger, Adam, 188n3
Koger, Gregor, 38, 39, 156–58, 160; on electoral penalty, 169; party unity scores and, 194n7; on tone, 162

leadership races, 4–5, 6, 104
The Lead with Jake Tapper (television show), 2
Lebo, Matthew J., 38, 39, 156–58, 160, 162; on electoral penalty, 169; party unity scores and, 194n7
Lee, Frances, 9, 55, 106, 187n9; on bickering, 50; on roll call record, 101; on teamsmanship, 11
legislative effectiveness, 6, *37*, 116, 134; bipartisanship relation to, 116, 176; ideological extremity relation to, 138; institutional resources and, 36; partisan intensity relation to, 117–18, 129–

30, *131*, *132*, 133, *134*, 135, 136, *137*, *144–45*; politicization relation to, 139; promotion-seeking behavior relation to, 129
Legislators' Ideological Extremity and Tone, *80*
Legislators' Partisan Intensity and Tone, *79*; by Total Number of Tweets, *90*
Lieu, Ted, 178
Likelihood Partisans Engage in Bipartisan Cosponsorships, *141*
linear probability model, 136
Lou Dobbs Tonight (television show), 2
Low-Ranking Party Leader, 98
Lugar Center, 122

Maddow, Rachel, 2
Madison, James, 17, 186n1
maintainers, 24, 157, 160; electoral penalty relation to, 42; home style and, 25–26; partisan intensity of, 39
Major Factors That Predict a Legislator's Partisan Intensity, *19*
majority status, 25, 42, 85, 96, 106, 187n9; partisan acrimony relation to, 84; partisan behavior and, 175; partisan intensity relation to, 186n2
major political disputes, 9
Malhotra, Neil, 156
Manchin, Joe, 67, 68, 166
marginal districts, 159–60, 162, 169, 177, 186n4
Masto, Catherine Cortez, 53
maximizers, 186n7; in competitive districts, 24, 25; partisan intensity of, 195n8; reelection of, 39; tone of, 41, 42
Mayhew, David, 186n7
McCarthy, Kevin, 82, 178, 192n13
McCollum, Betty, 2
McConnell, Mitch, 9, 46, 82, 93, 173; ACA and, 73; conservative judges and, 57; partisan intensity of, 67, 68
McMullin, Evan, 93
McSally, Martha, 193n20
Meadows, Mark, 2, 68
measurement error, 58–59
Measurement of Factors Used to Predict Partisan Tone, *85*

media interviews, 50
messaging campaigns, 25, 28, 29
Meyer, Chase B., 40
Michel, Bob, 45
minority party status, 26; credit-claiming
    opportunities and, 193n9; partisan
    acrimony relation to, 84
moderates, 71
Moran, Jerry, Roberts compared to, 23
multinomial logistic regression, 87
multiparty political systems, 57
Mulvaney, Mark, 81, 82
Murkowski, Lisa, 166
Murray, Patty, 192n14
Musk, Elon, 13, 186n9

national intelligence, 68
nationalized politics, promotion-seeking
    behavior relation to, 15
national party hierarchy, 31, 32
national support, for backbenchers,
    14–15
natural language processing tools, 64–65,
    66
negative nonpartisan tweets, 77
"negative partisanship," 190n2
negative partisan tweets, 77
Neguse, Joe, 35
net neutrality, 53–54
neural network, 65, 66, 77
Nielson, Howard C., Jr., 12
Noel, Hans, 55
nonpartisan rhetoric, 62
nonpolicy language, 152
North Dakota, 54–55
Number and Percentage of Strong Parti-
    san Types, by Congress, *82*

Obama, Barack, 13, 56, 178; on ACA, 73–
    74; on Graham, 94
Obamacare, 4, 73–74
obituaries, 45–46
Ocasio-Cortez, Alexandria, 115
off-the-record settings, 58
OLS. *See* ordinary least squares
omnibus procedures, 176
114th Congress, 60, 107, 109
115th Congress, 107, 109, 191n5;

116th Congress compared to, 67; on
    Twitter/X, 60–61
116th Congress, 191n5; 115th Congress
    compared to, 67; Tonko in, 115–17
117th Congress, 178, 179, 186n9
opportunists, 76–77, 82, 190n10; bicker-
    ing and, 175; cheerleading and, 89;
    partisan intensity and, 88; president
    relation to, 87; rhetoric of, 81; tone of,
    191n13
ordinary least squares (OLS), 84, 101,
    127, 130
Out-of-Sample Performance of Neural
    Network, *66*

partisan acrimony, 84, 195n1; bickering
    and, 96; in Senate, 106
Partisan Balance of Cosponsorship Coali-
    tions, *121*
partisan behavior, 10, 27, 83–84, 138,
    187n15; home style relation to, 160;
    majority status and, 175; partisan lean
    and, 25–26; reelection and, 103, 108,
    110, 111–12; of Republicans, 168
partisan bona fides: president and, 35; of
    Republicans, 107; tone and, 41
partisan brand: credit-claiming opportu-
    nities and, 49; party leadership relation
    to, 29; teamsmanship and, 11; on
    Twitter/X, 47, 189n18
partisan fidelity, 42, 83, 186n4
partisan intensity, 10, *19*, 43, *69*, *138*,
    148–50; bill development process
    relation to, 139–40; of committee
    leaders, 31; in competitive districts,
    6–7, 111, 180; cosponsorship relation
    to, 120, *120*, 121–22, 123, *123*, 128–29,
    176, 185n7, 193nn2–3; Determinants
    of, *113*; elections relation to, 6, 16, 20,
    22; floor voting relation to, 21; goals
    relation to, 19–20, 95, 97; of Graham,
    93; ideological extremity and, 101,
    134, 168; ideology relation to, 71, 173,
    174, *174*; impeachment relation to,
    181; for influence, 27–28, 39, 97, 165;
    leadership races and, 104; legislative
    effectiveness relation to, 117–18, 129–
    30, *131*, *132*, 133, *134*, 135, 136, *137*,

144–45; of maintainers, 39; majority status relation to, 186n2; of maximizers, 195n8; in 117th Congress, 178, 179; Party Accounts' Partisan, *70*; party brand relation to, 26, 95, 175; of party leadership, 29, 72, 98, 99, 108, 109; party unity scores and, 125–26, 194n7; party unity voting as, *127*; politicization relation to, 86–87, 177; presidential support scores relation to, 127, 128, *128*; president relation to, 104, 110, 124; primary challengers relation to, 167–68, *170*; promotion-seeking behavior and, 14–15, 97–98, 99–100, 105–7, 109–10, 111–12; reelection relation to, 83, 95, 96, 106, 109, 155–57, 168–69, 192n15; rhetoric and, 46, 60; roll call votes relation to, 124; Scatter Plot of, *71*, *174*; seat safety and, 37, 42, 96, 115, 159–60, 165, 186n5; tone and, 79, *79*, 81, 88, *90*, 162, 175, 190n8; Trump and, 67, 68, 70; on Twitter/X, 5, 12, 13, 61–62, 183; vote-based measures relation to, 59; voters relation to, 16, 19, 155–56
Partisan Intensity by Congress for All Members and Freshmen, *179*
Partisan Intensity's Predicted Effect on a Legislative Section Becoming Law, *137*
Partisan Intensity's Predicted Effect on Legislative Effectiveness, *132*
partisan language, 62, 63, *63*, 64
partisan lean, 23–24, 97; partisan behavior and, 25–26; tone relation to, 90
partisan links, 65, 66
partisan personas, 10, 26, 123–24, 174–75; in competitive districts, 169; cosponsorship and, 6; of Graham, 94; of incumbents, 39; of maximizers, 25; party brand and, 97; party leadership relation to, 14–15; party reputation and, 4; for political points, 29–30; primary challengers relation to, 191n5; reelection relation to, 34; on Twitter/X, 182
partisan polarization, 10, 51–55, 101
partisan policy labels, 63, 64
partisan reputations, 37, 133

partisanship. *See specific topics*
Partisanship's Effect on Party Unity Voting, *142*
Partisanship's Effect on Presidential Support, *143*
Partisanship's Effect on Probability Bill Section Is Enacted, *146–47*
Partisanship's Expected Electoral Consequences, *42*
Partisanship's Hypothesized Effect on Legislative Effectiveness, *37*
partisan tone score, 16, 78, 79, 83
Partisan Tweet Coding Rules, *63*
partisan warfare, 51, 74, 76
partisan warriors, 49, 190n10; bickering and, 76–77; tone of, 80–81. *See also* bickering
Party Accounts' Partisan Intensity Scores, *70*
party-based messaging, 67
party brand, 21, 96; cheerleading and, 74; credit-claiming opportunities and, 74, 76; partisan behavior and, 26; partisan intensity relation to, 26, 95, 175; partisan personas and, 97; teamsmanship and, 124, 180; tone and, 90
party caucuses, 14, 18, 28, 30
party cohesiveness, 188n5
party fidelity, 156; party leadership relation to, 105; public record of, 35
party image, 25
party labels, voters relation to, 7–8
party leadership, 18, 180; copartisans relation to, 97, 166; elections for, 4–5, 6, 30, 100, 104; fundraising and, 11–12; in House of Representatives, 192n13; impeachment relation to, 181–82; influence of, 50; legislative effectiveness relation to, 138; partisan brand relation to, 29; partisan intensity of, 29, 72, 98, 99, 108, 109; partisan personas relation to, 14–15; party fidelity relation to, 105; political ambitions for, 21; power-seeking legislators in, 28; roll call votes and, 48; team players relation to, 30–31, 97, 187n12; tone of, 84
Party Leader variable, 104
party line voting, 23

party loyalty, 31, 156, 176; national party hierarchy and, 32; primary challengers relation to, 166; vote-based measures and, 57

party performance rule, 25

party policy agenda, 25

party reputation, 4, 29, 35

Party Unity and Presidential Support Scores, *125*

party unity scores, 11, *125*, 157–58, 194n7; electoral penalty and, 40–41; partisan intensity and, 125–26, 194n7

party unity voting, 38, 124, *127*, *142*, 186n5

pejoratives, 56

Pelosi, Nancy, 67, 73, 81, 82, 192n13

Personal Factors' Expected Effect on Partisanship, *33*

Pew Research Center, 17

Pittenger, Robert, 40

policy appeals, 76

policy ideas, 135, 136, 138, 139, 151

political action committees, 30

political ambitions, 5, 16, 19, 21

political points, 25, 36, 124; partisan personas for, 29–30; politicization for, 6; president relation to, 126

politicization, 7, 116–17, 176; bickering and, 86–87; bipartisanship relation to, 37; cosponsorship relation to, 35; in hyper-partisan environment, 9–10; legislative effectiveness relation to, 139; partisan intensity relation to, 86–87, 177; for political points, 6; voters relation to, 8

position-taking opportunities, 117–19

positive nonpartisan tweets, 77

Potential Explanations for Legislators' Partisanship, *99*

power-seeking legislators, 28, 85, 97

Power Seeking's Expected Effect on Partisanship, *32*

Predicted Bipartisanship Score as Partisan Intensity Changes, *123*

Predicted Change in Partisan Intensity When the Least Competitive House Seats Become More Competitive, *111*

Predicted Party Unity Voting as Partisan Intensity and Ideology Change, *127*

Predicted Presidential Support as Partisan Intensity and Ideology Change, *128*

preference-based measures, 12, 59

president, 26, *125*, *143*; cheerleading relation to, 87; copartisans with, 139; DW-NOMINATE and, 193n7; elections for, 105–6; partisan acrimony relation to, 84; partisan bona fides and, 35; partisan intensity relation to, 104, 110, 124; political points relation to, 126; tone relation to, 83, 88, 89–90. *See also* Biden, Joe; Obama, Barack; Trump, Donald

presidential election endorsements, 188n2

presidential support scores, 126; partisan intensity relation to, 127, 128, *128*; party unity scores and, 124, 125, *125*

President's Party, 158

press releases, 60, 186n8

primary challengers, 6, 22, 156; ideology and, 40, 165; partisan fidelity relation to, 42; partisan intensity relation to, 167–68, *170*; partisan personas relation to, 191n5; party loyalty relation to, 166; teamsmanship relation to, 39–40; Trump relation to, 195n10

principal-agent relationship, 28

"profiles in courage," 176

progressives, 33

promotion-seeking behavior, 75, 82, 101, 104, 175; fundraising and, 12; influence and, 180–81; legislative effectiveness relation to, 129; partisan behavior and, 103; partisan intensity and, 14–15, 97–98, 99–100, 105–7, 109–10, 111–12; of team players, 95, 178

ProQuest Central database, 185nn4–5

Pruitt, Scott, 56

public image, 20–21, 25, 76

public opinion, 17, 156

public policy, 20, 28

public record, of party fidelity, 35

Putin, Vladimir, 46, 52

Quality Challenger, 158

Ratcliffe, John, 68

Reagan, Ronald, 49

Reed, Jack, 23
reelection, 19–21, 24, 42; bickering and, 87; of copartisans, 30–31; home style relation to, 22, 98; of maximizers, 39; partisan behavior and, 103, 108, 110, 111–12; partisan intensity relation to, 83, 95, 96, 106, 109, 155–57, 168–69, 192n15; partisan personas relation to, 34; tone and, 74–75
Reelection and Collective Party Goals Expectations, *27*
Reid, Harry, 73, 104
Republicans, 1, 30, 53–54, 182; ACA and, 73–74; Biden relation to, 178, 187n16; cheerleading and, 82; Democrats compared to, 84, 95, 96, 101; Gingrich relation to, 9; impeachment and, 2–3; Kavanaugh relation to, 41; partisan behavior of, 168; partisan bona fides of, 107; partisan polarization and, 51–52; party leadership of, 192n13; public opinion of, 17; SCIF and, 2; Tea Party, 33, 40, 55; tone of, 85; Trump relation to, 49, 166, 175, 188n6, 195n10; 2020 election relation to, 185n7
rhetoric, 67; of bickering, 74; for credit-claiming opportunities, 56; election-eering and, 68, 70; for goals, 165; for higher office, 87; ideology and, 53; of opportunists, 81; partisan intensity and, 46, 60; partisan policy labels and, 63, 64; for politicization, 86–87; in press releases, 60; seat safety relation to, 88; on social media, 50; tone of, 75–76, 90; on Twitter/X, 10, 62, 189n19; voters and, 169
Roberts, Jason, 139
Roberts, Pat, 23
Robustness Checks for If Partisan Intensity Is Associated with Section Passage Rates, *148–50*
Rogan, James, 182
Rohrabacher, Dana, 20, 56
Roll Call (news outlet), 100
roll call record, 101
roll call votes, 47, 48, 124, 158
Romney, Mitt, 56, 188n3
Running for Higher Office measure, 100

Running for Leadership Position dichotomous variable, 99
Running for Leadership Position variable, 104
Rush, Bobby, 2
Russell, Annelise, 12, 27, 84, 85, 96, 101
Ryan, Paul, 53–54, 81
Ryan, Tim, 192n13

Sanders, Bernie, 53, 54, 110
Sanford, Mark, 40
#SaveTheInternet, 54
Scalise, Steve, 1, 178
Scatter Plot of Partisan Intensity and Ideology Measures, *71, 174*
Schiff, Adam, 81, 182; on House Intelligence Committee, 1, 68; Trump relation to, 23, 57
Schumer, Chuck, 4, 23, 115
SCIF, 2–4, 185nn4–5
Scott, Tim, 94
seat safety, 22, 110, 158, 177; bickering and, 6, 75, 87; legislative effectiveness relation to, 138; maintainers and, 24; nationalized politics relation to, 15; partisan intensity and, 37, 42, 96, 115, 159–60, 165, 186n5; position-taking opportunities relation to, 119; primary challengers relation to, 167–68; rhetoric relation to, 88; tone relation to, 41, 89, 162, 163
Secret Service, 4
seersucker day, 50
self-presentation, home style and, 23
self-written content, 61
Senate: committee leaders in, 30, 98; House of Representatives compared to, 104, 105; impeachment relation to, 181; partisan acrimony in, 106; reelection for, 192n15; 60-vote threshold in, 176–77
Senate Finance Committee, 191n3
Senate Judiciary Committee, 93–94, 187n14, 191n3
shared interests, 5, 36, 129
Shutt, Jennifer, 30
Sinema, Kyrsten, 178
60-vote threshold, 176–77

SMaBERTa, 65

Smith, Jason, 107–8, 178, 192n17

Snowe, Olympia, 73–74

social media, 13–14, 20, 182–83; BERT and, 65; ill-advised posts on, 61; rhetoric on, 50. *See also* Twitter/X

Speaker of the House, 98

Spending Difference, 158

staffers, congressional communication by, 20, 61

Stanford CoreNLP project, 77

steering committees, 29, 30

#StopTheSchiffShow, 1

Stutzman, Marlin, 109

Supreme Court nominations, 53, 59

sycophants, 81, 93–94

Sykes, Charles, 94

Syria, 3

Taylor, Bill, 1

team players, 5–6, 22, 25, 93, 166, 184; cheerleading and, 39–40, 87; committee leaders as, 29, 180; electoral penalty for, 38; goals and, 157; Graham as, 94; Hastings as, 46; influence of, 27–28; partisan intensity of, 139; party leadership relation to, 30–31, 97, 187n12; party reputation of, 35; policy ideas of, 138; political ambitions relation to, 21; position-taking opportunities and, 118; promotion-seeking behavior of, 95, 178

teamsmanship, 34; fundraising and, 11–12; ideology and, 55, 157; party brand and, 124, 180; primary challengers relation to, 39–40; tone and, 90

Tea Party Republicans, 33, 40, 55

television, partisan personas on, 14

"Textbook Congress," 52

Theriault, Sean, 32, 33, 50, 96, 101, 187n15

Thune, John, 104

ticket splitting, 23

tone, 42–43, 51, 74, 163, *164*; of copartisans, 87; credit-claiming opportunities and, 49; Determinants of a Legislator's Partisan, *91*; Determinants of Strong Partisans', *92*; The Electoral Consequences of Partisan, *163*; electoral penalty relation to, 165; Factors That Affect a Member's Partisan, *86*; Factors That Differentiate Strong Partisans Based on, *88*; higher office and, 85; ideological extremity and, 80, *80*; Measurement of Factors Used to Predict Partisan, *85*; of opportunists, 191n13; partisan intensity and, 79, *79*, 81, 88, *90*, 162, 175, 190n8; of party leadership, 84; politicization and, 86–87; president relation to, 83, 88, 89–90; of rhetoric, 75–76, 90; unified government relation to, 176; voters relation to, 41, 158, 160, 162, 177. *See also* bickering; cheerleading

Tone and Partisanship Example Tweets, *78*

Tonko, Paul, 115–17

top-of-the-ticket races, 32

Total Tweets, by Congress, *68*

Tracking If Partisan Intensity Is Negative and Statistically Significant, *138*

Tracy, Thomas, Jr., 2

Treul, Sarah A., 40, 96

trolling, 56

Trump, Donald, 1–2, 3, 40, 45–46, 59, 178; Example Tweets About, *64*; Graham relation to, 93–94; hyper-partisan environment and, 174; major political disputes and, 9; North Dakota relation to, 54–55; partisan intensity and, 67, 68, 70; partisan polarization and, 53; Putin relation to, 52; Republicans relation to, 49, 166, 175, 188n3, 188n6, 195n10; Romney relation to, 56; Schiff relation to, 23, 57; Secret Service and, 4; Tonko relation to, 115, 116; on Twitter/X, 13, 182

Trumpcare, 4

#TrumpShutdown, 46

2020 election, 185n7, 187n16

Twitter/X, 14, 46, 60, 182, 185n1, 186n9; partisan brand on, 47, 189n18; partisan intensity on, 5, 12, 13, 61–62, 183; rhetoric on, 10, 62, 189n19

two-word phrases (2-grams), 135, 152

Ukraine, 1

unified government, 175–76

United States–Mexico–Canada Agreement trade deal, 3

US Code, 152
Utah, 12

Van Buren, Martin, 18
Van Hollen, Chris, 110
Volden, Craig, 129–30, 136
vote-based measures, 57, 59, 158
voters, 23–24, 25; partisan behavior and, 83–84; partisan intensity relation to, 16, 19, 155–56; party brand relation to, 175; party labels relation to, 7–8; rhetoric and, 169; teamsmanship relation to, 39; tone relation to, 41, 158, 160, 162, 177
voter trends, 23
Votes and Cosponsorship Opportunities for 12 Partisan Events, *58*

voting records, 50
V&W (Volden & Wiseman) approach, 136, 138, *146*

Walorski, Jackie, 107–8, 192n17
Washington, George, 17
Washington Post (newspaper), 3
Watergate babies, 33
wave elections, 32, 33
whip votes, 28
Whitehouse, Sheldon, 23
Wiseman, Alan E., 129–30, 136
within-party disagreements, 187n10
Wright, Ron, 4

Young, Todd, 109